Pulpits
AND Plain
Sailing

Getting to the top in the marine
engineering industry

Kevin Cooney

Pulpits
AND Plain
Sailing

Getting to the top in the marine
engineering industry

MEREO
Cirencester

Mereo Books

1A The Wool Market Dyer Street Cirencester Gloucestershire GL7 2PR
An imprint of Memoirs Publishing www.mereobooks.com

Pulpits and Plain Sailing: 978-1-86151-640-4

First published in Great Britain in 2016
by Mereo Books, an imprint of Memoirs Publishing

The address for Memoirs Publishing Group Limited can be found at
www.memoirspublishing.com

The Memoirs Publishing Group Ltd Reg. No. 7834348

The Memoirs Publishing Group supports both The Forest Stewardship Council®
(FSC®) and the PEFC® leading international forest-certification organisations. Our
books carrying both the FSC label and the PEFC® and are printed on FSC®-certified
paper. FSC® is the only forest-certification scheme supported by the leading
environmental organisations including Greenpeace. Our paper procurement policy
can be found at www.memoirspublishing.com/environment

Typeset in 9/14pt Century Schoolbook
by Wiltshire Associates Publisher Services Ltd. Printed and bound in Great Britain
by Marston Book Services Ltd Oxfordshire

CONTENTS

CHAPTER ONE

Happiness and heartbreak

⸻✳⸻

I have a story to tell. I don't know if anyone will want to read it, but I am going to tell it anyway.

I think my story has to start with the events that led up to my arrival on this earth in 1944. Dad came from Manchester; he'd travelled down to Bedford hoping to get a job at Vauxhall Motors in Luton but ended up working for A H Allen of Bedford, a company that produced ships' engines and generators. Mother lived in Bedford and they met and were married on 21st December 1935.

They were living in a council flat in Fenlake Road, Bedford. Terence was born on 17th October 1936, followed by Anne on 18th May 1938. Terence was lost on May 30th 1943 when he was six and a half. Anne was only four years old, but she remembers that someone knocked on the door and Mum just dropped her, and ran off. It was Barry Eaton's mother. Barry had taken Terry fishing. Terry had fallen in the river and Barry had run home to get help. I never saw Terry after that. I kept looking for him, but he never came. I kept looking for him in all the hiding places where we used to play hide and seek, although I was told he had gone to heaven.

All of the aunts and uncles came down from Manchester for the funeral; it's hard to imagine the terrible feeling of loss and grief that everyone must have felt. Mum, Dad, Grandma, Granddad and sister Anne just had to carry on with their lives. It must have been a strange time for Anne with her Mum and Dad racked with grief and trying to carry on as normal.

Anne remembers the nurse coming to the house, then a cry and the nurse came out and said "I have delivered my biggest and smallest today". It was me that was the biggest - apparently I weighed in at thirteen and a half pounds. Anne adored the new baby. She couldn't take her eyes off me and followed me around everywhere, worried that I might not come back.

My earliest recollection was lying in my pram in the garden at Grandma's house and Grandma coming out to fuss me. I used to call "oo-oo, oo-oo" and Grandma used to call back "oo-oo" and come bustling out to tend to me.

My infancy was filled with love and tenderness, and my mum, dad, big sister and grandparents doted on me. The first Christmas I remember I think the toys were probably home-made. I remember a wooden tractor or steamroller – one of the wheels broke after a very short time. During that Christmas suddenly it was noticed that I had disappeared, and everyone was frantically searching for me. Granddad eventually found me. I had crawled into the larder and was helping myself to the left-over goose carcass.

During the winter of 1947, one of the coldest in living memory, I remember being trussed up like an Egyptian mummy. I needed to be "wrapped up warm"! I seemed to spend a lot of time at Grandma and Granddad's. During that winter we had a visit from a relative with a motorbike and sidecar and he took me for a little ride. I was terrified!

After the snow came the floods. The river Ouse which meandered through Bedford, the same river that had claimed Terence, rose six feet and Cauldwell Street was under two feet of water. Grandma's house was flooded and they had to move upstairs. I remember seeing them talking to Mum and Dad through the bedroom window. We were living in a council flat in Fenlake Road at this time and I had a friend called Geoffrey who lived in the upstairs flat.

I was about four when we moved to Barford Avenue. I remember riding in the removal van in the front with Dad, and when the van went back for some more things I wasn't allowed to go. I was really upset and wanted to go with Dad. Mrs. Goldsmith, our new next-door neighbour, gave me some sweets to pacify me.

Dad worked as a toolmaker at Berkeley Coach Works in Biggleswade. The company manufactured caravans and was very successful after the war due to the shortage of housing. In those days Dad used to work very long hours. He would leave home at about 6 am and not get home until about 8 pm. I was usually in bed, but sometimes I used to get up early to see him and on special occasions, like birthdays, I was allowed to stay up.

In those days everyone went everywhere on bicycles. There were very few cars around. The road where we lived was tarmac and all of us kids used to have roller skates and spend hours skating or playing whip and top.

My first school was Silver Jubilee Infants. I remember when Mum took me I used to be heartbroken when she left and cry for ages. I don't think I learned much; we used to play with sand and water, making sand pies.

My sister was very clever; she passed her 11-plus and got a scholarship to the Convent School. She suddenly realised that I didn't know my letters and was behind with reading and writing, so she took it upon herself to teach me. I started to catch up and was soon as good at reading and writing as anyone in my group.

The next school was Kingsbrook, a newly-built school. I used to walk to school and home for dinner (lunch) every day, as it was quite safe to do so. There was corporal punishment, but it was not used often and it was certainly a deterrent.

At junior school I always seemed to be chosen for the lead part in the school play. Unfortunately I rarely liked the girl chosen for the part of leading lady, and this often caused a laugh in the audience when I had any lines of a romantic nature. On one occasion after finding my long-lost love I had to say "How I have longed for this moment". The audience were in stitches!

My time at Kingsbrook School was a happy one. Everyone was a lot poorer than they are today; the men had to have a job, as there very few benefits available, so people had to work.

The next school was Silver Jubilee Boys' School. Every morning we had to line up in class order while the headmaster bellowed at us through a megaphone. At the command we all had to "dress right", which meant look right and stretch your right arm out and put it on the shoulder of the boy to your right so we were equally spaced. We would then turn right and on command march in to our class.

The school was quite strict, which it needed to be with the mix of children, mostly from the large council estate surrounding it. The slipper was freely used for minor transgressions and for more serious misdemeanours there was the cane, two four or six strokes. Any boy caught smoking had six of the best on the stage at morning assembly in front of the whole school. In those days it seemed that everybody smoked, but very few got caught!

There were four groups divided into houses for each year, depending on ability, and I was always in group two (B stream). I consider that I had a good education. I left school with reasonable English and Maths and a knowledge of History and Geography that has stood me in good stead.

My last form teacher was a Mr Shelton, who was also our maths teacher, and he was very strict. In his class you could hear a pin drop. Everyone dreaded the shout "Get out, maggot!" As you walked to the front he would undo his briefcase take out his slipper, and as you reached the front of the class he would point the slipper at the floor, and you would bend over and be whacked twice across the arse. Quite often nothing more was said and you would just go back to your seat, or there would be a brief explanation.

Some of the teachers were strange characters and had served in the war. The art teacher had several sticks (canes) and had a name for each one. His nickname was 'Jumbo King' and he was a big man with a handlebar moustache. On more than one occasion I saw him chasing a boy round the classroom wielding his 'Big Bertha', a cane as thick as a broomstick.

In class the teachers would walk around looking at the boys' work, and if there was a mistake they would smack you round the back of the head. It didn't pay to answer back, as quite often you would get another smack round the back of the head followed by the slipper.

My favourite subject was metalwork. The first year I did it I loved it and did quite well. Dad was an engineer and I learned a lot from him without realising it. The next year I applied to do metalwork again; we were all lined up in our group of choice.

The different groups were woodwork, metalwork and gardening. I joined the metalwork group, but the Headmaster said there were too many in metalwork and I and a few others were made to stand in the gardening group. The headmaster then said "I realise that some of you may wish to change to a different group. If anyone would like to move to a different group do so now." I immediately moved from the gardening group back to metalwork. The Headmaster screamed at me, "COONEY, HOW DARE YOU! You were told to move to gardening!" He was apoplectic and gave me a right dressing down. Needless to say I did gardening that year. I realised afterwards that the metalwork teacher had taken a dislike to me.

The next year luckily I was allowed to join the metalwork class. I really enjoyed making things and did quite well on all the test pieces we had to make. At the end of the year there was an exam, comprising a practical test which involved making a test piece and a theory exam. When we were told our results I thought I had done quite well to achieve 96%. One of the other boys asked the teacher who had come top of the class, and he grudgingly admitted that I had.

Every Sunday we all put on our Sunday best and went to church, and we would then go and put flowers on Terence's grave. I always remember from a very early age the picture on the sideboard of Terence, my little brother, in heaven.

My parents decided that I should have swimming lessons. They used to take me to Newnham swimming pool, but I could only swim under water. I then went for lessons at Commercial Baths on the other side of town. The man who ran the pool was a Mr Nash. His method was to put a loop of rope round the swimmer and tow them along. After the first few minutes he had me swimming. He had a son Peter who swam like a fish and we became friends. Within a couple of weeks, I had swum a half mile. In the school summer holidays I used to spend most days at the pool.

I used to have various mates; there were lads that lived fairly close and some school
friends. Michael lived next door, David opposite, George and Johnny just down the road and various others came and went.

From a very early age I had an interest in guns. A lot of the other boys had air rifles and I pestered my dad to buy me one. At that time there wasn't the fear and paranoia regarding any type of gun that there is now. I remember the Christmas I got my first air rifle; it was the best present I had ever had. I kept looking at it and polishing it and I just couldn't believe my good fortune.

As I got older I graduated to shotguns. You could buy a gun licence for 10 shillings and cartridges could be bought over the counter at most hardware shops as long as you were over 17. There was very little gun crime in those days, probably because the courts were strict and crime was punished.

After the War there were a lot of guns around that had been brought back by returning soldiers. I obtained a Belgian automatic pistol from a boy at school for five bob and a couple of packets of sweets. I then sold it on to another boy for fifteen bob, making a good profit. At one time I had a Webley service revolver and then a German Luger, which we used as toys! One of my mates had a Sten gun (a submachine gun).

At the end of our street there were open fields and we spent hours playing in them. In the winter when they were flooded and frozen over we would be over there sliding and crunching through the thin ice. In the summer we would go all night fishing, camping out in small tents. The method was to rig up a cheap buzzer attached to the fishing line that would sound when there was a fish on the line. It was quite scary lying in the tent with the night sounds amplified in our imagination.

On one occasion I got back to the tent only to find it flattened, with a cow sitting on it contentedly chewing the cud.

As we got older we would cycle to a village called Willington and take our guns and fishing rods. We would camp out and catch pike and shoot rabbits, and we would cook the rabbits in a pot over an open fire.

Between us we had a variety of guns, from powerful air rifles to shotguns. On one occasion just as it was getting dark I was sitting round the campfire with some of the lads when another lad, Victor, was walking back from shooting to join us. He had a powerful air rifle and was swinging it around when suddenly it went off and shot Michael, who was sitting next to me, in the leg. In an instant Michael grabbed his .410 shotgun, which had been resting against a tree, cocked it and swung it towards Victor. I dived at Michael, grabbing the gun and deflecting the shot away. It went off harmlessly into the trees. There was a stunned silence as we all realised what might have been.

One of my best mates was Jack; he lived a bit further away, but for a time we were very close. He looked a bit like Elvis Presley and was very popular with the girls. There was a crowd of us that used to play in his street, and on one occasion we thought we would play a joke on one of the houses opposite. One of us crept up to the front door and tied a thread round the door knocker. We then retreated to a safe distance and pulled the thread several times knocking the door. The door opened but there was no one there. The man looked around and not seeing the thread closed the door. We then waited a few minutes and pulled the thread again. Once more the door opened and a rather puzzled man once again looked around and then closed the door.

We gave it a few minutes and pulled the thread again. This time the door flew open, as the man was obviously waiting for the knock. This time he saw the thread and grabbed hold of it, and started to run towards us following the thread. We all ran off and luckily he didn't catch any of us.

Dad used to like to bet on the horses – only a few pence but he used to be quite lucky. I remember when he won £60 on the Grand National, and with the money he bought our first television. It was the first one in the street and we had all the neighbours round to watch the Coronation in 1953 and the Cup Final that year. We were also the first house to have a telephone.

CHAPTER TWO

Young love

When Dad bought our first car in 1955, we had double gates fitted and Dad and Granddad concreted the drive and built a prefab garage. The car was an Austin A30. Dad bought it for cash. He did not believe in HP – his way was to save up for things and buy when you could afford it. It cost £475 and had no heater, radio, or any of the things that are now considered standard equipment. When Dad obtained his licence in the 1920s, there was no driving test, so to polish up his driving skills he had a mate who was a coach driver sit with him until he got the hang of it. I was so proud of my Dad's new car, but there was a lot of envy and many sarcastic remarks both from my mates and sometimes their parents.

Every year we used to go to Great Yarmouth on holiday. In

the days before we had a car we used to go by coach. One year we went to Caister holiday camp near Yarmouth, which was very 'Hi De Hi', but I thoroughly enjoyed it with all the organized things for kids to do. Other years we stayed in a caravan on the South Denes caravan site. There was no toilet or washing facilities in the caravan. There were wash houses and toilet blocks on the site that were kept fairly clean and respectable. But I was very fortunate that my parents could afford to take me every year to the seaside.

I read *Treasure Island* at a very early age, being far ahead of my year at reading, and always had a love of stories about pirates, buried treasure and sailing ships. One day on the beach at Yarmouth a pirate ship came sailing by. It tied up in the harbour and you could pay sixpence (about 2½ new pence) to go on board and look around. I was fascinated by all the ropes and rigging and couldn't understand why it had an engine!

Once we had the car we used to go camping, and Dad bought a load of gear from one of his mates and a 10 ft long ridge tent. We used to put it up on the beach at North Denes and use the facilities on the caravan site. We got away with it the first year, but then an official came and told us that we had to go to the proper site across the road.

We started using the camping site at South Denes, which was nicknamed 'the reservation' due to the enormous wall surrounding it. It was when we were staying on this site that I fell in love for the first time. I was 14 at the time and I had met up with one of the lads from my class at school. We used to go to the pleasure beach every night. We never had much money, just enough for a packet of cigarettes and a few rides on the roller coaster.

We got chatting to two girls, both a year older than us and working in an electrical goods manufacturing company down by the harbour. We told them we were fifteen and I said I was an apprentice bricklayer. We ended up snogging in the sand dunes and she let me feel her breasts, then at about 10 o'clock I walked her to the bus stop. We did this every evening, and all day I would be walking on air waiting for the moment when we would meet. Some days I would meet her at the factory gates at lunch time.

Unfortunately, on the last night at the funfair we had a disagreement about some silly thing to do with her friends, and I walked off in a huff and she went off with her mates. Back at the campsite I realised it was our last night and I felt such anguish – I had never felt that way before. I went rushing back to the funfair to try to find her. When at last I saw her she was having an argument with her best friend; she wanted to come and find me, and her friend was trying to dissuade her. We fell into each other's arms as her mate went marching off in a huff. We ended up in the sand dunes again!

We had exchanged addresses and promised to write to each other. A few days after we got home a letter came; my dad got to it first and opened it, thinking it was for him. I managed to get it off him before he had a chance to read it. It started off 'Dear Kevin, I love you, I love you, I love you, I can't wait to see you again...' The letter was full of this type of thing. One of the sentences said "I came on my periods yesterday, thank goodness." I wrote straight back with similar sentiments, but I never received another letter from her. I always wondered just how much Dad had read of the letter and whether any further letters were intercepted. I was, after all, only 14.

I couldn't wait to leave school. During the last year I played truant a lot. One of the lads from my class called Roy, whose mum and dad were out all day, used to meet up with one of the girls from the girls' school and we three used to go to his house and take it in turns with the girl on his sofa.

On the last afternoon of the term I went fishing. I have always hated goodbyes, and the thought of parading round the school with the other school leavers saying goodbye to the teachers didn't appeal.

In Bedford there was a Youth Employment Bureau. We would go along and look at the jobs on offer and discuss them with one of the staff to decide which was most suitable. Different jobs required different qualifications. I wanted to join the police force, but you had to be 16 years old to become a cadet. Anne, my sister, was a police officer at that time and I was influenced by her. I used to be so proud of her, so smart in her uniform.

The job I chose was as an apprentice at the International Stores, an early supermarket chain. The job was a stopgap until I was old enough to join the police. They were a great crowd to work with. At Christmas customers used to hand in bottles as tips or presents, and these were saved up for the Christmas party. It was Christmas Eve, and when the shop closed the party began. We all got sloshed, and goodness knows what we got up to. Eventually two of the staff, Maureen and Jim, put me in a taxi to take me home. I was sick in the taxi and all over myself. The taxi driver was furious and Jim gave him some money to calm him down and to clean up the taxi.

Maureen decided that I couldn't go home in that state and she and Jim took me to her flat. She lent me some of her husband's clothes and put mine in the washing machine. When her husband who was working late arrived home, as they were going to another party which was on the way, they walked me home.

The shop was fairly central in Bedford and we had quite a few people calling in to buy snacks for lunch. Quite a few were young female shop assistants and there was a lot of friendly banter and flirting with them. There was one called Julie who

I really fancied, who worked in a bank. She was gorgeous, nineteen years old and let it be known that she fancied me. I asked her for a date and she accepted. I told her that I was 19 as well and was hoping to join the police. We went out a couple of times, but she eventually found out I was only 15 and dumped me.

It was around this time that my big sister Anne got married, to Tony, who she met whilst stationed in Luton. Tony was a painter and decorator and was working at the police station when they met. His mates dared him to ask her for a date and the rest is history.

They were the first couple to marry in the newly-built Catholic church. One of Dad's mates, Ron Jemmet, had a recording device which looked like a big tape recorder but used a wire instead of a tape. He sat at the front and tried to record the ceremony, but although the priest spoke in quite a distinctive voice the recording was barely audible.

The priest, Father Galvin, was a wonderful man. He stood over 6ft tall and had a very commanding presence. He was very good at raising money and building churches. Everyone liked and respected him.

It was decided that as I was going into the police I needed to polish up my English, so I found a course at the local collage that was on a Thursday afternoon, and as Thursday was early closing I arranged with the manager, Mr Goodship, to start early on a Thursday morning and finish early at the shop in time to go to college for the course.

The entrance exam for the police was held in the police station and there were half a dozen of us hopefuls. I felt that I had done quite well in the exam and seemed to do all right in the interviews. One morning there was a letter in the post, the envelope marked Police. I was quite excited, but on opening the letter I found that it was a rejection. The reason given was that

I didn't have a good enough educational background.

I was bitterly disappointed. I had really looked forward to being a police cadet. I suppose being a bit of a rebel at school probably made the Headmaster reluctant to support my application. I think I would have made a good copper, but it wasn't to be. I had gone to the International Stores as a stopgap – I had no intention of staying a shop assistant.

That year we went to Southwold for our summer holidays, staying in a caravan owned by one of my sisters' colleagues. I was quite shy and did not make friends easily, so I used to sit around the caravan reading. One day a man came over from one of the other caravans for a chat. He said I looked lonely, told me he had two daughters and wondered if I would like to go with them to the cinema. They were a Jewish family, quite well off, and I spent the rest of the holiday with the two girls. The younger one, Bernice, I was particularly fond of. She was 13 and her sister Jackie was 16. I had never known a kinder and friendlier family. Bernice was bubbly and full of fun, and her sister a bit more serious.

They had a friend, Carol, who was tall and, slim with long dark hair and my age, and we soon became a little more than friends. On the last Friday I took her to the cinema, and we spent the whole film snogging in the back row. When we left the cinema I suggested that we should take the way back across the fields, but she said she would prefer to go back via the road. I wonder why!

We all exchanged addresses and promised to write and keep in touch. I wrote to Carol for over a year, but we never met up again.

It was around this time that I took up judo. There were two clubs in Bedford, the BJA, British Judo Association, and the AJA, Amateur Judo Association. I started with the BJA. The training was really tough but there was a great atmosphere of respect. The sessions used to start with warm-up exercises, then instruction and practice of the moves you had just been shown and then Randori. This involved fighting everyone in the room one after the other. You would form two lines facing each other and move down the line with the one on the end running round to the other end. I trained with the BJA on and off for several years.

On one occasion there was a competition and I managed to get into the final. The Mayor of Bedford was there to award the prizes and there was a photographer from the *Bedfordshire Times*. I fought hard but got beaten by Tony, one of the instructors, so I didn't win any prizes but my picture ended up in the local paper. It was amazing how people's attitudes changed towards me. I seemed to be respected more – people seemed to think I was some sort of prize fighter!

There was a girl who used to train with us called Peta. I used to get on very well with her and she used to train just as hard as any man. Some of the instructors didn't like training with a woman, although she never asked for special treatment and was as dedicated as anyone. In the end she was told not to come any more, which I considered to be so unfair. She then went on to join the AJA club and achieved her Dan grade (black belt).

CHAPTER THREE

Apprentice

I had now decided to try to get an apprenticeship in engineering, so I went to the Youth Employment Bureau and they got me an interview at Fords Finsbury Ltd, which had nothing to do with cars. They made dairy equipment, everything generally manufactured in stainless steel, aluminium or non-corrosive materials, as was necessary for food use.

I had arranged the interview for a Thursday afternoon, although it would mean I would miss my Thursday college lessons. Fords were in Kempston, which was about seven miles from where I lived, but one of the lads I worked with, Mike, agreed to come with me for something to do on his afternoon off. The weather was foul, there were several inches of snow and there was a blizzard, with the snow blowing horizontally.

Fords were on the other side of Kempston, and with the weather conditions we had difficulty finding it. Our bikes were sliding about a bit, but we eventually found the way.

When I arrived I was directed to the Works Manager's office, which was in the main workshop. When I walked into the factory, covered in snow and not knowing what to expect, there was a cheer and everyone started banging their lockers. I walked up to the Works Manager's office, which was raised up about 10 feet above the factory floor.

The interview was held by the Works Manager, Mr Lowe, and Mr Mortlock, one of the directors. Fred Lowe was a gruff, no-nonsense engineer who didn't suffer fools gladly, but he had a kind way with him. I think he was perhaps impressed with the fact that I had turned up for the interview despite the weather conditions.

As my dad was an engineer and I had done metalwork at school, I understood some of the jargon. I was asked several questions on decimal equivalents, like 'what is a quarter of an inch as a decimal' and a trick question, "how many thousandths of an inch in one inch?" I knew all of the answers and did very well in the interview, telling them that one day I hoped to be a manager myself.

When I got home my dad was furious with me for missing an afternoon at college and said the interview was just an excuse not to go. But a couple of days later a letter arrived in the post offering me an engineering apprenticeship. It came with one day a week day release. Dad was quite pleased at this. The hours were 7. 30 till 5 Monday to Friday with one hour for lunch, and I found that if I left home at 7. 00 I had plenty of time to cycle the seven miles to work. You were allowed up until 7. 33 and then you were docked a quarter of an hour's pay. If you were late twice in a week you could be sacked.

Fords did not have Union recognition, although quite a few

did belong. I joined the AEU as my dad had been a lifelong member. At Fords the wages were higher and conditions far better than the local big union firms.

My first department was sheet metal, where I was put with John, one of the most highly-skilled craftsmen, who also had an evening job taxi driving, using his own car. When I went to be introduced he said "I remember you! You were the c**t that puked up all over my f***ing taxi last Christmas Eve!" Not the best start to a beautiful friendship!

The thing that most surprised me about working in the factory was the swearing; every other word was the F word. At home my parents never swore and even when I was out with my mates I avoided such profanity, but I soon became as bad as all the others.

I originally left school on April 6th 1959, four days after my 15th birthday, and started work at International Stores the following Monday. I started at Fords around March 1960. Fords was a very happy place to work, and quite often the guys in the machine shop would be singing. If one of the machines was making a regular noise, such as a lathe with a big casting turning slowly and making a regular clonk or squeak, they would incorporate this into their song. One of the centre lathe turners had a particularly good voice.

I felt a bit out of my depth in the first few weeks. I was working in the sheet metal department and the verbal abuse and practical joking was dire, although I soon got used to it. Some of the chaps knew my dad, having worked with him at AH Allen during the war or Berkeley Coach works after. I used to cycle to work every day, as did most of the other blokes in all weathers. When it was raining it was quite difficult keeping a fag alight, but I always seemed to manage.

Every morning it was my job to go round the factory taking orders for rolls and sandwiches and then ring the order through to the sandwich shop, so the order would then be delivered in time for tea break. There were quite a few apprentices and at 10 o'clock every morning some of us would bring out enormous trays full of cups of tea. A klaxon would then sound, signalling tea break.

Fords had a sports and social club and a small subscription could be stopped out of your wages. This covered the cost of a day trip to the seaside and the annual Christmas party – other people could come along but they had to pay. On the buses there was a lot of camaraderie and as everyone got stuck into the beer, some singing.

One of the older apprentices had his sister Pat and her friend Julie with him. I and some of the other lads were chatting to the two girls in the pub. We all decided to sit on the back seat of the bus on the way home, and Julie and I got very friendly indeed!

I enjoyed my day release course and learned an enormous amount. There was no CNC in those days and all the machines had to be worked manually, tools set and ground by hand.

It was around this time I noticed cracks appearing in my parents' marriage. Mum worked at Cardington Camp, an RAF station, and I could tell she was unhappy. Sometimes I would come home and catch her crying, and I didn't know what to do. Apparently Dad was always questioning her, looking in her handbag etc. Mum was a heavy smoker and she often came home from work with cartons of 200 cigarettes that she had been given.

On one occasion old Joe, a guy she worked with, came to the house. Joe was the one who gave her the cigarettes. They asked me to take some parts off an old bike frame that was in the garden, probably to get me out of the way. I tried to smooth things out between them, but one day on my way home from college I saw Dad in his car heading into town. He slowed down and shouted out of the car window, "We've got problems, I'll see you at home in a few minutes. "

When I arrived home, a letter was lying open on the kitchen table. A feeling of dread came over me as I picked up the letter and read it. It said she was leaving and Dad was not to try to find her.

Dad came home in a dreadful state. He kept breaking down in tears. Someone had said that she might be staying with a woman she worked with who lived at the top end of town. We went to pick up her mum, who was also distraught, and we all went looking for her. I went and enquired at the New Inn, which was near where she was supposed to be staying, but to no avail. The strange thing was that my grandmother went straight to the house where we afterwards found out she was staying, but it was all in darkness and there appeared to be no one there.

The next day we went to see Minnie, Mum's half-sister – she was not a blood relation but had been brought up with Mum. She said she did not know Mum's whereabouts. Minnie and her second husband had an antiques shop. My sister Anne found out where Mum was living and arranged for me to go and see her, but I was sworn to secrecy regarding her address. She was living with a spinster called Nan. I pleaded with her to come home but she refused and asked me to leave as Nan was due home and she had to get her tea ready!

I went back with my sister. Mum wasn't there, but there was another woman there who knew all about it, and was saying things about Dad that Mum had obviously told her. She said a big problem was the sexual side. Most men got 'better' as they got older, meaning they didn't want sex so often, if at all, but Dad had got worse, wanting it more. I really didn't want to discuss my parents' sex life, especially with a stranger!

Mother used to run a mail order club and Anne my sister got roped in to wind it up by collecting any outstanding monies and sending back unwanted items. Anne and Dad had a disagreement about one of the items and Dad and I left with my sister in tears, Dad upset and me very sad.

Mum had left a few weeks before Christmas. Dad and I cooked a turkey on Christmas Day, and Gran, Granddad and Anne and Tony came over, but it wasn't a happy time. Dad tried to put on a brave face but he and Grandma were heartbroken.

I visited Anne after Christmas. She had seen our mother and had exchanged Christmas presents. There was a present for me, but I refused it. I knew that it would upset Dad if I had accepted it. When I arrived home I told Dad about the present, and he said "wasn't there one for me?" I said no, and he burst into tears.

At Fords it was against the rules to have personal phone calls, but one day there was a call on the Tannoy for me to go to the office to answer a call. I was quite embarrassed as I went up to the office switchboard. It was Mother, and she wanted to talk about things. The girl on the switchboard knew what was afoot and pretended to be deaf. I'm afraid I was a bit short with her and told her we were not allowed to accept phone calls and not to ring again. The girl on the switchboard had a tear in her eye as I walked away.

Mother was 46 when she left and was a very attractive woman. Dad was 10 years older. We found out that she had moved in with a 26-year-old man and moved to St. Albans.

I decided to support Dad as much as I could. I never had any further contact with Mother; Anne stayed in contact with her and used to see her regularly, and I didn't have a problem with that. Girls always have a special bond with their mothers and it was nice to know Anne was keeping an eye on her. I decided then and there that I would never put my family through the heartache of a marriage break-up.

In Bedford there was a dance hall called the Court School of Dancing, and I used to go there some Friday or Saturday nights. At the start of the evening they would line everyone up and try to teach a dance step, then they would pair people up to practise, with the instructors going round and correcting where necessary. After this it turned into a normal dance with the boys encouraged to ask the girls to dance. Sometimes during the course of the evening there would be a break to learn another dance. Some of the really good dancers would help out with the teaching.

I started going out with a lovely girl called Marilyn, who was blonde, beautiful and an excellent dancer. My dancing improved no end!

There was a café that sold coffee and soft drinks, but no licensed bar, so there were no alcohol-related problems. This was a very good way to meet and interact with the opposite sex. However, at a lot of dances, all of the boys would be on one side of the room and the girls the other, and everyone too shy to dance.

There were several dance halls I used to go to on a Saturday night and my mates would sometimes be in awe as I would ask one of the prettiest girls in the room for a dance and then march round doing a waltz or a quickstep. Most of them would get plastered and then pluck up courage to ask a girl for the last few slow dances!

For my 17th birthday my Dad bought me a provisional driving licence and I started having driving lessons with the British School of Motoring. I failed two driving tests and then decided to go with Dad. I used to drive everywhere with either Dad or Tony (my brother-in-law) sitting with me. I went for another test but failed yet again; I could drive fine, but as soon as the examiner got into the car I went to pieces.

In the next test I thought I had screwed up when I got into the wrong lane at traffic lights. After that, convinced that I had failed yet again, I just drove without caring. I couldn't believe it when the examiner said I had passed!

I spent a few months in the polishing department at Fords. Most things were made in stainless steel or aluminium and had to be polished to either a mirror finish or sateen, which is the finish used on most stainless domestic appliances. I worked on most of the machines and became a fairly competent machinist before going on to fitting.

One of the chaps I worked with was into photography and I became interested too. My first camera was a Halina 35mm which I bought from a mail order club. I bought some processing equipment and started developing and printing my own photos. Fords had a camera club and we used to meet once a month; the company photographer used to give talks and there were competitions. Mr Geoffrey Ford, the managing director, was a keen photographer.

As I became more competent I sometimes used to accompany service engineers on visits, and sometimes if a director was visiting a client who required a demonstration I would go along to assemble and run the equipment. I went to work with a guy called Jock Lees, and we were building the Fords' KA presses, which had a cast stainless housing and were the top end of Ford bottle-capping presses. Whilst talking to Jock I found that it was he who had pulled my brother Terence out of the river in 1943. Apparently he and some of his mates were swimming in the river when someone told them a little boy had fallen in. They dived in to rescue him, but by the time they found him it was too late.

I learned a lot from Jock. He was very precise and everything had to be spot on. He was also very strict and would give me a dressing down at the slightest provocation. When he left I took over the building of the KA presses.

As I had a driving licence I used to be asked to sit with guys who had not passed their driving tests, and I was invited to quite a few good parties. On Saturday nights there was a dance at the Conservative club, and one of my mates asked me if I wanted to go to a party in Leighton Buzzard – there should be plenty of girls there I was told. That party was to change my whole life.

My mate Pete had an MG Magnette, quite a large saloon car, but had not passed his driving test, so I was in the car to make it legal. The party was in the back room of the White Horse pub in Linslade, and never ones to turn up empty-handed we took with us some crates of beer. Ann still remembers me walking in carrying a crate of beer with a fag in my mouth.

There were four of us from Bedford, Pete Lovell, Alan Brown, Steve Saunders and myself. There were a lot of girls and some Americans from the Chicksands base.

Pete came up to me with a girl in tow and said to her "Ann, this is Kevin, he's been dying to meet you all evening". I spent the rest of the evening with Ann, and I gave her my phone number, as there wasn't a phone at her house so I couldn't ring her. Ann rang me the following week and I arranged to pick her up the next Saturday, but when I arrived at her house she had already left for the party. I went to the party, only to find her with someone else! One of the Americans from the air base also fancied her. I won in the end, no contest really I was much better looking than the Yank!

I used to see Ann two or three times a week after that. I would borrow Dad's Austin A30, and could get to Ann's house in about 20 minutes from leaving home.

Ann's brother worked for SAH accessories, a company that modified sports cars to make them even quicker. They also sold new and used vehicles, and one day they had for sale an Austin

Healey Sprite which they had taken in part exchange. I managed to raise enough money for the deposit and did the deal, and I was so proud of my new car.

When I first drove the Sprite the engine started to overheat, so I took it back to SAH and the salesman said, "That will be all right, stick a tin of Radweld in the radiator". I did as he suggested and it did the trick. I came to realise that the engine was well worn. Although the car performed well enough I realised that it needed quite a lot of work on the engine.

When I came to the end of my apprenticeship I moved into the Development Department. There were three of us in the department, Tom, who had an artificial leg, Brian and me. Our job was to work with the designers and draughtsmen making prototype machines and testing different sealing methods for food containers. Fords were the forerunners in the heat sealing of plastic yogurt pots.

A lot of the dairies had problems with bottle cleanliness. The bottles all went through a washing plant and were then visually inspected. The problem was that quite a few bottles were missed and ended up on the doorstep with a problem, and the dairies were having a lot of complaints. Everything from paint to plastic toys was ending up going through the system, so Fords developed a 'dirty bottle detector'.

The chief electronics engineer, Geoff Sainsbury, was into judo, so we had something in common. He used to train at the AJA club and invited me to go and train with them. Peta was there, my pal from the BJA club, and for a time I trained at both clubs. I was asked if I would join their team for a competition in Cambridge; I was a bit reluctant but was persuaded to go. I don't think their team leader liked me and he was a bit abrupt with me. When it was my turn to go on the mat my opponent was quite cocky and overconfident. When the referee said 'hajime' ('start'), I went in and my opponent didn't know what hit him. I won the contest, and had two more, winning both. After this the team leader suddenly became very matey!

CHAPTER FOUR

Going away to sea

About this time I decided to rebuild the engine of my car. There was an area in the development workshop that had lifting equipment and as long as I worked at weekends and in my own time I was allowed to use this space. The access to the engine was quite good and I soon had the complete engine unbolted and lifted out of the car. I then stripped the engine down, and the head went for grinding and the cylinder block went to be re-bored. I decided to have the block bored out 20 thou oversize and I bought oversize pistons to fit. Luckily I could get this work done at Fords, but the crankshaft had to be ground elsewhere.

At last everything was ready for reassembly. The head was rebuilt with new valve guides and springs, and the oversize pistons and reground crankshaft with new bearings fitted. The engine was now ready to go back into the car. When I fitted the engine back into the car it needed a shaft turning up to line up the clutch in the bell housing with the end of the crankshaft. This was quite easy to do and I soon had it all put back together. One of the fitters was quite good at tuning up engines with SU-type carburettors and I soon had the car back on the road.

I became quite involved with the electronics boffins on the DBD and learned quite a bit about the optics and electronics involved. The machine scanned the bottom and sides of the bottle and would automatically eject any bottle that had imperfections. When the prototype machine was ready to go into a dairy for trials, Fords had arranged to install the machine in Express Dairies in London. We had to make special legs which would enable the machine to be jacked up to go over the bottling line and be set up in position before the filling machine. There was a large team comprising electronics engineers, designers and technicians involved in the installation of the machine and we had to work through the night so as not to disrupt production.

At last the machine was ready. The problem was that it was so efficient it rejected far too many bottles and wouldn't allow any blemish through no matter how small. I suppose this was a good problem to have in a way, but it was quite difficult to desensitize the scanning mechanism. However the machine was a great success and was installed in several dairies.

I had a very good lifestyle – a doting girlfriend, a good job which paid very well and a nice car – but always a dreamer, I wanted something more. One of the chaps that worked at Fords had been to sea as an Engineer Officer and used to tell of trips to exotic places. Apparently there was a shortage of engineers in the Merchant Navy and if you were a time-served engineer you could get in as an engineer officer.

I went up to London and managed to get an interview with Furness Ship Management in Leadenhall Street. I knew I had done well in the interview and the letter confirming my appointment came a few days later. All I had to do now was tell everyone! When I told Ann she took it very well and promised to wait for me. Dad was sad that I was leaving but proud of me for joining up. Everyone else seemed surprised but pleased for me. I had never been out of the country before, so for me it was a great adventure.

A telegram arrived telling me to join the RMS *Amazon* in London, lying in King George V Dock. So I said my goodbyes. I remember going over to see my sister Anne; her two sons Ian and Michael were fast asleep tucked up in bed. I was setting off on this great adventure and felt quite sad to be leaving.

When I went over to see my girlfriend Ann with the news, I had mixed emotions – partly excitement, part sadness at leaving Ann and slight apprehension, wondering what I had let myself in for. When I arrived at Ann's house she had been working in the temporary dark room that we had set up in the cupboard under the stairs in her parents' house. I had given her all of my photographic equipment as I was going to be away at sea possibly for long periods.

We had a tearful farewell and the next morning Dad took me to the railway station. I had directions for the Underground and had to get off at Aldgate East tube station. I arrived at the docks and was directed to Amazon. As I walked out of the dock sheds I thought it was foggy and then I realised that the wall of white in front of me was the side of this enormous ship!

I walked up the gangway and was directed to the chief engineer. The engineers' cabins were all on the boat deck. My cabin was quite adequate. It had a bunk, a day bed, desk and wardrobe and small washbasin. There was a porthole so the cabin was light, but as the ship was air conditioned this had to be kept closed.

The representative from the uniform suppliers came on board. I already had my basic uniform, but as the ship carried passengers I needed mess kit. The whites for the tropics were called 'No 10s' and comprised a white jacket, trousers and shoes. The mess kit was a short white jacket, white shirt, black bow tie, black trousers and black shoes. I was a bit green and I think the guy sold me a lot of things I didn't really need, but I did look good in uniform, even if I say it myself!

Amazon was 20,000 tons and there were three similar ships in the fleet. The other two, the Aragon and Arlanza, were referred to as the "A" boats, and were all diesel powered. There was one other, a steamship called the Andes. Amazon was a cargo/passenger ship that carried about 500 passengers and 5000 tons of frozen meat, mainly beef from South America.

Before we set sail there was "boat drill", when we all had to don lifejackets and go to designated boat stations all dressed up in our uniforms. The ship was equipped with davits which were designed to lower the lifeboats level. I thought the design was quite good. it meant that more or less anyone could lower the boats without them tipping up.

I didn't know my way around the ship, which was so big it was easy to get lost, so I made sure that I stayed with my group.

In the mornings I thought there were women in the alleyways from the sound of the footsteps. I queried this with one of the other engineers and he said "No, it's the alleyway stewards, they're all queers".

We were bound for South America, calling at Santos, Brazil, Montevideo, Uruguay and Buenos Aires, Argentina. We also had a few ports of call on the way, first Boulogne and then Vigo in Spain. There were three classes on board, First class,

Cabin Class and Tourist. Being an officer, I was allowed to socialize in all three areas. We ate in the Cabin Class dining room and the food and service was excellent, although I think some of the stewards resented serving us.

When we set sail, although it was a fairly large ship, the motion made me feel a bit queasy. I remember lying in my bunk with the sound of the engines and with the motion of the ship waiting to be called for my watch. I was on the 12 to 4 watch, and there wasn't a lot to do. It was my job to do the engine room log. This consisted of checking literally hundreds of thermometers and recording the temperatures in the log book.

There were three officers to each watch, a senior a middle man and a junior, plus two 'donkey men', who looked after the boilers and kept the engine room clean. Halfway through the watch the donkey man would bring a jug of coffee and some food, which could be anything; quite often it would be chicken legs. It all depended what he could forage and what was on the dinner menu the night before. I couldn't eat a thing for the first few nights, but the others all tucked in with gusto!

At the aft end of the boat deck was the officers' smoke room, where we used to go for pre-dinner drinks. It had glass doors and windows that looked out over the stern of the ship. We could invite guests but they were not allowed to buy drinks. There was a veranda, and it was quite pleasant having a drink looking over the aft end of the ship with the creamy wake stretching out into the distance.

In the engine room there was a workshop which had a lathe, milling machine, pillar drill and various other engineering kit. On my watch we had the Inter 2nd engineer, 4th engineer and me as 4th junior engineer. Being on the 12 to 4 watch was quite good. I could go to dinner and then to whichever lounge had entertainment. We were allowed to buy drinks at the bar in Tourist or Cabin Class, but in First we weren't allowed to go to the bar but had to be served by a steward.

I was always fairly popular because I wasn't afraid to get up and dance, which the lady passengers appreciated; a lot of the officers would just sit there and watch. But it was very tiring, going on watch at 12 o'clock until 4 am after socializing all evening. I came to realise that I needed to get at least some sleep before going on watch and found that as long as I had about 20 minutes' kip before the watch, that was enough to get me through.

On one watch Mack, the Inter 2nd, was working on the lathe attempting to make a new shaft for the bypass valve. He obviously didn't have much idea when it came to turning as the bar was sticking out of the chuck far too far. I tried to advise him, but he shouted that he knew what he was doing and could get a job anywhere as a turner! Eventually, after scrapping several pieces of bronze bar, he sheepishly asked if I could do it. The shaft was about 12 inches (300mm) long with a button on the end to locate into the gate valve, and it was turned down to various diameters along its length, with a threaded section. There were no dies to cut the thread so it had to be screw-cut on the lathe. This involved synchronizing the saddle of the lathe with the chuck so that as the chuck turned the saddle moved along, with the tool cutting the thread. With the lathe was a set of gears called change wheels which had to be changed to set the speed of travel of the tool to cut the thread. I remembered the calculation from my college days: 'drivers over driven', which roughly means the number of teeth on the lathe spindle is divided by the number of teeth on the motor spindle, which should work out to the number of threads per inch.

As the shaft needed to extend quite a way out of the chuck it needed to be supported by a "centre" in the tailstock of the lathe. There were several centres with the lathe tools but no centre drills for the shaft. The angle needed for end of the shaft for the centre was 90 degrees. All of the drills on board were ground for drilling metal and should have had an angle of 118 degrees. Over the years most of them had been re sharpened and were all shapes and sizes, however I needed a 90-degree drill so had to grind one up myself by hand.

It took most of the watch to make the shaft. Although the workshop was reasonably well- equipped, most of the kit had been abused or could not be found without searching for ages. Several of the watch came to see the new shaft taking shape, and I got the impression that they had never seen a turner in action before. When I'd finished I gave the new shaft to Mack, and he took it away.

During the morning watch I went back to my cabin to pick up something and as I was walking down the passageway I saw the Chief Engineer walking towards me with the new shaft in his hand. I thought he was going to compliment me on a job well done, but he said "Kevin, when you go back down into the engine room, could you fit this new shaft into the bypass valve, Mack made it during last night's watch." I found it difficult to say nothing!

My first run ashore was Vigo in northern Spain. I had never been abroad before and as I wandered around with some of the other lads listening to the Spanish music coming from the bars and cafés I thought life couldn't get much better.

We left Spain heading for the Canaries to take on bunkers (filling fuel tanks) as fuel oil was tax free there. However we only fuelled up at the fuel terminal and didn't have a chance to go ashore. Next stop Santos, Brazil!

Once under way we relaxed into a certain rhythm, or so it seemed, being called for watch about 15 minutes early, doing the watch and then having a few beers after. We were all writing home, and looked forward to getting our mail when we docked at the various ports of call.

On each ship there was a purser's office. Their job was to sort out money issues and deal with the incoming and outgoing mail. On large ships such as *Amazon* this was quite a large operation with the department, almost like having a bank on board. I fell out with the clerk (purser) who dealt with the engineers' affairs. I wondered why I had not received any mail from the last port of call. Ann wrote to me often and I usually had a lot of mail from her, my dad or sister or granddad, or anyone else I was writing to. I felt a bit abandoned – you can't imagine how important mail is when you are away from home.

One night there was a get-together in one of our cabins. The Chief Engineer was there and the engineers' purser. I couldn't understand his smug, sneering attitude as he cosied up to the chief. Suddenly the chief went apoplectic. It turned out that the purser had been holding back my mail, thinking it was hilariously funny! I was then given all my mail and discovered that Ann did love me after all.

The trip down to Santos was for me a great experience. When you get into the routine of watches and free time you don't want it to end. You make friends and build relationships and although you can't wait to arrive you almost don't want to, because that part of your life will have passed.

The ship had four large generators and there were usually two running, one spare and one being serviced. The main engine propulsion was two enormous heavy oil engines. The fuel oil had to be heated up to about 90c and it was quite important to keep the temperature about right. The six cylinders were about 1 metre diameter, and spare piston rings and bearings were stored on board. Sometimes a liner would crack or develop a leak. If this happened, it was necessary to shut down that particular cylinder so the engine would run on five remaining cylinders. On arrival in Santos a team would come on board from a company that repaired the cracked liners. There was quite a bit of stripping down of the main engines and maintenance to do.

At sea we had to rebuild the generators after so many hours of running. The generators were like enormous car engines, each cylinder about 300mm diameter. The generators had six cylinders and each cylinder had its own head, which was solid cast iron and weighed about 200kg. The head had to be unbolted and craned off and the valves ground in. The piston would be removed and if necessary new piston rings fitted. The bearings were white metal and had to be hand-scraped to fit the crankshaft. This involved smearing blue onto the crankshaft journal offering up the bearing and hand-scraping the high spots until the bearing fitted snugly, which often took some time to achieve. Sometimes it was necessary to change a liner. These had to be craned out of the engine and it was quite a job!

Rio de Janeiro came after Santos. I loved the scenery. The city was stunning and Copacabana beach was breathtaking. Drinks were very expensive, so we tended to drink on board.

When we arrived in Buenos Aires we were there for about 10 days going to different Frigorificos to load meat. We adopted a different watch system to allow more time for sightseeing. Some of us did 12 hours on and 24 off, which gave us lots of shore time. A few of the officers had regular girlfriends who they used to meet up with and bring on board to canoodle in their cabins.

The main street we all headed for was called the Venticinco de Mayo (25th May) and this was where all the bars and flesh pots were. In one bar the old lady that ran it used to have a dice game going. If you won you got a drink, and if she won you gave her the price of a drink. She didn't lose very often!

I tried to learn some Spanish and managed to get around and order drinks in the bars, but a lot of the bar staff could understand the Spanglish of ships' crews.

The main engines and generators were started with compressed air. There were two large compressors and massive compressed air tanks, which had to be serviced regularly. This mainly consisted of rebuilding the compressor valves. On board there were spares for just about everything including compressor valves. The problem with the ones I had to fit was that the threads were not cut deep enough and they wouldn't screw in. There was nothing for it but for me to screw-cut the valve bodies again. This was not as easy as the shaft for the bypass valve, as the tool needed to be retracted manually just before the thread ended. Once again I had an audience as I recut the valve threads.

I enjoyed my two trips on Amazon. I was the new boy and the piss-taking was merciless, but I held my own and gained respect because I was good at things nobody else could do. I learned as I went along, and although the engineering I had been trained in was more precision than heavy I enjoyed the different environment and took to it.

When I first told Ann I was going to sea she said she would wait for me. Looking back I wonder what everyone thought. I had already got the job and was going to sea before I announced it to anyone. It must have come as a shock to Ann, as well as my dad, granddad and sister. All my friends must have thought it a bit odd that suddenly I was going off into the sunset.

One of the reasons/excuses I gave was that I wanted to save up to get married. The problem on Amazon was that the socializing used up all my income and I couldn't save much money, so I decided to leave the A boats and transfer to cargo ships. On board uniforms were worn most of the time, and for the engine room watch we wore a white boiler suit. I was proud

KEVIN COONEY

of the fact that I was qualified to wear the Merchant Navy officers' uniform.

After each trip you had about two weeks' leave. One day, as a surprise, I walked into the bank where Ann worked unannounced, in full uniform. The surprise on the faces of her colleagues was something to see. The bank manager invited us both into his office for a chat. I think Ann was very proud, and it raised her profile no end. I think everyone realised that we were a serious proposition.

When I moved on to cargo ships I arranged a standing order at the bank to transfer most of my salary into a savings account. I still had enough to do what I wanted or needed to do with the limited socializing available. The Chief Engineer was quite miffed that I wanted to leave the A boats, as I had proved to be a good team player and had become competent at the work necessary to keep the engines running, and was often in demand on the social evenings because I liked to dance.

I remember my first Christmas away on Amazon, which was also my first Christmas away from home. I wondered what everyone at home was doing. I felt so homesick. There was a special meal and all the senior officers were decked out in their best uniforms with medals they'd won for serving on convoys during the war (special small ones for their dress uniforms). They went round to the different tables wishing everyone Merry Christmas. Everyone ended up in the Cabin Class Lounge, where there was a disco belting it out and everyone was having a great time. Most times around 11 pm the party would finish, but as it was Christmas the party
was still in full swing when the Captain walked in to close it down. The record being played was Yellow Submarine. Everyone started singing 'We all live in a White Amazon, a White Amazon, a White Amazon' and the captain's stern expression eased into a smile. Suddenly the third officer

shouted "Three cheers for the captain!" and the cheers rang out. The captain smiled, gave a stiff little bow, turned around and walked out! The party carried on.

Crossing the line (the Equator) for the first time for me was a bit of a non-event. For the passengers one of the crew dressed up as King Neptune and there was a ceremony involving a lot of larking about and ducking in the swimming pool. "King Neptune" was a deckhand with shoulder-length hair and a long beard nicknamed "Jesus" due to his appearance. With his crown, robes and trident he really looked the part.

Shipboard life was like life in general – with some of the people you had friendly relations and with some you didn't. One of the watch leaders couldn't stand me. Luckily I was never on his watch. It all stemmed from the fact that he really fancied one of the female passengers. She worked as a model for an Argentinian model agency and was stunningly beautiful. She took a shine to me and came as my guest to the officers' smoke room on a couple of occasions. We used to dance together and became friendly, but not I may add romantically involved. It really used to piss him off, as he was chasing after her and getting nowhere whilst I, the new boy, seemed to be succeeding without trying. After a time we started playing on this. I liked her and she knew that I was engaged, so we had a good relationship. In a way I protected her from unwanted attention due to my close friendship with her.

I will always remember my two trips in Amazon. I learned so much. about how life really is. It is what you make it!

CHAPTER FIVE

Across the Atlantic

The *Albany* was my next ship. She was one of the "Y" class – there were three in the fleet and it was said that *Albany* was the happiest ship in the fleet. When I joined her she was in Pembroke docks, which at that time was full of ships. I stopped one of the dockers and asked if he knew where *Albany* was lying and he said, "she's the one down the end, you can't miss her, she's the one that's on fire!"

Albany had just returned from a trip to Mexico with a cargo of sulphur and had a fire in one of the holds. Luckily the local fire brigade soon had it under control.

The first trip on *Albany* was over to the Caribbean, through the Panama Canal, down the west coast of South America, through the Magellan Straits, then up the east coast of South

America and then home. All in all, about four months. The cargo we were collecting was fishmeal, which was used as fertiliser.

On *Albany* there was a really good atmosphere. We had two alleyway stewards who were West Indian. The deck officers' steward was Smithy, a larger-than-life character who was always singing. Many was the morning when I was woken up by the sound of Smithy doing a Tom Jones.

The engineers' steward was Eastman, a much quieter man, also West Indian. The chief cook was a Mr Brown, a very dignified West Indian with a droll and wicked sense of humour.

At this time in the UK there was a health scare regarding parrots' disease and all crews were ordered not to bring parrots back from South America – quite a few were brought back by returning sailors.

The captain's clerk (purser) and the chief steward were into photography, so I had something in common and got on well with them. The captain's clerk was into telephoto lenses and was always being ribbed about this. One day I said to him, "I reckon your long lens must be a phallic symbol". He replied, "don't you mean a facsimile?"

I was on watch with the 4th engineer, who was responsible for the refrigeration plant. *Albany* carried some frozen cargo, though only a small amount compared to Amazon. The "fridge flat" was down aft, at the stern of the ship, and during the watch I had to go aft across the open deck to do the log. Quite often the decks would be awash with the ship rolling quite violently. There was a lifeline rigged down the deck with safety lines attached which you held on to to stop yourself being washed overboard. It was quite stimulating sometimes, and quite exciting.

The Captain and Chief Engineer ware heavy drinkers, and every night before dinner they would have a few in one of their cabins. When they rolled down the alleyway with their beaming red faces to the saloon for dinner, it wasn't the rolling of the ship that made them unsteady on their feet. We would meet up in one of our cabins and drink rum and orange. The rum was Appleton's Estate, at 10 shillings a bottle (50p). I remember sitting in the cabin looking out of the porthole. One minute all I could see was sea and the next minute all I could see was sky as the ship rolled along, with the fumes of the rum in my nose. I was getting greener by the minute.

The plumber poked his head round the door and said "Have you been eating corned beef and peas?"

"Why?" I asked.

"Someone has" he replied, "they've just puked it up in the alleyway".

That finished me off. I couldn't get to the heads quick enough and only just made it. But I did get used to the motion of the ship after a few days, and used to quite enjoy it when the sea was rough.

We called into the Azores, outward bound for bunkers (filling fuel tanks), but did not go ashore. The next port of call was Hamilton, Bermuda. We were there for about a week. Bermuda was very British and we used to go to the Hog Penny Pub, which was very English with a dartboard and English beer. As Bermuda was in the middle of the Atlantic quite a few interesting characters seemed to have congregated there.

The Hog Penny was always full of interesting people. One guy, John Riding, had sailed all the way from France to Bermuda in a 12ft sloop on his way to the USA. The boat was called the *Sea Egg* and it did look a bit like an egg. John sailed all the way to New York and wrote a book detailing his exploits called *The Voyage of the Sea Egg*, which was published in 1968.

We left Bermuda and headed for Nassau in the Bahamas. It was very expensive in Nassau, and beer was about four times more expensive than Bermuda. If you went into a bar and sat down, you were charged for the seat. It seemed that everything was geared up to extort as much money as possible. Nassau was very American, whereas Bermuda was British.

It was beautiful weather and several of us would go to the beaches. When off watch we tended to drink on board and there were some girls who came on board who knew some of the other officers. Some of them had done this trip several times and got to know some local girls. I chatted one up called Diane, and we decided to go ashore. She knew a good bar where the locals went and she said she would give me a lift on her scooter, which was a bit like the Lambrettas that were popular in the UK around that time. We parked the scooter and walked to the bar; there were a lot of young people there and they were interested in me and the stories I had to tell. I was made very welcome and was bought a lot of drinks.

We left the bar and were walking down the street when we were confronted by two black youths demanding money. I told them to f*** off, but they became more aggressive and snatched Diane's handbag. I waded in, trying to be a hero, and landed a few blows on our assailants, but then one of them struck me a violent blow on the head with a blunt instrument, which slowed me down somewhat. I fell to the ground and Diane was screaming "leave him alone" and they ran off, but with her handbag.

I went to the police station to report the mugging and two plain-clothes officers drove me around in a police car to see if I could identify the attackers, but to no avail. Diane had 20 dollars in her handbag, so I gave her 20 dollars the next time I saw her.

We left Nassau and headed south for Baranquilla, Columbia where we off-loaded cargo and stayed for a couple of days before heading for the Panama Canal. As we transited the southern coast of Cuba, we were buzzed by American military aircraft. It was only a short time after the Cuban Missile Crisis and the Americans were still very suspicious of ships in this vicinity.

We arrived at Colon at the Atlantic/Caribbean end of the canal. The canal was owned and run by America at that time. Ashore it was a bit wild. All of the bars had lots of girls and as soon as anyone walked in they would be accosted by them. It was 9 dollars for a bottle of beer and a 'short time' with one of the girls, and if the girl liked the look of you it was possible to knock the price down. One guy managed to get it for 5 dollars! The exchange rate at that time was 3 dollars to the pound.

The Panama Canal bisects the isthmus of Panama between the Atlantic Ocean and the Pacific. It is about 51 miles (75km) long. It was completed by America in August 1914, having taken 34 years to build and cost the US 350 million dollars. It is estimated that over 30,000 people died during its construction. It stretches from Colon at the Atlantic end to Panama City at the Pacific end. There are three sets of locks, and small but powerful locomotives escort and tow the ships through them. Going through the locks the engine room was on standby, which meant we were on duty for two hours before the start of the watch and two hours after. Depending on the situation, the time in the engine room could be up to eight hours, although standbys rarely lasted that long.

Once through the canal we made for Guayquil in Ecuador, which was very hot and humid. We were provided with a night watchman and food was left out for him in the mess room next to the engine room, where there was a small electric cooker. The watchmen didn't have a clue when it came to cooking. They would just throw everything into a frying pan and mix it all up together so that it looked a disgusting mess, and then eat it out of the frying pan.

Next stop was Trujillo, Peru, known internationally as the 'city of eternal spring', due to its temperate climate. The temperature is around 19c all year round. The city was quite a change from some of the ports we visited, with a large beach that we used to visit for swimming.

From Trujillo we sailed down to Calleo, the port for Lima. I had hoped to visit Lima and go to a bullfight, but none of the other lads wanted to go and the public transport seemed a bit of a nightmare as I could only speak a smattering of Spanish. The bars in Calleo were very similar to other South American bars with the girls and cheap rum.

One night we found our way to a "night club", which had a solid door with a flap in the top. When the door was knocked the flap would open and the bouncer would weigh you up and ask a few questions. He then told us that inside everyone paid the same for the drinks and the girls. There were all walks of life there, including professional people, doctors etc. Any trouble and you would be thrown out.

There were a couple of other ships' officers in there and they had girls with them. The price for the girls worked out to about £4.50, far too expensive, and the drinks were £2. At home at that time a pint of beer cost, as I remember, less than two shillings (10p). I would buy one drink and make it last all evening in the club, but mostly I would go to a different bar. The girls in this place were quite classy compared to the usual bar girls. The two officers that were with these girls became quite attached and would meet up with them in the afternoons to go to the beach.

The night we were due to leave there were a few of us in the club and the girls were quite tearful saying goodbye. The guys that had befriended two of the girls were professing undying love, and it was almost embarrassing knowing that they would never see them again.

After the lush green landscapes of Ecuador and Peru the Chilean coast was quite featureless, with mile after mile of desert. Our first port of call in Chile was Arica, which at that time seemed to be a town in the middle of a desert. There was not much to do or see and we looked forward to the next port, Antofagasta. The third engineers' pet name for this port was Owtofukfaster!

There were a lot of bars around the dock area and it was generally "a good run ashore". In the bars there were the usual bar girls and music to get the party going. In one of the bars, as well as the girls there were some that didn't look quite right. One of the engineers, Paddy, got quite friendly with one of them and decided to go with her. I said "Are you sure she's a girl?" and he said "I don't care, it's near enough for me"!

When he came back I said "how did you get on?" He said "not very well, it was a bloke and he just wanted to stick his dick up my arse!"

By this time several of the crew had obtained pet parrots, but the captain announced that this was not allowed and they had to be got rid of.

Once a week we had captain's inspection, when the captain would go round the ship and among other things check that cabins were being kept tidy. On inspection day whilst doing the engine room log I noticed some strange noises coming from the back of the engine, so I went to investigate and discovered that the area had nine cages hanging up and the noise was the parrots. The engine area was full of parrots in cages! As soon as inspection was finished the parrots were all returned to their owners' cabins

There were several small ports on the way down to Valparaiso, just a small harbour and a few houses surrounded by desert. The area seemed so desolate with animal skulls lying around, all bleached white by the sun. Valparaiso is the second largest city in Chile, but seamen tend to stay around the dock areas.

There were the usual bars around the docks. One night the third mate suggested that we should go to a particular bar. When we arrived the bar tender said, "we have one of your officers here already". He told us which room, and the second mate and I went to look. When we looked into the room, there was his boss in bed with a young girl. We went back to the main bar and suddenly as we sat there the doors burst open and the whole crew came dancing into the bar doing the conga. As they went round other people joined on the tail end of the column. They went round the bar singing at the tops of their voices, blind drunk but loving every minute of it! I have a lot of happy memories about the trip, and that has to be one of them.

The next port of call was Talcahauno, which was the home of quite a large fishing fleet. We did not go alongside and anchored off. To go ashore the local boatmen would take us in long clinker-built rowing skiffs. There wasn't a dock as such, so we had to swing ashore on a long rope. This was fine when going ashore sober, but it was a bit interesting when you were returning a little worse for wear. The boatmen would sleep in their boats waiting for us to return.

We carried on south until we reached the Magellan Straits. The deck officers were keeping a wary eye out for ice, and the engine room was on standby. We were a long way south and just north of the Antarctic Circle. We docked in Punta Arenas, which as well as a commercial port is a Chilean naval base. Several of us took our cameras ashore, but we suddenly found ourselves surrounded by armed naval personnel who thought we were spies. We were taken to the guardroom and interviewed by a lieutenant of the Chilean Navy. Speaking perfect English, he explained that we must not take pictures around the naval base. His name was George and we all got on well with him. He came on board for dinner one night and invited some of the deck officers back to his ship for dinner.

I found the Chilean people that I came into contact with to be charming. Quite a few spoke some English and they were very helpful. In one bar in Punta the owner spoke about 10 languages; learning and speaking languages was his hobby. When we arrived he had a most peculiar accent, but by the time we left he was speaking and swearing fluently!

To the south of the Magellan Straits is the island of Tierra del Fuego (Island of Fire). It got its name from the many campfires of the Yanama tribesmen who inhabited the island, which were visible to ships passing through the Straits. Magellan, who discovered the island in 1520, was convinced that the many fires were made by the natives lying in wait ready to ambush them! The capital city is Ushuaia, the southernmost city in the world.

At last it was time to leave Chile and head back north towards Europe and home.

CHAPTER SIX

Coasting

From the tip of South America back up to England is many thousands of miles, and it took a few weeks. But it was good getting back into the seagoing routine again as we plodded through the Southern Ocean, the "Roaring Forties" and the Horse Latitudes, eventually arriving in London in early June.

Customs came on board and cleared everyone in. I had some boxes of cigars that I didn't declare. It was customary when leaving a ship to wait for a relief complement of officers to take over. We would then get taxis, with four officers to each taxi. We would each give the taxi driver five shillings together with our dock pass, which he would then give to the copper on the dock gate. This worked out to £2 per taxi. It ensured that we would go straight through and not have our bags searched.

My relief was late arriving, so when I left the ship there were no taxis. I struggled to the dock gates laden with bags, along with an oil painting I had bought from an artist in Calleo, to try to find a taxi, only to be pounced on by the dock police. They searched my bag and found the boxes of cigars I was taking home for Dad. I was marched off to customs and they fined me £9 and confiscated the cigars.

I then found a taxi. I told the taxi driver what had happened and pointed out the copper that had searched my bag, he said "You should have given him some money, he always lets us through if we give him some cash!' The problem of course is that if you try to bribe the wrong one you could end up in even more trouble.

I eventually arrived back at Bedford railway station, rang Dad and he and Ann picked me up at the station. The leave seemed to fly past and he last few days waiting for the telegram with joining instructions were filled with apprehension. Although it was wonderful being home I looked forward to going back to sea.

The leave lasted for nearly three weeks, and then it was summer. When I rejoined *Albany* we were informed that we were going to Africa on a French charter. There was a French "supercargo" on board who was bringing his wife. The wife was a very attractive lady and I wondered how she felt being the only woman on a ship with 45 men.

Numerous cases of wine came on board; this was the Supercargo's private stock and every night at dinner he provided wine for the Captain's table.

Our first port of call was Dunkirk, and it was interesting to visit the infamous beaches and war grave cemeteries. It was June and the weather was beautiful, so we went to the beach most days.

Next port was Le Havre and the beach there was stony and

not as pleasant as Dunkirk. Some girls came aboard advertising the local bars and knocking shops, which would never be allowed in British ports, but the French seemed to have a much more relaxed attitude to such things. We did not see much of Supercargo or his wife except at dinner – they tended to keep themselves to themselves.

La Pallice was next, a good run ashore with a beautiful beach with lots of bikini-clad girls playing volleyball. After picking up cargo at La Pallice/La Rochelle we cleared Biscay and northern Spain, heading down the Portuguese coast towards the Straits of Gibraltar and the Mediterranean. It was quite misty in the Straits but I managed to see Gib through the mist as we sailed past. It was uneventful as we sailed along the Spanish coast and then up to Marseille.

It was quite strange in Marseille. The Mediterranean French dialect seemed quite different from the French we had learned in northern France and even simple phrases like 'short time', 'all night' and 'how much' needed to be relearned!

After leaving Marseille we headed out of the Med and back through the Straits and then south down the African coast, round the Cape of Good Hope and up to Beira, Mozambique. I was amazed at the poverty and living conditions of the black people there. They had absolutely nothing and the men working on the ships wore just a loin cloth or a pair of shorts. A notice was posted on the alleyway notice board saying that it was not allowed to strike or abuse the men working on the ships. In the bars there were the usual bar girls, all colours, shapes and sizes, and most of the black girls wore wigs which they used to take off and hang on the bed post. It cost just £1 for a short time or £1. 50 for all night!

There was a naval blockade operating at the time, and a British destroyer was patrolling offshore to enforce an embargo on Rhodesia (now Zimbabwe), whose Premier, Ian Smith, had declared UDI (Unilateral Declaration of Independence). I met up with a party of naval officers in a bar and we went on to a night club, where the floor show was a scantily-dressed woman dancing with a python entwined around her body. I ended up dancing with them and to the cheers of my new buddies became part of the floor show. Although there was an embargo on Rhodesian goods, we were loading tons of Rhodesian copper in long cigar-shaped ingots.

After Beira we headed for Dar es Salaam In Tanzania. The people here seemed a lot better off. There were the usual bars, but the place to go was the disco on the top floor of the Kilimanjaro hotel.

After Dar es Salaam we headed for Zanzibar, where we anchored offshore. We were not allowed to go ashore, but there were "bum boats" coming alongside selling just about everything. The harbour was absolutely teeming with fish and fishing became a popular pastime. At night there was a lamp shining into the water and it was possible to put silver paper on the hooks and pull the fish out of the water as soon as the hooks were thrown in. They were mostly mackerel, and the cooks took them to serve up for breakfast.

One chap caught an enormous sucker fish. It had a large suction pad on the back of its head and he had great fun swinging it by the tail, whacking it against the bulkhead and sticking it there. I bought a fishing rod off one of the bum boats – it cost me £7, which was a lot to spend. It was a two-part rod made of split cane and very nice.

The third engineer was a keen fisherman and liked to rubbish everyone else's equipment. He would be out there with his really nice equipment and not catch much at all. One night I caught an enormous eel, which was about two metres long and had a large mouth with razor-sharp teeth. While I was attempting to get the hook out of its mouth it grabbed my shoe and the teeth bit right through the leather. Luckily I was able to kick the shoe off in time! The third was so jealous of my success he kept muttering that he couldn't stand "schooner rigged" fishermen.

Mombasa came next, and it seemed a lot more civilised than the other places we visited in East Africa. We were docked in Kilindini harbour, which is Kenya's only large seaport. Mombasa is a major trade centre and was the centre of the ivory trade in the 19th and early 20th century. You could still buy ivory figurines in the shops, but they were very expensive.

During our watches there was quite a lot maintenance to do. On one occasion I was working on the main engine and needed to remove an inspection hatch on the water jacket. One of the bolts was very stiff, and I needed to use a spanner to undo it all the way. Suddenly it became loose and the hatch fell from the engine, landing on my big toe. The pain was unbelievable and the toe swelled up to twice its normal size. I had difficulty walking for over a week!

It was soon time to head back south round the Cape of Good Hope and then north up the west coast of Africa and home. On the way home the Supercargo provided wine to have with dinner most nights as he wanted to use it up before returning to France.

After several stops in the Mediterranean we headed back to England. It was a funny feeling heading back to what most people considered normal, with no more bar girls (or so I thought) and the English winter to look forward to.

Several of us had 'channels' for the last few days, a purely psychological condition where you can't sleep no matter how tired or drunk you are. I spent hours wandering around the deck with my brain in overdrive.

We docked in Swansea on 3rd November and were there unloading cargo for four days. We left on the 7th and made our way round to Hull, paying off on the 13th. I had decided to move on from *Albany*, and during the leave I waited for the telegram telling me which ship would be next.

There was a rumour that one of the company ships, *Deseado*, a cargo passenger ship of 10,000 tons, was going to Vietnam. At this time the war was in full swing and the company was offering double wages whilst the vessel was in Vietnamese territorial waters. I went to the company's office in Leadenhall Street and volunteered for the trip, thinking of the extra cash and adventure. Unfortunately they already had a crew and the ship was due to leave imminently. I was told that I would probably be sailing on *Ebro* after some coasting trips on other ships.

My leave seemed to flash past. Most of the wedding arrangements were in hand and it was good to catch up with friends and family. My wedding to Ann was arranged for September 14th 1968, so I hoped for short trips up until that time.

The telegram, when it came, ordered me to report on *Amazon* for a trip 'coasting' – travelling round the coast loading and unloading cargo. It seemed a bit strange to be going back on an "A" boat again. There was largely the same crowd on board and there was the usual banter, but when I told them of my trips down the Chilean coast and to Africa they seemed quite envious.

A new crew came on board for the trip around the coast and the 2nd Engineer, as he was new to A boats, had me as his no. 2, which was perhaps a promotion. There was a foot and mouth disease epidemic and all imports from Argentina were banned. We took the ship over to Boulogne in France for a couple of days, came back and then unloaded our 5000 tons of Argentine beef!

When I left *Amazon* on 2nd December I was looking forward

to Christmas and seeing the whole family. Ann and I had been looking at houses to buy. The houses in Bedford were very expensive and we thought we would probably get a nicer one for less money if we looked in Rushden, which was only about 15 miles away, up the A6. One of Dad's colleagues had a son, a policeman, who lived in Rushden and was thinking of moving. Dad, Ann and I went to view the house. It was quite nice, had three small bedrooms and was on a fairly new estate. The asking price was £2950, which I thought was a bit high. I offered £2850 and the vendor accepted. Ann and I thought we had a good deal, and excitedly started making plans.

A couple of days later I had a message to say that the vendor had changed his mind and wanted the asking price. we were so disappointed. The house was probably worth it, but on principle I decided against it. We then started looking at plans for new houses, and eventually decided on a new build that was due to be finished, we hoped, before we were married.

When we went to view the site with the estate agent, there was only the road and the concrete foundations completed. I asked the agent if the rectangle of concrete was for the garage, but he informed me that no, it was the house. It looked so small.

The telegram when it came ordered me to report to *Ebro* for a coasting trip. *Ebro* was a larger version of *Albany* and carried general cargo and some frozen She was lying in Liverpool. The 2nd engineer was probably one of the nicest I sailed with, and the crew were a good crowd. I got on well with Wally, one of the other engineers, and we quite often went for a drink. A lot of the ports were quite dead in the evenings with the docks quite a way from any lively pubs. When we docked in Middlesbrough the good pubs were a fair distance from the ship, but the fact that there were no police on the dock gates more than made up for it. It was possible to pick up a girl and then take her back to the ship!

There was a pub called the Robin Hood which was full of women out for a good time. It often had a small group playing and some of the girls would get up and sing. One girl, Janet, had a particularly good voice and used to sing pop songs. She did a very good 'Puppet on a String' and sounded just like Sandie Shaw. But I soon came to realise that most of them were "on the game" and they were a lot more expensive than the bar girls abroad. A lot of the stewards were queer; the chief steward was queer but it was not at all obvious and he was a nice chap.

When we arrived back in London we were due to be there for a week or so, and as Ann was in London with the bank doing a computer course, we decided to get together and arranged to meet at the Monument tube station. She was staying with a lady in Ladbroke Grove. Neither of us realised that the tube station had four entrances and we managed to miss each other. The next morning I sent Ann a telegram at the place where the course was being held naming another meeting place and this time we found each other. I had arranged for her to come back to the ship to dinner and had arranged for a few drinks in my cabin.

Ann thought the other officers were a most peculiar bunch. The second steward came in and said "Alec the chief steward has just fallen down the fu... the gangplank". He just realised in time that there was a lady present.

We had a nice dinner and then Ann came back to my cabin for a kiss and cuddle, which was to be the last for a few months. She could have stayed on board, but she didn't fancy it as she thought the other officers a bit strange. On the way back to Leighton Buzzard on the train she fell asleep and missed her stop, not getting off until Bletchley. Luckily her dad was there as he worked on the railway, and he was able to give her a lift home.

The few days before setting sail it seemed that no one knew

exactly when we would be leaving. I went ashore for a haircut and the barber informed me that we would sail tomorrow. How he knew before any of us was a mystery, but his information was always fairly accurate. We eventually sailed on Monday 5th February 1968.

Before we left there was the Boat Drill. This is where we all put on our uniforms and practise lowering the lifeboats. My job was to start the emergency fire pump. This was a diesel-powered pump and to start it the decompression lever was lifted and the starting handle rotated furiously and then the decompression lever released, and with luck the engine spluttered into life. It took two or three attempts, but I soon had the pump engine running sweetly with water gushing over the deck. It always seemed a shame that after all of the effort to start the bloody thing it would run for five minutes and then be stopped!

On this trip I was determined to pack up smoking, cut down on drinking and save as much as possible. Cigarettes were ten bob (shillings - approx 50p) for 200 and beers about 12 bob (60p) for 12. A bottle of spirit was ten bob. This trip we were going to the Caribbean for sugar; at that time to, help out the Caribbean islands we were buying their sugar, and most of it came from Jamaica.

On 6th February we anchored off Gravesend to load explosives. This was quite a stressful time as there were regulations in place regarding smoking on deck and until this cargo was safely loaded everyone had to be very careful. I was on watch with the 2nd Engineer and we worked well together. We were doing the 4-8 watch, which I considered to be the best. The 2nd Engineer electrician and I would have breakfast in my cabin. This usually consisted of two fried egg sandwiches and tea or coffee.

We all had to do our own washing. There was a washing

machine in our washroom and I used to wash my boiler suit and plimsolls about once a week. I found if I didn't I tended to have black feet! I was looking forward to getting into a proper sea-going routine. I intended to study most days so that I could take the exam for my 2nd Eng. ticket as soon as I had the required sea time.

We went on standby at about 1600 and were full away by 1620. We had another standby at about 2100 to drop off the pilot. We had been at sea a couple of days, and the Captain had called by to introduce himself, the first time that this had happened. I'd complained about the state of the carpet in my cabin and was surprised when there was a knock on the cabin door and the steward brought in a roll of new carpet. I had to fit it myself, but this only took about an hour.

The weather seemed to be getting warmer, but it was still very cold at night and when I took the fridge log, I wore a duffel coat and took a good torch with me because there was quite a lot of deck cargo and at night it was a bit dangerous.

I was still not smoking and studying quite hard for my ticket. My plan was to take the exam in September after we were married. I was also off the booze and rationing myself to three beers a day.

We had been working on No 1 generator since we had set sail, but that was nearly finished so I wondered what the Chief had lined up for us next. I had decided to have one night ashore in Kingston, and I would go to the Buffs (RAOB) lodge. That should consist of a good booze up and no whores to tempt me. Apparently they were quite good looking in Kingston and only charged about ten bob (50p) for all night and half a crown (12.5p) for a short time!

I had arranged for Ann to receive a card and flowers on Valentine's Day – the radio operator used to do it through Marconi. We changed into "whites" on 15th February and everyone looked very smart in freshly laundered uniforms. Cargo whites consisted of white shirt with epaulettes, white shorts, long white socks and white shoes.

On Sunday 18th February 1968 I wrote in my diary:

I was on deck this morning to watch the sun rise. The thing about the sea in the tropics that I like is the wonderful fresh clean smell that seems to be everywhere. The weather is fabulous now and I did a little sunbathing this morning.

I am sure that Ann would love this weather, and I can just see me rubbing Nivea over her sunburn.

I will never forget the last time I did it, and it makes me feel rather strange when I think that we will be married next year.

Monday 19th Feb: The days seem to be much the same now, the sunrise at about 0600, the early morning heat building up to its intensity at about midday and gradually cooling off towards evening time. I bought a bottle of gin yesterday, the Gordon's we get at sea always seems better than shoreside Gordon's. I got quite suntanned today and feel a bit sore. Tomorrow I will buy some Nivea for my legs, they seem to be the worst.

I think this is going to be one of the hottest trips I have ever done. It should stay hot until the Azores homeward bound. I am looking forward to going swimming in Kingston, by the time we arrive I should have quite a tan.

It was estimated that we would arrive at Port Royal at about midnight on 20th Feb, but on our evening watch we had a six-unit scavenge fire which slowed us down and delayed standby by approx two hours. We went onto six hour watches from midnight. We were anchored in a bay just off Port Royal to unload explosives, the bay surrounded by hills topped by fluffy clouds and beautiful blue skies. We then moved the ship alongside to a berth next to the oil refinery. I decided not to go ashore as I had the midnight till six watch. I came off watch at

0600 and was watching the sun come up and it was quite amusing to see all of the lads coming back from ashore. They'd all had women at prices varying from ten bob to two quid. In the afternoon some of us took a taxi to the Myrtle Bank hotel, which had a large pool surrounded by tables on three sides and the sea on the other. There were palm trees for shade and a steward to bring drinks to the tables. While we sat having a rum and coke after a good swim an old lady came over and complimented us on our swimming.

We left fairly early as I was on watch at 1800. We had a problem with the main engine exhaust piston on No 4 cylinder, which was bolted on with four large nuts, the thread being about 70mm dia. There were enormous spanners on board and no matter how we struggled the nut would not shift. We tried whacking the spanner with a sledge hammer, but to no avail. The three other nuts came off OK but the fourth would not budge, so it was decided that the nut would have to be split. To do this it would be necessary to saw down the length of the nut next to the thread.

The second engineer took the lead, setting an example, and spent two hours sawing with a hand hacksaw. We all took turns, but cutting through 4 inches of solid steel with only a hand hacksaw was a daunting prospect. It took 12 hours continuous sawing to split the nut and when the job was done we took a case of beer onto the promenade deck to celebrate and unwind.

On the 25th February we left Kingston and headed for Santo Domingo in the Dominican Republic. We were at sea for about a day and the standby to get into the harbour only lasted about half an hour. Santo Domingo was very Spanish looking, and there were soldiers everywhere carrying self-loading rifles. Most of the buildings were pock marked with bullet holes. There were armed guards on all of the banks.

Ashore there were preparations for a festival and I decided to go ashore with some of the lads. As soon as we stepped ashore we were accosted by a pimp who insisted on being our guide. The 2nd engineer got quite annoyed and told him to bugger off but he wouldn't, and as things seemed a bit unstable or even dangerous ashore we had to put up with it. There were crowds of street kids begging for money and cigarettes, but it was not wise to give them anything – if you did you would be surrounded by groups of them. They would say "Hey mister, you give me one cigarette" or "Hey mister, what's your name?" I was getting annoyed so I said "bollocks!" the kid then said "hey bollo, you give me one cigarette!"

In the evening there was a local military brass band playing. A woman accosted us and persuaded us to go to her bar. The place was really jumping; there were a lot of Norwegian sailors in the bar and they were quite rowdy prancing around with the bar girls. I got into conversation with one that claimed to speak English, and everything I said to him got the reply "Well how about that" or "Jesus Christ". I suddenly realised they were the only two English phrases he knew!

The rum was only about £1 a bottle and we drank a bottle each; it wasn't that strong and we were leaving early the next morning. I tried to round up our group but could not find the third engineer. I eventually found him with a girl, absolutely plastered, both stark naked on a bed, and he refused to come with us. I was a bit concerned, but he was there on watch the next morning.

We left the Dominican Republic and set out for Venezuela, La Guaira first and then Puerto Cabello. Although this seemed to be one of the cleanest places we had visited this trip, there were still the street urchins scrounging cigarettes. The kids here seemed a bit less aggressive and we chatted and got to know some of them. I was still not smoking, although I was drinking a fair bit.

On Sunday 4th March 1968 I wrote in my diary:

We have decided to stay on six-hour watches until we return to Jamaica. I went ashore with John this afternoon to have a look around and to post a couple of letters, one to Ann and one to Dad. I asked one of the local lads where the post office was in my best Spanish and he directed me to an office where they weighed the letters and wrote something on them in red pencil. I then had to take the letters up the road to buy some stamps, and then back to the other place to post them. After that we wandered around and in the course of the afternoon took some photographs. The subjects I thought were quite good. It's nice to be in a country where it is safe to take a camera ashore. We ended up in a bar and had a couple of beers, the local grog is not bad.

The night watchman here is not a bit like the English night watchmen, who are usually about seventy-five and read the paper and sleep all night. The night watchman here is about twenty-three, wears a steel helmet, and patrols the decks carrying a sub-machine gun in the crook of his arm! I received two letters today, one from my love and one from Dad.

Tuesday 6th March: We arrived Curacao this morning and I stayed in bed until about 0900. After my customary egg sandwich and black coffee I went down to see the Bum Boat down aft. I bought some underwear, two pairs of trousers, a pair of flip flops, cushion cover and a set of unmentionables for my love which stirred up all sorts of thoughts about when she was aboard the Ebro. I received a rather morbid letter from Ann, which was surprising.

She must really get sick sometimes when she reads about these hot places and rum and cokes in the sunshine, but now I would much rather be with her than stuck in this hothouse, and if I wrote about the other things like working all hours in all sorts of conditions and heat she would be worried anyway.

Wed. 7ᵗʰ March: I did my watch from four to eight but have spent most of the day in bed. I got drunk last night and did not feel too hot this morning. I am not looking forward to the week on the Jamaica coast. It hardly seems possible that in three weeks I will be home with my dewdrop once more. I am on deck at the moment and I can just make out land to stbd. there is a bit more breeze today and in a minute I will stretch out and enjoy the sun.

I was not involved in the standby and was on deck to watch the deck watch perform. Embarking the pilot was amusing. The pilot boat was a tired-looking old launch that had seen better days with an engine that sounded like an old tractor.

In the post there was a letter from Westerley Marine Construction, forwarded from Liverpool, enclosing the details of the Westerley Windrush Sloop and asking if I would like to go for a demonstration sail. Having seen small yachts in the various harbours just about everywhere, I had this dream of one day owning a yacht and sailing to distant places. When at home I often bought a yachting magazine and sent off for details of yachts featured in them.

On arriving at Black River we anchored off and barges would come out to the ship laden with bags of sugar which would then be emptied into the hold. A lot of the crew were West Indian and had connections ashore and we saw a lot of stuff going ashore, probably ships' stores, but we turned a blind eye.

One of the cooks jumped overboard with a lifebelt and swam around the ship. We were all warned against swimming around the ship as there were sharks in these waters! The ship's carpenter constructed a "thunderbox" for the West Indian workers – this was a small shed with a toilet seat positioned over the water on the side deck for the workers to use as a lavatory.

The weather was deteriorating and for a couple of days it was too rough to work cargo. There was a two-masted schooner tucked away in its safe anchorage. As the weather improved the local sailing club were out dotting the anchorage with their small white sails.

The next port of call was Montego Bay and the sugar berth where ships are loaded was the "Crab Cay" where the James Bond movie 'Dr No' was filmed. I was getting a super tan and spend a few hours "bronzing" each day on the smoke-room roof. The second mate was often up there in the nude – he used to cover his balls with a facecloth to stop them getting sunburn!

Sunday 18th March: The Engineers' Steward was adrift all day. There was a booze-up in the alleyway when I came off at twelve that ended up in Joe's cabin. They were all in good voice until about three thirty apparently, but I turned in at about one thirty. I got up at about eight thirty and asked the steward for my usual, but the idiot put sugar in the coffee. Anyway the alleyway steward came back at about nine so I suppose we will soon be back to normal.

We move to Ocho Rios this evening and should arrive early tomorrow morning. Many believe that although he landed in many spots along the Jamaica coast, Christopher Columbus first set foot on land on Ocho Rios. A few miles north is the James Bond beach where the famous scene was filmed where the young Ursula Andress comes out of the sea to see James Bond (Sean Connery) waiting there.

At last it was time to leave paradise and head back to England. It was rumoured that we would dock in Liverpool but I hoped it would be London. It should take about 14 days and we should arrive on April 4th.

On 24th March I wrote:

It is 1330 at the moment and the lunch was a badly cooked morsel of tough leather about 2 1/2 inches x1 1/2 inches x1/2 inch that the catering department had the effrontery to call steak. In about 9 days we should be reaching UK and now it is said that Liverpool will be the port of discharge. In a couple of weeks' time I will be looking back on this lot thinking about the marvellous time I was having stuck in the middle of the bloody ocean. I did have two hours bronzing this morning and today so far has been quite nice. I think I will have a look at my pictures of Dewdrop now before turning in.

As we plodded further north the weather got cooler and the seas a bit rougher.

26th March: Nothing spectacular happened today, I did not go in for lunch but had some rolls brought round to my cabin. the days seem to be cooling down quite fast and the after deck is awash. As we are well loaded the old tub does not roll much, but the waves are coming right over the ship and at lunch water was coming through the saloon windows as they don't shut properly. It is quite a bit colder now and we will soon have to be using our cabin heaters.

The greasers' alleyway is awash and their mess room is flooded although it has not reached any of the living accommodation yet. Lunch was pork chop and it was quite tasty. I did some exercises but it is dangerous to use weights in this weather. I got a tin of cocoa from Flint the steward and had a couple of cups before turning in.

31st March: Quite an uneventful day. I did not turn in after lunch and enjoyed my steak. Apparently we are going to pick up a ditched aeroplane pilot tomorrow morning. Only three more days and I hope we will be home.

1st April: Picked up the ditched pilot from a weather ship. He is an American civilian and apparently missed the Azores. He was not in for lunch due to sea sickness.

2nd April: I am 24 today and I don't feel a bit older. I bought a case of ale for the lads and ended up drinking that and my docking case also.

We went to the Isle of Man to pick up the Liverpool pilot and we eventually docked on 4th April.

CHAPTER SEVEN

Getting hitched

⚜

The leave flew past and all of the wedding arrangements were finalised for September 14th. I rejoined *Ebro* for a coasting trip towards the end of April. I was hoping for fairly short trips as *Ebro* did tend to have engine problems that delayed progress. I was eventually told that the ship was doing the South America trip, similar to the trip I had done in *Albany*. I was concerned that a four-month trip would possibly overrun and I went to see the Chief Engineer, who said that I needed to go to the office in Leadenhall Street and talk to Joe Oliver, who was in charge of officer placements.

I went to London and explained my predicament, but Mr Oliver he didn't seem at all sympathetic. The first thing he asked me was "have you signed articles yet?" (if you have signed articles you are legally bound to sail). I had not and asked if I could perhaps be moved to another ship on shorter trips until September. He said that this was not possible at such short notice and if I wouldn't sail I would be sacked!

I went back to the ship and packed my gear. I was in a bit of a daze, as I couldn't believe that my career in the Merchant Navy was finished. I thought that perhaps I could join another company doing shorter trips, but thought that I needed to talk things over with Ann first. I knew she was waiting for me to phone from the ship to tell her when we were sailing. I decided to catch the train to Leighton Buzzard and go and see her.

When the train arrived at Leighton Buzzard I took a taxi to Ann's Mum and Dad's house. When her dad opened the door he couldn't believe his eyes – he thought that I should be miles away on the high seas and that I would be gone for a month or two, but here I was standing on his doorstep.

Ann's mum and dad didn't have a phone but there was a phone box on the corner not 50 yards away. Ann was at her brother's house babysitting their son Paul and was waiting for my phone call. Her dad went to the phone box and rang her, saying that she needed to come home at once, but he wouldn't tell her why. Luckily her brother Ron and his wife Kate had returned from their night out so she was able to leave at once to return home. When she walked into the front room and saw me standing there in my uniform she was speechless. We fell into each other's arms, and when I explained that I had left and the reasons why she seemed so happy. I wondered if it was perhaps the greatest mistake of my life so far!

My Dad was a bit peeved that I had gone to Leighton Buzzard first, but he enjoyed having me home.

The spring weather was beautiful, with lovely hot days and warm evenings. I used to sunbathe in the back garden, but I already I had a super tan from the time I had spent in the tropics. However, the next problem was finding a job.

The manager of the Anglia Building society summoned Ann and me to his office and told us that as I was now unemployed the mortgage offer on our new house was being withdrawn! I applied for several jobs and attended various interviews, and was offered a job at Sound Engineering in Rushden as a centre lathe turner. The job entailed turning lead screws. I didn't think much to this, but it was a job and I needed to have a job to justify the mortgage application.

I went to Unilever Research Laboratories in Sharnbrook for an interview, as this was the sort of job that I was most suited to, making prototype food processing machinery all in stainless steel. It was similar to the work that I had been doing at Fords. The interview went very well, and the works manager, Les Turner, was ex Royal Navy so we had something in common. I had to meet the Union representative and agree to join the union should my application be successful.

The job offer from Unilever came two days before I was due to start at Sound Engineering. I wrote to Sound telling them I had decided not to take the job.

Unilever were an excellent company to work for. They provided transport in the form of coaches that picked people up in various locations including Bedford, where I lived, and Rushden, where I was moving to after I was married.

There were two of us starting on the same day, Brian Harris and me. Brian was of similar age and was married to Carol who was heavily pregnant. We became friends and used to go out as a foursome. Brian was friendly with one of the other engineers and they used to do work in the evenings and planned to start a business. The other guy, Nick's, parents had a property in Cornwall with a workshop and Brian and Nick planned to eventually move down to Cornwall. I used to have plans to do something similar, as I had always had dreams of working for myself and starting a business and used to discuss plans with Brian. I was looking at simple things to manufacture, with the minimum of equipment as I had no money. As I now had a job, the Anglia Building Society renewed our mortgage offer and I was looking forward to getting married in September. The new house was well under way and we just hoped it would be finished in time.

Although we had enough saved for the mortgage deposit, we had little money for anything else. My dad was buying carpet for the ground floor and Ann had obtained some second-hand kitchen furniture, which she repainted. Ann's mum and dad donated an old three-piece suite. Ann's cousin was going through a marriage break-up and we had a cooker and various bits of furniture from him, so I hired a big van and moved a lot of furniture to his new house for him as payment. With what we were given and picked up cheaply second hand, we were gradually getting a home together.

The job at Unilever went very well, and I enjoyed the type of work making experimental food processing machines. The working day started at 8.30 am and finished at 4.30 and the bus picked up about 8.10, and although it was quite a walk to the pick-up point in Bedford, it was very convenient.

At that time Granddad (Mum's dad) lived with her in St. Albans. I had seen him from time to time at my sister's with his lady friend Daisy and they were both looking forward to the wedding.

In July Ann's Mum and Dad were due to fly to Spain on holiday, but unfortunately her maiden aunt May died and Ann's dad, being the only living relative, had to make the arrangements for the funeral. He wanted to cancel the holiday, but Ann said she would go to the funeral in his place and I arranged a day off work and agreed to accompany her.

It was arranged for a car to pick us up from Leighton Buzzard and take us to Islington, London, where the funeral was to take place in the Salvation Army Citadel. I had never been to a Salvation Army service before and was quite interested in the proceedings. The minister said a few words and then gave out a hymn number. He had a baton to conduct the music as the organ struck up and everyone started singing.

Then he noticed that Ann and I were not singing. He stopped the hymn by banging his baton on the lectern and looked directly at us, pointing the baton and starting the hymn again! Ann and I started singing with gusto, bellowing away like the best of them. The ceremony was quite moving and although a sad occasion almost joyful. We were delivered back to Leighton Buzzard and I decided to stay over. I think that was probably the night our daughter was conceived!

Brian's wife Carol had her baby, a beautiful little girl, and Brian was absolutely besotted with her. They asked if Ann would be Godmother. They also asked Geoff, another colleague, if his wife would do the same, but she declined as her family were Irish Catholics.

At the christening there were various family and friends, including Carol's mum and dad, Mr and Mrs Player, who was nicknamed John, after the cigarette manufacturer. The Godparents said their bit and then came the hymns. Ann and I, after our practice with the Sally Army, burst forth into song. Mr Player looked at us aghast and then burst out laughing!

The few months up to the wedding seemed to fly past. Ann had arranged to transfer to the branch of the bank in Rushden, and we both went in to meet the manager, a rather pompous character called Brown, and she looked forward to starting there after we were married. We used to visit the building site at weekends and it soon became apparent that the house would not be ready for us to move into in September, so we started to look for somewhere to rent. We saw an ad in the Bedfordshire Times for a house to rent in Harborough Road, Rushden, and arranged to view it. The owner was a Mr Bayes, a builder who was also the local undertaker. He was a man of big stature but a kindly disposition and a lovely wife who was quite charming and helpful. The house was next door to the Bayes' and had been renovated and decorated to a high standard, and the rent was reasonable, so we arranged to move in after returning from honeymoon.

While we were away Ann's brother Ron agreed to move our few pieces of furniture into the house for us. I decided to have my stag night the week before the wedding and my dad and all of my mates came along. I suspected that my drinks were being spiked so I tried to moderate what I drank, but became hopelessly drunk.

On the night before the wedding I went down the pub with Dad, which seemed a bit of an anti-climax. All of the arrangements had been made, the honeymoon organised, and I had arranged for a minibus to take us all from Bedford to Leighton Buzzard.

The wedding was on 14th September 1968, and on the morning of the ceremony various neighbours came round to wish me well, and some brought presents. The minibus arrived – the driver was Barry, who by coincidence, had been in my class at school – and we all set off to Leighton Buzzard. We called in at Midland Road railway station to pick up Granddad who had come from St. Albans, where he lived with Mother. His lady friend Daisy was there also.

We arrived at Leighton Buzzard in plenty of time and on the way to the church, we stopped at Ann's house and I left her a Gonk (a small shapeless cuddly toy) for good luck, making sure that I didn't catch sight of the bride before the allotted time. We were quite early and luckily opposite the church there was a pub, so we all went in for a drink. Unfortunately it had started to rain. I walked into the church and waited for the love of my life to arrive. We had decided not to have the Wedding March, but soon the organ struck up and Ann's dad, chest stuck out, bursting with pride, marched her to the altar.

The rain was now pouring down and after the ceremony it was a struggle to get the photos done. They were finished in double quick time and consequently we arrived at the venue for the reception quite early. Ann had made her own wedding dress and it had a long train, which by this time was saturated.

The wedding cake did not have conventional pillars. On each corner there were decorative flowers and the idea was to put upended sherry glasses over the flowers as a feature. The host and hostess were very grumpy. They said" You're far too early, we are not ready for you yet and the cake came with no pillars, but we managed to find some. " They had assembled the cake with these pillars and it looked fine but not as good as intended. When we tried to explain about the flowers and sherry glasses the hostess pooh-poohed the idea. In the end Ann's mum put the cake together as it should be.

The afternoon seemed to fly past. Ann's cousin took us to Ann's mum's house to change into our going-away clothes and then we returned to the reception to say our goodbyes. I went to the minibus driver to pay him but he said someone had already paid and would take no money, not even a tip. I never found out who had paid. Ann's brother Ron had arranged for a car to take us to the hotel for the first night, a riverside hotel near to Gatwick from where we were flying the next day on honeymoon.

The rain was still pouring all the way to London. When we arrived at the hotel they had a private party in the dining room and would not let us in until about 10 o'clock. We ordered T-bone steaks and a bottle of Beaujolais to wash it down. By this time we were both hungry, although as soon as the food was put in front Ann she felt queasy and ate very little, so I had to eat two steaks.

All night the rain was pounding on the roof, although it wasn't the rain that kept us awake! Someone had put lots of confetti in our cases and there was a tell-tale trail of confetti from our room to the bathroom. The next morning a lot of the hotel was flooded and the dining room where we had been the night before was under about two feet of water. The water stretched all the way to the road, which was choc a bloc with cars and buses. The nearby river had burst its banks and there were half-submerged cars in the car park. Parts of Gatwick were submerged and there were long delays to all flights. The taxi company couldn't get through to the hotel, so we wondered what to do. The road past the hotel was slightly higher and the traffic seemed to be moving, although at a snail's pace.

I decided to wade to the road and see if we could hitch a lift on one of the buses going near Gatwick, so I rolled up my trouser legs and waded through the water to the road. Luckily there was a bus stuck in the traffic that was passing by Gatwick and the driver said he would give us a lift. One of the residents of the hotel had a large car and had offered to drive through the standing water on the hotel driveway to get us and our bags to the road.

We got onto the bus and it crawled its way to where we were to be dropped off. All of the people on the bus seemed quite excited and happy for us and wished us good luck. The bus driver would not accept any money and seemed amused by our plight and only too happy to help us.

It was quite a walk to Gatwick Departures, but we chatted to quite a few people in similar circumstances. There was almost the "Dunkirk Spirit", as we were all in the same boat. We went to check in over two hours late, but luckily due to the weather the flight was delayed and had not left. The aeroplane was a Viscount propeller-driven aircraft; I had never flown before and it was quite an experience. There was standing water on the airport but the runway was clear and we landed in Jersey about three hours after taking off.

The hotel we were staying in was the Mandalay hotel in St. Helier, which was comfortable. The couple who ran the hotel were quite young and were both actors – they had worked as film extras and also appeared in some TV adverts. The hotel had a function room with entertainment several nights a week, and we joined in with everything that was going on including the Knobbly Knees contest and all sorts of silly games. Although it rained continuously, we had a wonderful fun-filled carefree week. We hired a car for a few days and toured the island. We went to a night club at the Bay hotel and Chico Arnez and his orchestra were playing. We bought one of their long-playing records, called 'This is Chico'.

As we toured round the different harbours, we saw yachts in different places, and I said to Ann "One day we will have a yacht and sail it over to here." I used to dream of travelling to exotic places in our own yacht.

All too soon the honeymoon was over and most of our money spent. We said goodbye to the people we had befriended at the hotel and flew back to Gatwick. We had left ourselves with just enough money to get home. A bus company operated from Rushden called Birch Buses, and we had a timetable that showed that they picked up in London daily. We got the tube to the pick-up point and just hoped that the bus would turn up. We had just enough money for a drink in the pub and our bus fare. The bus arrived, much to our relief, and we had a lazy ride back to Rushden nodding off to the soporific drone of the engine. At the end of our road was a bus stop, which was very convenient.

We struggled up the hill with our bags and let ourselves into our first home to begin our married life. The house had an electricity meter that took coins, so we had to make sure that we had a plentiful supply of coins. Although Ann was pregnant it didn't show yet, and we had to decide when to make it known to everyone.

Although we had the basics in the house, there were a lot of odds and ends needed to make the home complete and it was nice to go into the shops to buy things for the home. We didn't have a car, so we walked everywhere or used the bus. Mr and Mrs Bayes were very understanding and helpful.

The house had no heating, only a fireplace in the front room. We had a two-bar electric fire, but the house was bitter cold and often had ice on the inside of the windows. Mrs Bayes felt sorry for us and said we could help ourselves to the coal in their coal shed, but we didn't take her up on her offer. Dad came to stay once or twice but he must have been frozen, sitting in front of the electric fire, and to cap it all we had no television. We were looking forward to moving into our new house, which had warm air central heating!

CHAPTER EIGHT

My own business

I stood at the bus stop waiting for the Unilever bus to pick me up. It was a dull chilly morning, and the other people at the bus stop stood around with the resigned looks on their faces, not looking forward to the working day ahead. I however was quite looking forward to going back to work, and was filled with optimism and enthusiasm.

On arrival I was summoned to the manager's office to explain why I hadn't turned up the day before the wedding. I had taken the day off to avoid any embarrassment. It was customary when people got married for them to be presented with a wedding present, and as I had only been there a few months I thought that I probably wouldn't qualify. On that day, my last day of freedom, I had gone into town and wandered round the shops. I had gone into a sports shop and bought a fishing reel – I don't know why, I never went fishing! Perhaps I remembered when on the *Albany* in Zanzibar and I had to borrow one. I had gone for lunch in the Greyfriars pub next to the bus station and met up with Dave, a lad who had been apprenticed to me at Fords. Since leaving Fords he had started his own cleaning business. He had started by cleaning the windows of the Technical College and within three years had 80 women working for him doing office cleaning!

I soon got into the routine of going to work every day. The bus picked me up at 800 and work started at about 830. I was working on some very interesting projects, working closely with the designers. One of the charge hands didn't like the way I worked with the designers, making suggestions regarding technicalities and different ways of doing things, so I had to be careful and make things seem like their idea.

Unilever used to hold social events and there would be a meal followed by a disco and dancing – they were very good and well attended. We used to go with Brian and Carol and became good friends with them. Brian and Nick, the guy Brian was doing evening work with, were not getting on very well and eventually there was a falling out. Brian was quite upset, as he had contributed a lot of ideas and was really keen to start something.

Eventually Brian and I formed a partnership. Ann, through working in the bank, had some idea of how things worked and her best friend was an accountant. We called the new partnership Harris and Cooney. To start with we needed premises to work in, but as we had no money it was difficult to find anywhere. Eventually we managed to talk the landlord of the Cock Inn in Denford into hiring out his stable, for a very low rent. We both put in £50 (my share was Ann's maternity grant) and bought a small arc welding set from a mail order club. I made a jig for bending scrolls to make up wrought iron products, including telephone tables, coffee tables, gates and porch canopies and anything else we could think of that required curly bits of metal.

Everything was cut using a hand hacksaw – we couldn't afford a power saw but soon managed to obtain an angle grinder and a bracket that turned it into a disc cutter. For the tables we bought the glass tops from a local glass company – they were rough-cast glass and looked very nice. We were buying 1/2" x 1/8" mild steel bar, which was fairly cheap. We then started getting it sheared at the required width from sheet, which worked out cheaper.

Most of the things we made were painted black or white, and initially were hand painted, which took ages. Brian obtained a spray gun that worked off a vacuum cleaner. It had a can underneath for the paint and the spray nozzle on the top connected to the vacuum cleaner hose. There was a hole in the top and to activate the spray it was necessary to place the thumb over the hole. This speeded up the painting process, but it wasn't very efficient, and Brian and I used to end up plastered in paint.

We sold a few telephone tables to Peter Crisp's, a local hardware shop, and advertised wrought iron gates and storm porches in the local paper. We also looked for simple sub-contracting work, and picked up a few jobs from local builders.

With both of us working full time and spending all our spare time working in the stable, there wasn't much time for socializing or anything else. We had no spare money, as everything was ploughed back in. Brian had a particularly hard time as he was running a car. I didn't have a car and Brian did all of the running around. We were banking at the bank where Ann worked, and Ann did the book keeping and kept everything above board. Her friend Janet, who worked as an accountant in a large accountancy practice in Birmingham, advised us how a partnership should be run.

We decided to leave work and run the business full time on 1st January 1969. We had practically no money and not a lot of knowledge. All we had was the confidence in ourselves and the determination to make it work.

Our new house was nearly finished and we were looking forward to moving in. I had decided we would move ourselves, as we had no spare money and Ann's dad offered to help. I hired a Ford Transit van and we did it over a weekend. We didn't have much – an old three-piece suite handed down from Ann's mum and dad, a kitchen table and chairs, a room divider to separate the dining area from the lounge area and a cupboard for the kitchen. My dad paid for the carpet for a wedding present so the house was quite cosy with the warm air heating.

Ann, working at the bank, had made several new friends. The partnership bank account was at the Rushden Bank. As we were starting the business full time in January we needed better premises, and there was a workshop advertised in the local paper that included various items of machinery. Brian and I went to view the property, a small workshop behind a house in Hallwood Road, Kettering, which had been run as a business making turned parts during the war. The proprietor had died and his widow, Mrs Southwell, who was living with her bachelor son David, was keen to let the workshop. It had several small lathes, a pillar drill and benches, and was ideal for what we wanted, apart from being very small.

The rent was £7 per week and we agreed to take it from 1st January. The workshop had no heating, so we purchased a space heater from a mail order catalogue. This was a very basic heater, just a circular steel drum about 400mm wide by 500mm high. It had a valve in the top that dripped paraffin (kerosene) onto a steel plate which burned quite smokily, and a chimney that went out through the wall. The heater wasn't very efficient and the five-gallon tank didn't last very long, so we decided to put a larger tank on the roof, which we did without consulting the Southwells. We obtained a 40-gallon drum, which was bright red with a broad white stripe round its middle and fixed it onto the roof. Mrs Southwell was furious and ordered us to take it down. She said "It looks Just like a space ship sitting on the roof!"

I could see she was getting emotional. Then she said "It's awful and in the terms of your lease you are not allowed to ornament the building, take it down at once!" We agreed to take it down as soon as it was empty, as it was too heavy to handle when full, but every morning in the early hours we used to refill it with cans. They suspected what we were up to and one morning they lay in wait for us and pounced just as we were going up the ladder, jerry can in hand. The 40-gallon drum had to come down!

The lathes were quite small but we were getting turning work and some small toolmaking jobs from the leather and shoe trade as well as some small fabrication jobs. Brian and I worked together quite well, but money was a big problem. The bank manager wasn't very sympathetic and as Ann worked there, things were a bit awkward. He wouldn't give us any leeway and although we were getting our money in from customers, due to miscalculation sometimes there was not enough in the account to cover cheques written out. Ann did very well juggling finances, but it was clear we needed help.

One day Brian came up to me and said "My bank account has run out". Ann, with her bank connection, would never write out a cheque we couldn't cover. We decided to ask the bank for help, but Mr Brown the bank manager flatly refused – he was annoyed that Ann had been pregnant when she started to work there. Ann suggested that we went to the bank in Leighton

Buzzard where she used to work and see if Mr Morris could help, so Ann and I went to see him. We agreed to a second mortgage on our house as security and Ann's dad and Mr Player, Brian's father-in-law, both agreed to be guarantors. In the end he agreed to give us a £750 overdraft limit with a safety margin of £250, making it £1000 in total.

When I told Brian he could not believe it, it was almost like winning the pools. Brown was not amused and seemed really annoyed that we had moved the account, but we didn't have much choice in the matter as he had flatly refused to help!

Ann was getting very large now and would soon have to give up work. She needed maternity clothing, but we had no spare money. She bought a maternity dress for £7, which to me seemed extravagant, but I didn't have the heart to say anything. Although the new overdraft facility made things easier, we still needed to keep a very tight rein on things; we only allowed ourselves £20 per week wages. Some of the subcontract work was very tightly priced. We were getting work from Baker Perkins of Peterborough, which had a fixed price that was worked out for their machines, which were far more powerful than our small lathes. I got some subcontracted work from Fords, my old employer, Unilever, and Kismet where Dad worked. Although money was tight everything seemed to be going OK and we were enthusiastic and confident that we were going places.

We needed some more machines. A machinery dealer in Kettering called P. L. Pilling came to see us and we did a deal to buy a Wicksteed power saw and a new more powerful welder. Pilling had a small office and storage unit in Grafton Street, Kettering that he rented from Neil Stephenson, who ran a carpentry and joinery business. Stephensons' employed about eight people and their workshop was adjacent to Pillings. He took us to look at the saw to a company called Electro Motion in Leicester that reconditioned old plant, and we agreed to buy it. While we were there we saw a reconditioned Herbert No. 4 chucking capstan lathe – it was love at first sight and we had to buy that too. Pilling arranged the finance; the interest rate was 14 per cent, which was normal for around that time.

Then one of our former colleagues, Geoff Allison, said he would like to join us. We weren't too keen, as the pressures of a two-way partnership were bad enough and Mr Morris the bank manager warned me of the pitfalls. Geoff offered to invest £500 into the business and as he was a highly-skilled sheet metal worker we agreed to let him join us. He started in March and his £500 investment was very welcome. Geoff soon got into the routine of working all hours seven days a week.

We were running a Mini Van and it was the partners' only transport. Ann was getting closer to having the baby, but officially still had two months to go. One morning she was up early doing the ironing and seemed a bit agitated. I went into work as normal. I got a phone call to say she had gone into labour soon after I arrived at the factory. We never had a phone at home so Ann had to walk down to the building site office and call an ambulance.

When I told my partners that Ann had gone into labour and was in hospital they didn't believe me. Geoff said "A bit soon isn't it?" with a sneer on his face. I told them "I'm going to the hospital now!" Ann had been picked up by the ambulance at about 9 am. When I arrived at the hospital I was told to come back later, so I went back to work. Then I had another call to say she was about to give birth. I sped to the hospital, but when I arrived the baby was already born. The baby was in a room with a lot of other babies and the nurse lifted her up and said "You have a beautiful baby girl".

I looked at our daughter and can't describe the feelings of love I felt for this precious little bundle being held up by the nurse. I rang Ron, Ann's brother. Ann's Mum and Dad were there; they all thought our daughter was premature.

"What did she weigh?" asked Ron.

"Eight pounds four ounces" I said. Ron burst out laughing. Kate his wife came on and said, "What was the real birth weight? Ron said it was eight pounds four".

"That's right" I said. More laughter! Ann's mum came on the phone and said "That was a bit soon". Of course, we had only got married in the September. I said, "I think perhaps the less said about it the better" and it was never mentioned after that, but I do think we did a good job keeping it quiet.

Ann was in the hospital for five days and Ann's mum and dad took me to the hospital to pick her up on the Sunday. My dad was there and it was a wonderful time. I just had to keep going over to the cot to look at my beautiful daughter.

CHAPTER NINE

A toe in the water

When the workload allowed we used to try and have Sunday afternoons off, but often we had to work all day. We needed larger premises, and Pilling agreed to rent out part of his warehouse. It was very basic, with an old pot-bellied stove, and we found that if we filled it with sawdust and poured in a gallon of paraffin it would burn for most of the day. It was decided to keep the name Harris & Cooney as this was already established. Geoff, with his contacts from Unilever, pulled in some fabrication work, which was a welcome addition. We were still doing some wrought iron decorative scrollwork and also some copper canopies. We would do anything in metal within our capabilities and sometimes beyond. If we didn't have the correct plant or equipment for a particular job we used to get round it somehow, but some of our methods were crude and unconventional. The chucking capstan increased our capacity significantly. It would take up to 2-inch diameter bar and had the advantage of the chuck.

Brian's father-in-law, Mr Player, worked at the Skefco ball bearing company in Luton and in their stores the storemen used to move the bearings around in steel trays which were exceptionally heavy. They used small trolleys called Shays which were manufactured with rollers for wheels, and the ones they were using were worn out. We got an order to make ten replacements, which was an ideal job for our lathes. I had two machines working at the same time, one skimming the outside diameter whilst I turned the internal bearing surfaces.

We were keeping the two workshops going but decided to move everything up to the Grafton Street workshop. There had been complaints from local residents around the machine shop about the welding plant causing interference on TV screens, so we had to move the welding to Grafton Street. We needed to escape from the lease on the Hallwood road workshop, but I think the Southwells were keen to see the back of us.

Money was very tight. We were still under equipped and kept having to buy pieces of equipment which were a drain on finances. Ann kept the books fastidiously, and sometimes she told us that there was not enough in the bank for us to pay ourselves any wages. When there was enough we paid ourselves £20 per week each, which was less than we had been earning when we were employed but enough to get by on.

In June money became even tighter and I told Brian and Geoff that there was not enough money in the account for us to have any wages. We decided to take just £5 per week each, which was just enough to buy food. I used to have 50 pence spending money, just enough for about four pints of beer.

In Grafton Street there was a small workshop run by a man called John Bagshaw which made components for the shoe trade, and to earn some cash we worked a few hours for him on piecework, making parts for shoes. The rate was very poor, but we were desperate for cash. This only lasted for a few weeks as we became busier with our engineering work. We designed a manually-operated fork lift trolley for Skefco, and it worked quite well, enabling their storemen to take six trays of bearings around the stores at once instead of just one at a time. We were very busy and had some good customers. At last money started to become a bit easier and we started to have a small wage again. I had a meeting with the building society, who agreed to allow me to pay interest only on the mortgage until things picked up.

Then Skefco called us in for a meeting, and we were quite curious as to the reason. One of the directors questioned us about why we wanted to work for ourselves, and seemed almost amused at the hardship we were putting ourselves through. The reason for the meeting was to offer us all jobs at Skefco! I said I would rather continue working for myself, Geoff said the same, but Brian seemed quite keen to go and work for them. Brian left in August 1969 and Geoff and I worked every hour available to try and get the overdraft down and things paid off.

We needed a vehicle and ended up buying a 1947 two-litre petrol Land Rover from Eady Bros in Burton Latimer. It was a bit of tank and I don't really know why we got talked into it.

Then we were contacted by a company called Caswell and Co. in St. Peter's Road Kettering that manufactured adhesives. In their factory they had several large drums that were mounted horizontally with a shaft running through on which were mounted large paddles. To make the glue they would put rubber in the top and then pour in solvents such as Acetone. The shaft was driven by overhead shafting and there was a crude clutch arrangement on the end. They had several problems. The main one was the paddles coming loose, which made it necessary to get inside the drum to tighten them back onto the shaft. this was a very messy job and the fumes in the drums would make you feel quite drunk!

Another problem was the gland where the shaft went through end of the drum. This had a seal similar to the glands on the ships pumps, which I knew how to fix. Some of the shafts were badly worn where incorrect gland packing had been used and we were able to sleeve the end by welding on steel collars.

The pressures were building up between Geoff and me, which is normal in partnerships. Some days we would hardly speak to each other, although we did socialize a bit. Ann and I never had a television, so on July 19th 1969 we went round to Geoff and Theresa's to watch the Moon landing on their telly.

One Sunday Geoff took the vehicle to deliver a copper canopy to a customer he knew. He was supposed to pick me up at lunchtime and take me home. when it got to 2 pm I thought I would ring to find out where he was. He never had a phone but said it was OK to ring the next door neighbour, who would get him round to answer a call. When the neighbour answered he said, "I'm afraid they're not in, they've all gone out in the Land Rover for the afternoon".

I was furious that he had left me at work and gone out with his family. I managed to get a bus from Kettering to Rushden, where I lived, but my anger at being left with no means of transport was getting worse the nearer I got to home. I got off the bus and was walking towards home when he drew up all smiles, looking rather sheepish, with a cock and bull story as an excuse, not realising that I had spoken to his neighbour. I tore into him, which took him a bit by surprise. I had always tried to be calm and reasonable and it was unlike me to lose control.

Things started to get more awkward as time went on. He said he wanted to see the company books, and he thought his mother should be our book keeper. She was doing the books for a chap who mended washing machines and he thought she would be more capable than Ann. He came to my house and was poring over the books. Ann offered to explain anything that needed clarification, not realising that he couldn't read that well.

One day we were at Caswell's fitting a new motor for a new type of glue-mixing machine. We were barely speaking and nearly came to blows. I said "Look Geoff, it's no good carrying on like this, I think we should consider going our separate ways". We then had a discussion and agreed to both work together to pay off the company debts and then part company.

With the decision made we seemed to work much better together. Geoff started using his old Morris Minor and I resurrected Dad's old Austin A30, which only needed a tidy up and an MoT. We obtained orders for some quite big jobs from Unilever, some exposure chambers for animals, and we also worked for Huntingdon Research Laboratories, making animal cages.

I needed to find premises to work in, so I was looking for places to rent and put feelers out with all of the local estate agents, without much luck. Geoff Allison and I had decided that the partnership should finish around the end of 1970, and at that point we had built up assets of around £2000. When it came to the split, Geoff's share worked out to £809 and my share was £638. Most of it was in plant and machinery, and we came to an agreement as to which of us should have which pieces of equipment. I ended up with the lathes, a milling machine, various pieces of engineering equipment and the Land Rover. Geoff ended up with the guillotine, folder and various sheet metal equipment. I had also bought a new

Bridgeport milling machine that was to be delivered as soon as I had found new premises.

I looked at an old shoe factory in Rushden, a converted Baptist Chapel of about 3000 sq. ft. made up of several rooms on the ground floor and a large room on the first floor. One of the ground floor rooms was about 500 sq. ft., which would be ideal for me to work in and the rest could be rented out. The asking price was £6000, which was out of the question, but I heard that an offer of £3750 had been accepted but the deal had fallen through. I made an offer of £3800, which was accepted. All I had to do now was find the money!

I went to see Mr Morris the bank manager, who knew Rushden quite well having worked in the bank there previously. He told me I would need a £1200 deposit. To me this seemed an enormous amount of money. He suggested that if Ann's dad would agree, the bank could lend him the deposit, using his house as security, and then we could pay off the loan account. Ann's dad agreed without hesitation, as he had every confidence in my abilities and would do anything for his daughter.

The deal was done and I was so excited. I needed to find tenants for the first floor and the ground floor areas, which I wouldn't be using. Before I moved in, my workshop floor needed to be concreted and a large door was needed in the end wall. The existing floor was wooden planks and I needed some help to rip them up. There was a void under the planks which needed filling with hardcore. One of the draughtsmen from Unilever had a mate who was a builder and we agreed a price to hardcore and concrete the floor and put the door in the end wall. I bought a length of RSJ (rolled steel joist) for the lintel and an "up and over" garage door. When the work was complete I was quite proud of my workshop.

I had some turning work, but not much for the new Bridgeport milling machine. I obtained some toolmaking work from Nene Valley Homes, the local caravan manufacturer, but their production parts, which were mass produced, were so poorly priced that we couldn't compete. I obtained some small fabrication jobs from Unilever and employed a few men part time, usually in the evenings.

It was around this time that Brian Kidd started working for me part time. He used to start his full time job at 8 am but work for me from 6 am till 7.30 in the morning and then from 5 pm till 8 in the evening. Sometimes if we were very busy we would work till 10 pm, as well as most Saturday and Sundays.

I found a tenant for the redundant ground floor rooms. Reg Wheeler, a former RAF Spitfire pilot, had an electrical business and needed storage space. The rent was £23 13s 4d. per month. This was one of the last payments in pounds, shillings and pence; decimalisation day was 15th Feb. 1971.

Money was very tight. I borrowed £200 from my father to help out, and had some work from Caswell's the glue company, Mercier Charvo Services, a company that imported and serviced French tannery equipment, and some toolmaking from the Batten Manufacturing Company. Mr Morris came over to visit – I think he was a bit concerned at the apparent lack of work. The problem was that when I knew he was coming I cleaned the workshop and tidied up so the whole place was spick and span, giving the impression that there wasn't much going on. He then went to see Ann and our daughter at the house. I think he had a soft spot for Ann as she had gone to work in the bank straight from school and she knew his daughter Kate. The whole of British industry was in recession, and militant trade unions seemed determined to bring the country to a standstill. I was desperate for work and would have done anything to keep busy. Rolls Royce, one of the best known names in British industry, went into receivership and the future looked bleak for industry on the whole.

Ann and I went to visit Ann's brother Ron, who at that time had a garage business in Grendon Underwood. He was doing very well, with a Leyland dealership, petrol pumps and repair workshops. He had several employees and was quite successful living in a large four-bedroomed house next to the garage.

I asked him if he knew of anyone who wanted engineering work doing, and he said "You can work in stainless steel can't you?"

"Yes," I said.

"Well" he said, "there is a chap down in the village that builds boats and he is always moaning that he can't get stainless deck fittings. If you like I will give him a ring. He's building a sailing boat called the Sea Wych, and he's selling quite a few. His name's John Sadler."

I went down to meet John Sadler, little knowing that this was to be the turning point of my life. John had a beautiful thatched cottage and had workshops in the garden, which he'd made from packing cases bought from Stansted airport. The Sea Wych was a 19ft sloop designed by John for the home completion market. You could buy just hull and deck mouldings or various kits of parts to finish the boat. At that time building your own boat was becoming very popular as it seemed a cheap way of getting a boat.

I looked at the stainless fittings that he had and they seemed uncomplicated. We seemed to talk for ages and I agreed to make a sample batch for 10% less than he was already paying his existing supplier. Although I had the machines capable of making the parts, I had no polishing equipment, so I bought a second hand polishing spindle from Clifton Engineering in Thrapston for £12.50p. I rang Jack Bowers, the buyer at Fords where I used to work, for the name of the company that supplied polishing compounds. At first he was reluctant to speak to me, no doubt thinking I was touting for work, but when I explained what I wanted he was only too happy to help.

A sample set of fittings was made with toolroom precision and polished up to a mirror finish, as at that stage I didn't know what I could get away with regarding quality. I delivered the first set and John was quite impressed with the quality and workmanship and ordered six sets for delivery as soon as possible. He also agreed to pay on delivery for an extra 5% discount! The rudder fittings were not stainless but manganese bronze castings and I had patterns made and bought the castings from Hobkirks of Bedford.

During my discussions with John he told me about Russell Marine, who were based at Southend in Essex. They were building Vivacity and Alacrity sloops in large numbers, so I went to see them, taking with me a set of Sea Wych fittings. Peter Waghorn was the buyer and I came away with an order for 100 bow roller fittings!

At this stage I was only doing the plate work for the small deck fittings and I needed some tube-bending capacity to make bow and stern rails. I couldn't afford to buy a pipe bender, so I made a hydraulic one using a hydraulic car jack. The formers I fabricated from sheet metal. I used this to put in the large radius for the bow and on old plumber's bender for the smaller bends. Although crude, this system worked, and I was soon supplying all of the Sea Wych fittings and pricing up all sorts of deck rails for other boatbuilders. It seemed that if you could offer stainless steel for boats, instead of the frosty reception that was normal when visiting companies for the first time, you would be welcomed almost with open arms.

I also found a tenant to take the first floor workshop, a company called Multi-Weld which was run by a larger-than-life figure called Arthur Johnson. Arthur was an expert welder/fabricator and for a time we did work for each other. In order to access the upstairs workshop, we removed one of the large gothic-style windows and fitted steel doors and a gantry with a block and tackle for lifting items too heavy to carry up the stairs. In my workshop I had a small oven for hardening press tools and we used to use it for warming up meat pies. Sometimes we would forget the pie and end up with just a pile of ash.

Multi-Weld bought an 8ft x 1/4" guillotine which I agreed to them installing at the back of my workshop if I could have the use of it. I ran an armoured cable down the back wall which was not clipped to the wall and was not very straight. This machine was just what I needed for shearing the plate for the yacht fittings, and every day Brian or I would spend hours chopping up stainless steel plate.

One morning I had a visit from the local council's environment officer accompanied by an irate neighbour. Our factory backed onto the garden of the local bakery. The baker lived above his shop and used to get up at four o'clock every morning to bake his loaves. He then used to catch up with his sleep later in the day and the rumbling of the guillotine used to keep him awake. He'd told the council officer that the machine had caused the wall to crack! They thought the armoured cable down the wall was a crack in the wall. We agreed times to run the machine so as not to cause problems for our neighbour, but sometimes if jobs had to be done we just had to run it anyway.

Although we were now extremely busy, I wanted to move away from general engineering and concentrate more on the yacht fittings side of the business. Money was still very tight and we were working all hours. Quite a few people thought I was a bit of a dreamer to try and get into what at that time was seen to be a slightly exotic market. My old partner Geoff, when I met up with him, sneered at the idea of being in the marine industry and I heard Reg my tenant discussing it with one of his workers and roaring with laughter at the prospect.

Me, aged one   Growing up

My first car

In uniform

RMS Amazon

RMS Ebro

Sister Anne with family

CHAPTER TEN

Pulpits and powerboats

Our neighbours in Masefield Drive, Linda and Kevin, were thinking of putting their house on the market at an asking price of £4650. This seemed an enormous sum and I suggested to Ann that we put an ad in the local paper for our house to see what would happen. Linda and Kevin said, "You'll never sell privately, you need to put it with an estate agent". Within a week we had an offer at the asking price!

The house we moved to was in Denton Close, Irchester, and the price was £5200. The building society was slightly reluctant to give us a mortgage due to our previous problems, but as we'd kept them informed when we'd been unable to pay and had paid off all arrears they decided in our favour. I decided that we would move ourselves again and hired a Transit van, and once again Ann's dad helped with the move.

The house in Irchester had an enormous garden and it was quite a bit bigger than our old house. The neighbours all had young children and we got on well with everyone. Ann was heavily pregnant again at this time and used to do deliveries.

I bought a Ford Cortina from Ann's brother Ron, an estate and ideal for delivering large quantities of bow rollers to Russell Marine and Sea Wych fittings to Sadler's. I traded in the Land Rover, which was only firing on three cylinders and kept backfiring and making loud farty sounds! I noticed that the steering tended to wander a bit and took the car into Warners Garage in Rushden, with whom we had an account. They declared that the vehicle was unroadworthy because the front shock absorbers had rusted away from the bodywork. I took it back to Ron's and he welded it back together. Another problem was that the starter motor kept stripping the ring gear on the engine and then the car wouldn't start. In the end I used to always park on a slight hill. Once I got it rolling I could put it in gear, drop the clutch and it would start. If Ann did any deliveries, she used to keep the engine running.

On one occasion when we had a particularly urgent delivery, I was insistent that she should take a load to Sadlers. She started out but came back in floods of tears. I then realised it was far too much to expect an eight-months-pregnant woman to do deliveries in an unreliable and barely roadworthy vehicle! Luckily the garage on the side of the house was at the top of a sloping driveway, so once I got the car rolling I could start it.

One morning at about six o'clock Ann started having pains. By eight I realised I needed to call the ambulance, which was fairly quick to arrive. Ann was in a bit of a state by this time, but the ambulance men were brilliant. They got her on a stretcher and into the ambulance and I was afraid she was going to give birth there and then, but they drove off quite calmly. I was in a bit of a panic as I needed to get our daughter Teri to Ann's friend Nicky, who had agreed to look after her, and then on to the Maternity unit.

I got Teri dressed and into the car, but it wouldn't start. I went out into the road and there was a chap walking past the house on his way to work. I said to him "Could you give me a hand? I need a push to get my car started, my wife has just been taken into hospital". He was quite a weak-looking individual and he started to push, but nothing seemed to be happening. He said to me "I'm sorry but it won't move and I'm going to be late for work". I was furious and shouted at him "DON'T JUST STAND THERE, PUSH THE F***** G CAR!"

"Oh all right" he said. He must have found some inner strength, for he pushed, the car started to roll and then burst into life!

I dropped Teri off at Nicky's and sped off to the hospital, but once again, by the time I arrived it was all over. James, impatient to arrive, popped out just as the ambulance went past Wicksteed Park.

I was so pleased to have a son and to know that Ann was OK. I drove to Nicky's to tell her the news and to tell Teri that she had a new baby brother, but Teri wasn't there – apparently Nicky's cooker had caught fire and her kitchen had been gutted. Nicky had taken Teri to Carol's house in Harborough Road. When I arrived at Carol's, Teri had a black face from the smoke but was otherwise OK and was delighted to have a little brother. James' unscheduled arrival made the local paper, and there was a lovely picture of mother and baby on the front page.

Multi Weld were having problems and owed us for supplies and rent. They had some plant in their workshop which I was going to take over, but the biggest problem was their creditors.

Some of them, thinking I was part of Multi Weld, became quite nasty and refused to supply me!

The guillotine had to be sold, and to get it out I decided to take the roof off the lean-to shelter so it could be craned out. I was up on the roof removing the asbestos sheeting when suddenly one of the sheets shattered and I fell through the roof, landing badly on my right leg. The pain was excruciating, but I managed to hop round to the workshop. I tried to carry on working, but the pain was too much so I drove myself to the doctor's. He suspected the leg was broken and called an ambulance to take me to hospital. I had to wait in casualty, but when I eventually saw a doctor and had X rays it was confirmed that I had a broken tibia and heel bone. I was plastered up to the knee and taken home.

This was all I needed, as there was quite a lot of work to be finished off. I found I could get around with one crutch and went into work. I didn't seem to have a lot of pain, just a dull ache all of the time.

I needed to see the bank manager. By this time John Morris had retired and the new manager, a Mr Sorrel, was not as sympathetic. When I limped into the bank on crutches he laughed and implied that I was trying to get sympathy!

There was a delivery to do to Russell Marine. I dreaded doing it in the Cortina, with not much chance of starting it if it stalled. When I arrived and got out of the car on crutches and with the leg in plaster I told Peter Waghorn that I needed to leave the engine running because of the leg!

Working together, Brian Kidd and I were getting most of the work out. There was one very wide pulpit for a racing catamaran that was required for the Round Britain race, and we needed to deliver it by the end of the month.

I had to go back to the hospital for a check-up after a week and when the doctor, a Mr Gupta, saw the state of my leg he was most annoyed. When the plaster came off the leg was badly swollen. He said he needed to keep me in hospital for a week with the leg elevated until the swelling went down. I was admitted into the hospital and was in a ward with two farmers who had replacement hip joints. They were good company and the nurses were cheerful, but it was so frustrating having to lie there when we had work to get out for the end of the month.

Ann and my dad came to visit and Brian came in to give me an update on production. James was only three weeks old, so Ann had her work cut out to keep everything going. The next time Mr Gupta came to see me I told him that I wanted to leave, but he said he could only agree if I promised to go home and stay in bed for a week with the end of the bed propped up. I agreed, as I couldn't bear to stay in there any longer. The physiotherapist gave me some exercises to do and Ann took me home.

Teri, although she was only three years old, wanted to mother me. It was a novelty for her to have Dad home all day, even if I was in bed. I propped up the end of the bed on two large books, one of them being Reed's Mathematics for Marine Engineers – I knew this book would be useful for something one day! I felt so frustrated being stuck in bed but decided that I needed to get the leg mended and abided by Mr Gupta's orders.

There was an urgent delivery to do to Sadler's. The Cortina starting problem seemed to be fixed and Ann said she would do it and left me with Teri and baby James in a cot next to my bed. She was still breast feeding James but left me with a full bottle should he need it. While she was gone I fed James to quieten him down, but when Ann got back she was bursting with milk and wanting to give him a feed. James was fast asleep, so Ann had to get into a hot bath to try and get relief. When I went back into work the large catamaran bow rail was finished and was delivered on time. Brian had worked all hours to make things happen and it had paid off.

Polishing was a continual problem. It is a dirty job but also quite skilled. Ann's friend Nicky was married to Joe, a French teacher at the local school, and I used to get on well with him. He used to do work for me in the evenings and at weekends. He had a mate called Fred who had done some polishing and was unemployed. The polishing machine was in the stairwell and had no hoods or extraction. Fred made up a cloth mask – it looked like a Ku Klux Klan hood but he still got filthy! It used to cause much hilarity seeing Fred lurking in the stairwell with his Ku Klux Klan hood plastered in black polishing compound. I bought some steel hoods for the polishing machine, which made the job a bit less unpleasant, but there was still no extraction on the machine. Janet who did our accounts suggested that I should contact Oundle Marina, which she used to drive past from time to time. I went to see them and the buyer, David Wills, was quite pleased to have a potential supplier so close. I measured up their Fairline Fury pulpit (bow rail). The Fury was 25ft. long and quite a large boat at that time. I made a sample and delivered it, quite proud of our efforts, but when the managing director came to look at it he said "No, I don't like it, it's bloody awful, I'd rather stay with our existing supplier!"

Fairline were producing two boats, the Fairline Family, a small 19ft. cruiser. and the Fury. I got an order for a sample pulpit for the Family. This had a bend at the front that I did on the hydraulic bender, but the side bends were a gentle curve. I found the best way to achieve this was to jam the end against the wall and then bend the side bends across my back. This worked very well and we started producing six of these pulpits per month.

By now we were doing quite a wide range of yacht fittings. I used to have long conversations with John Sadler, and his advice and encouragement were invaluable. During the discussions, John suggested that there was a need in the market place for a jib reefing system. He suggested that a slotted tube over the forestay could be rotated to reef the jib. I had several ideas on how to do this. There was a dinghy system on the market made by Holt Allen, a manufacturer of sailing dinghy equipment, which had a slotted tube that rotated around the forestay, and there was a furling system called the Wickham Martin system, but this was used for stowing the sail and could not be used for reefing it.

Around this time I decided to try and get into a decent car. There was an advertisement in a Sunday newspaper for new cars, offering to take in part exchange any old car plus £50 and allow this as HP deposit. I was running Dad's old Austin A30 and he agreed to let me use it to do the deal on a new Hillman Avenger estate. I sent off the £50 together with details of the A30 and waited expectantly for more information.

After several weeks of hearing nothing and not getting any sense when contacting them, I asked for my money back. In Rushden there was a car dealership which had a new Hillman Avenger estate in stock in 'sundance red'. I went along and did the deal, it was a beautiful car, capacious, quick and looked gorgeous. When our old neighbours Linda and Kevin came to visit and to show off their new car, they were surprised to see that we had a new car on the drive as well.

Around this time there was a boom in the housing market and I decided that I would get the house valued, although we had only been there for a year. The valuation came out at £10,200, almost double what we had paid. If we moved we would need a house of a similar size, but we started to look around to see what was on the market. We found a house in Woodford, a new build, one of three, built to a very high specification. The father of the builder lived in the end one, a Mr Shortland, a very nice man with a charming wife. We took the one in the middle and on the other side were Angela and Paul Brinkman. By moving we were able to pay £200 off the business overdraft, but I always wondered if it was worth the effort for such a small advantage.

Angela and Paul became firm friends and we socialized with them quite a bit. We had a baby alarm so we could go to dinner at their house and hear if the children became restless.

At the end of Mill Road was Essams' Garage, run by Bryan and Valerie Essam. We had an account there and they did our repairs and servicing. They had two daughters and the younger, Diana, used to babysit.

We were getting more and more marine work and the representative of one of our steel suppliers, a chap called Tony, suggested that I contact Shetland Boats at Bury St. Edmunds, who were making small powerboats. I met the four directors, Jack Stokes, John Hardy, Bernie Reinman and John Stevens, who were producing 200 boats per month and buying a lot of stainless. The main product was a pulpit which they fitted on all of their boats, and I took one away to cost it up. I did a rough price but needed to know what they were paying. Tony, who supplied their existing supplier with steel, said he would find out.

To produce the pulpits economically I needed to make some press tools to flatten the feet and a welding jig to hold the legs in place for welding. I made a simple jig for the milling machine for machining the legs to fit the main tube. I produced a prototype that was identical to the sample apart from the polishing, which I did myself to a much better finish than the original. Tony told me they were paying £10.25, so I arranged to pay them a visit with the prototype. I saw Jack Stokes, John Hardy and Bernie Reinman and they were impressed with the quality. We went into the office and they sat me down with my back to a radiator and the sun in my eyes and gave me a talk about how money was tight and their need to buy as competitively as possible. I said I could make the pulpits for £9.50, and they shook their heads and said that they couldn't possibly afford to pay such a high price. I said to them "Look, I could have come in with a higher price and let you knock me down but this is the lowest price we can possibly produce this item for."

I came away wondering if Tony's information was correct, and thought perhaps I had overplayed my hand. But the next morning on opening the post there was an envelope with the Shetland postmark, and on opening it I saw it was an order for 200 pulpits! I was delighted, and told Brian that we would work all hours to make sure the order would be completed on time. But the next day an order came in for another 200 pulpits, and then the next day another, so now we had 600 pulpits to produce as well as all of our other work!

I called in some part-time labour and Brian and I were working day and night to produce everything for the end of the month. The jigs, although crude, did the job, the problem being we only had fly presses for flattening the feet and it was very hard work. I badly needed a power press and found a very old Rhodes press. Although it was well used, all the guards were working and I modified the jigs to fit. At this stage the fixing holes had to be drilled and I made up crude drilling jigs that worked very well. There were pulpits everywhere in different stages of completion. Brian was doing most of the welding and I was machining the legs and flattening the ends of the tubes on the press, which was exhausting work.

At last we had 200 ready for delivery with the next 200 well on the way to completion and the third 200 stacking up as well. The Hillman Avenger estate with the back seats down had a very large cargo area and I was able to fit 200 pulpits into the back, although the weight made the rear suspension groan. I drove over to Stanton to deliver the first 200. Several were unwrapped and inspected. The goods inwards could find nothing wrong with them and commented on the quality and high standard of finish. When I got back to the factory the next 200 were finished, so I loaded them up and prepared to deliver them the next day. The stores people were surprised to see me again so soon with another 200, but accepted the delivery with no problems. While I was away doing this delivery, Brian was determined to get the next 200 finished for me to deliver by the end of the month, and when I returned to the works they were just about ready. I delivered the next 200 and by this time they were taking up quite a lot of space in their stores, but they accepted them and I was relieved to get them all delivered and invoiced. The invoice was to make such a difference to our cash flow. VAT had yet to be introduced and boats were exempt from purchase tax. This was a concession left over from the war and the Little Ships at Dunkirk.

The next morning I had a frantic phone call from Bernie Reinman of Shetland's. He shouted down the phone, "Kevin, is that you? Look for f**** sake don't send any more bloody pulpits, we can't move for the f*****g things!"

It turned out that after my meeting with Jack Stokes, John Hardy and Bernie Reinman, they had agreed to place a trial order of 200 to see if I could perform. The problem was that each of the directors had raised an order for 200!

With the demise of Multi-Weld I needed to find another tenant for the first floor workshop, as the rent was needed to pay off the loan on the property. I advertised, but as it was on the first floor there did not seem to be much interest. I had an enquiry from a company that made hockey sticks called the MCC company. In the past they had manufactured many types of bats, including cricket bats, hence the company name. There were three directors of the Bedford based company and their existing premises in a built-up area were to be demolished to make way for housing. They used to import the basic blanks from Pakistan and then finish them off and customise them.

I dealt with Harold Alsop, the managing director, and they agreed to take a 10-year lease at a slightly higher rent than I was getting from Multi Weld. They built a small office in one corner and constructed a spray booth with an extractor fan. One of the directors was an engineer and he rigged up a lathe for turning the shafts of rounders bats and baseball bats. Their main product however was hockey sticks, and huge lorry loads of the bent wooden sticks were delivered every few days. The directors all worked on the production and they had an office lady and one or two other employees, all of whom commuted from Bedford.

With the factory now fully let, my workshop was now far too small. Fairline had introduced a new boat, the Fairline Family 22. David Wills asked me to do a sample pulpit for the new boat and indicated that it would probably fit the Fury as well. By now we were a lot better at tube work, but with the Shetland work, Sea Wych, Russell Marine and various others the workshop was bursting at the seams!

I delivered a sample and it fitted both boats. Fairline were producing three Fairline Furies a month and four of the new Holiday. I picked up an order for these two boats and was also producing 12 pulpits a month for the 19ft Fairline Family. We desperately needed more space.

On talking to an estate agent, I realised that at that time if a property was sold as an investment with tenants in place it could achieve a price of up to ten times the rent. If I were to take a lease back on the property, as I was getting about £1000 per year from my two tenants and allowing £500 per year for my workshop, I worked out that I could sell the factory for perhaps £15,000. I should have no problems letting the workshop as it had good access and would lend itself to many different trades.

I put the Park Road factory on the market as an investment for £15,000 and was prepared to take a lease back with a rent of £1500 per year. The local estate agents laughed in my face and said "You'll never get that for it", so I advertised it in the *Daily Telegraph*. I had a few enquiries and one man said he would like to view. He came from London and was due to arrive on the train at Wellingborough Station. He was wearing a long black overcoat and a bowler hat and looked a bit intimidating, but was pleasant enough. I showed him round and he asked me what my plans were. I told him that I wanted to sell the factory, take a lease back on it and use the money to buy another factory. He was quite open and said that he would not be interested in that arrangement. He said that he would only be interested if I was going to take a lease back, stay in the unit and invest the money in the business.

I was looking at old shoe factories in the area; at that time there were several on the market. I looked at an enormous one in Moor Road, Rushden and several in Kettering. The most suitable was a property in Green Lane, Kettering, with a three-storey factory of about 10,000 sq. ft. with a rear ground floor unit of about 3000 sq. ft. It looked quite run down. Most of the windows on the ground floor were broken and it looked somewhat ramshackle. The interior was quite reasonable; there was a working lift to service the three floors and some reasonable offices on the first floor.

I was lent a key by the selling agent and spent some time planning the layout, which parts I could let and which parts I could occupy. I took Ann's mum and dad round to view. I suppose to them it seemed an enormous project and when I took my dad to view the property he said "You must be mad to take this on when you have a perfectly good factory already". But it was just what I wanted. I could rent out the three-storey part and the rear ground floor workshop would give me plenty of space for the yacht fittings.

The asking price was £15,000. I agreed to buy it, but now was quite desperate to sell the Park Road property. I had an enquiry from a Mr Gerald Moulton, who was looking to invest. Mr Moulton had two companies, Ridgewood Joinery and Atlanta Marine; with the marine connection we had something in common and he came to see me. Atlanta Marine were building the Atlanta 28 sailing cruiser and a 22ft fishing boat. I had details on the boats they produced with a view to quoting on their stainless requirements. I had a long conversation with Moulton praising his boats and when asked what my plans were I told him that I wanted to sell the property, take a lease back and invest the money in the business.

We eventually agreed on a price of £13,750, which gave me a profit of over £9,000. I still needed some help from the bank to do the deal to buy the Green Lane factory, but they flatly refused. Mr Sorrel the bank manager never liked me! Our accountants suggested I try the Midland in Kettering, who agreed to help just as soon as I had exchanged contracts on the Park Road factory. There was a lease to be drawn up and the solicitors seemed to take ages as it went back and forth from them to us and I was under a lot of pressure from the vendors to exchange contracts on Green Lane. The yacht fittings work was pouring in and I had quite a lot of part-time workers working all hours. I had to be there while there were men working, so I didn't get much spare time. Brian Kidd was my only full-time employee and we devised a method of pricing jobs and recording the time on each job, with time sheets divided into 15-minute slots. All jobs were priced and had job cards. The system worked well, but often jobs took longer than the allotted time. Some jobs were much better priced, but on the whole we were quite profitable.

I called into Fairline to look at a new job, and as David Wills and I walked into the workshop we met Sam Newington, the Managing Director. David said "Morning Sam, this is Kevin, he's come over to look at the new pulpit". I remembered the last time I'd seen Sam and the "bloody awful" remark. Sam said, "You're Kevin? Pleased to meet you old boy, lovely work, you're a most valued supplier." I was a bit taken aback after the reception I had received the last time!

In 1971 Sam had joined the family business, which owned the Oundle Marina, with several hire cruisers on the river Nene. He had left the RAF, where he had been a fast jet pilot with over 700 hours on Hunters. They started fitting out Seamaster hulls for their hire fleet and then became boatbuilders and started Fairline Boats Ltd.

At last we were able to move into the Green Lane Factory. It only took a couple of days and I did a lot of the heavy work. I hired a mobile crane to lift the machines onto large flatbed lorries. The crane then followed the lorries to Kettering to offload at the back of the Green Lane factory. I bought a Tirfor, a piece of equipment for dragging heavy plant, and with skates and crowbars soon had the machines in place. I soon had the place shipshape and in production.

The first person to be employed was a polisher. He only lasted a few days, but we picked up some reasonable fabricators. One of Brian Kidd's former colleagues came to work for us. He was a skilled polisher who had worked in London polishing brass musical instruments. He had been working with Brian at Brian's former employers, polishing stainless fabrications, and the quality of his work was excellent.

I had by now finalised the design for the jib roller reefing extrusion and had ordered tooling to be made by British

Aluminium Company. BAC were keen to get into the marine Industry and were involved in the production of an aluminium-hulled sailing cruiser called the Sarum 28, a beamy fast cruiser designed by Robert Tucker; the aluminium hull and deck made a very light and strong structure.

John Sadler was keen to fit a jib reefer on his Sea Wych sloop, so I knew that at least I could sell them to him. It was still a bit of a risk, as although the tooling was relatively cheap I had to commit to several thousand meters of extrusion for it to be worth BAC producing it. Now we were in the new premises I was trying to persuade Ann that we should buy a set of Sea Wych mouldings and build a boat! I eventually won her over and picked up the boat in kit form from Sadlers just after moving into the factory. There was a covered over entrance between the main factory and my workshop and the Sea Wych fitted in nicely. How I ever won Ann over is a mystery, as we still needed furniture for the house.

I had a visit from another Sea Wych builder who lived in Kettering, Glen Thomas. He'd done a lot of sailing and knew a lot more about small boats than I did. I started to increase the workforce and soon there were about 20 employees. I was still very much hands on. I used to work a lot harder than most to set a good example and always unloaded the delivery lorries.

I started building the Sea Wych in April. Drawings were supplied with step-by-step instructions and I could call on John Sadler for help and advice at any time. Glen's boat was more advanced, as he had taken delivery before me, and he was a great help when it was time to join together the hull and deck. He also did some part-time work in exchange for stainless steel parts for his boat; quite a lot of the parts he made himself as he was a very capable engineer.

Now I needed a tenant for the three-storey part of the factory. I had managed to find a tenant for one of the small workshops, Alan Harris, a local builder. I had a call from a Mr Plews, a local businessman who had a company that made lampshades, called Anglian Lamps. Jim Plews came to see me to discuss renting the main part of the factory. He seemed disappointed that I had bought the factory and said that he would have bought it himself, and implied that I had done a dodgy deal with the estate agent, which was absolute nonsense!

We agreed on a rent of £4000 per year, payable quarterly, but when I went to the bank the manager advised me not to take on Anglian Lamps as a tenant – he wouldn't say why. The local estate agent also advised me against taking them on, but a few days later I was amazed to find a gang of men working in the factory putting up lights and doing various alterations. I threw them out and angrily rang Plews. He apologised and came to see me. He said, "Don't worry, I'll give you a grand" and he gave me £1000 cash for the first quarter's rent, and a few days later the balance of the first year's rent in advance This was before a lease had been agreed!

Anglian Lamps moved in on 22nd June 1973, and although I found Jim pushy he seemed to be a reasonable tenant. Soon the factory looked industrious again. It lost its dejected air with the broken windows replaced and signs up advertising the various companies. Most of the wire frames for the lampshades were dipped in paint and there was an old Belfast sink full of white cellulose paint in a small first-floor room. When the local fire prevention officer came round to do a survey for the fire certificate, Plews and I went round with him and he pointed out various areas for improvement. In the end Plews got quite exasperated. He said, "Look, would it help if I bought a f*****g fire engine and parked it in the back yard?" Although the fire officer wasn't happy with the facilities for dipping the wire frames, they eventually issued a fire certificate.

To comply with the fire certificate, in one of Anglian Lamps' offices there was a door that led into one of my upstairs offices which I gave permission for them to use as an emergency fire escape. It was fitted with a special door bar that would allow people to exit through our offices in an emergency. The agreement was that at all other times it should remain closed. One day, sitting in my office I heard noises from upstairs, and on investigation I found that the fire door was open and some of Plews' employees were wandering round my upstairs rooms. I told them to get out and went to see Plews, who pooh-poohed my objections. He said "It's a hot day, they only wanted a bit of air." I told him not to let it happen again and he grudgingly agreed.

A few days later the same thing happened. This time his workers were quite belligerent and Plews was un co-operative. I knew he wouldn't be around that coming weekend as he was due to play in a cricket match, so I arranged with Alan Harris, the builder, to come in and brick up the doorway. When Plews saw the bricked-up door he was furious, and was marching around shouting at everyone. I'm afraid I had a little chuckle to myself and all my blokes were smiling.

CHAPTER ELEVEN

Messing about with boats

⊰✴⊱

I was getting on quite well with the construction of the Sea Wych and was looking forward to launching it in August. Glen's boat was a bit further on than mine and he was due to launch a few weeks before me. He offered to tow my boat down to Wells-next-the-Sea, Norfolk, where I had arranged a mooring with the harbourmaster. The cost of the mooring was £10 per year, which was cheap even for those days. Wells harbour was tidal and the boats were only afloat for about two hours either side of high water, but when the tide was out the harbour was sand and ideal for children to play.

We christened the boat *Aleric*. I don't know what possessed us to choose a Nordic name, but it seemed to fit the boat. I'd bought an old Seagull outboard motor which was just about powerful enough to push the boat along in calm weather. Glen towed the boat down to Wells. I had never handled a small boat before and when it floated off the trailer I had mixed feelings. Due to the state of the tide we couldn't quite reach our mooring, so we put the boat on a mooring as close as possible. On the next tide we had to move the boat to its proper mooring, which was quite daunting to us novice boaters but we did it OK.

Paul and Angela, our neighbours, came to stay on the boat and Paul and I put up the mast and rigging. The weather was foul, with sheeting rain and a gale blowing, but the rig got erected. The next day Glen took us for a sail in his boat. The weather had moderated and we planned to sail out of Wells on the morning tide, down the coast and then back on the afternoon tide. This trip was my first-ever sail and I loved it. I helmed quite a bit and thought it was easy and was looking forward to taking my own boat out.

The next weekend I decided to take my boat out for a sail. Paul came with us, along with Janet, Ann's friend, who used to do our accounts, Teri, who was now six, and one-year-old James. Ann, Janet and Teri were to sleep in the forecabin and Paul, me and baby James in the saloon, with James in a carry cot between the bunks. We set out from the mooring and as soon as practical the mainsail was pulled up and the jib unrolled. I had fitted a prototype of the new jib reefing system and it worked very well.

We sailed down the main channel and out through the bar, and the weather was idyllic with a gentle breeze and a light swell. Paul was an experienced dinghy sailor, and as we put the boat through her paces I soon felt confident about sailing her. It was late afternoon and as the tide turned it was soon time to return to the mooring. The wind by now had increased and with wind over tide it was quite rough on the bar.

We fired up the trusty Seagull outboard and headed back over the bar. The boat was by now pitching and rolling quite violently. A sudden wave slopped over the transom and the engine spluttered and died. Then, before we could do anything, we were blown sideways out of the channel and went aground. I threw the anchor over the bow, but the tide was going out and we were soon firmly stuck.

As soon as the water level had receded, Paul went over the side and laid out the anchor and chain so that when the tide returned we would float off. I cleared the water out of the Seagull outboard and got it running; all we had to do now was wait for the early morning tide. It was quite a pleasant evening, so when the tide had gone right out I walked to the harbour and bought fish and chips for us all, which we sat and ate on board.

The next morning I took some photos of the jib reefing to use in our advertisement in *Practical Boat Owner* and also for an article in the Sea Wych Owners' Association magazine. I thought my Sea Wych was a tidy-looking ship, and all the stainless deck fittings were of the best quality, as I had made them and polished them to perfection. The interior fit out was not so good, but I intended to re fit the interior over the next winter.

During that summer I learned a lot about sailing and seamanship. Wells, being a tidal harbour, was a good place to learn as well as great for the kids to play when the tide was out. I always insisted that whenever we took the boat out we all wore life jackets. I took the boat out as often as weather permitted, there was a small and friendly group of sailors at Wells and we all helped each other out.

On one of the first occasions when I took the boat out, when she was safely back on her mooring Glen rowed over in his dinghy and said " The boat looked nice out there sailing, but when you go about it's better if you tack and not gybe each time!" Wells was a good place to learn and there was always someone to give advice or lend a helping hand. Most of the boats were under 25 feet in length. One of the nicest was a Macwester 26 called *Perfect Lady*. She was beautifully finished off with a small wheelhouse and looked a lot bigger than her 26ft. length. At the back of the factory was a shop called Owen Smart the Jeweller's, and Owen had a Seamaster 27ft power boat at Wells.

I discovered that it was possible to buy what was called a 'weather cowl' for the Seagull outboard. This was a simple rubber moulding that went over the air intake hole on the carburettor to stop the engine being swamped by a wave. Although this improved things, I realised that I needed a more reliable outboard and ended up buying a Chrysler 4 HP, which we could barely afford as money was still very tight. In the year to 31st December 1972, company turnover was £7557. 1973 was proving much better, and we turned over more in the first three months than in the whole of 1972. This was due to a massive increase in marine work and working all hours to fulfil customers' requirements.

The new premises with all the extra space were working well and I set up a crude production line to produce jib reefing systems. I was buying the reefing drums from a local die casting company. All they needed was the central hole pressing out to fit the aluminium extrusion and some slots milling for fixing eyes. Sadler started supplying Cooney Jib Reefing as standard equipment on his boats and was soon buying 8 units per month, and with other customers and direct sales we were soon producing 50 units per month. Fairline did not have a design department at this time and used to call me in to design any deck equipment they required.

There were a lot of regulations regarding the placement

and height of navigation lights and as the boats were getting bigger and able to venture further, this became more important. Shetland were also keen to comply with regulations and we started making small light masts for them – this was good business for us as they ordered 200 at a time!

Although the Sea Wych was a super little boat, it was a bit small and I was looking out for something bigger. I wanted something over 25 feet. I could probably have done a deal with one of my customers, but the cost would have been too high. I didn't know whether to build another boat or refit an older vessel. I looked at various options but they were all just out of reach financially, and by the time the boat had been finished the cost would have been in the region of £7500.

At the end of the season I managed to get the Sea Wych into the workshop to re fit the interior and I put it on the market at £1350. It had cost about £700 to build. I saw advertised in PBO a Kingfisher 30 sloop for £4500, which was about as much as I could afford with the addition of a marine mortgage. It was in a Kingfisher 30 that Chay Blyth made his first attempt at a solo circumnavigation, the attempt being abandoned off the coast of South America due to damage sustained in a collision with a press boat as he left UK waters.

Paul, my neighbour, said he would come with me to view the boat and we set off one Saturday morning down to Hayling Island, where she was laid up ashore. After the Sea Wych, the boat looked enormous, although it looked quite forlorn and was in a bit of a state. Kingfisher boats were nearly all fibreglass with the minimum of wood trim. This one, *Agape*, like all Kingfishers, was soundly built. The engine was an Albin 10 hp inboard petrol with a three-bladed propeller. Paul thought it seemed OK for the money as new boats were over £8000, and although it had been built in 1966 and used for charter it didn't seem too knocked about.

I decided to make an offer and went in at £3500, eventually doing the deal at £3700. I paid a deposit of £1300 and the balance was on a marine mortgage. I completed the purchase of the Kingfisher on 20th May 1974. She was berthed at Hayling Island and for a time we sailed from there.

The first time I took her out the engine lost its drive. I didn't know what to do so I sailed it to the Hayling Yacht Co. moorings and dropped anchor. The anchor didn't want to dig in and I had no working engine. The harbour dries out to horrible sticky mud and I dinghied ashore to talk to the harbour master, who said "You can't leave it there, the mud is nine feet thick!"

I spent all night in the dinghy laying out the anchor and getting plastered in mud. Ann was suffering from a bout of flu and could not help. By morning I was exhausted, and wondering what I had let myself in for. I was thinking of getting a tow to my mooring, packing up and going home.

There was quite a lot of activity around the harbour. A dinghy came alongside and the owner asked if I needed help. He told me his name was Howard and he was living on a house boat, one of several tied up ashore. I told him our problems and he offered to tow *Agape* and lay her alongside his houseboat, which was an ex-Navy MTB, and leave it tied alongside until the engine was fixed.

When we arrived alongside Ann and the kids went on board and met his charming wife and four children, three boys and a girl. They looked after Ann and Teri and James and made us all at home. I will never forget Howard and family who helped us when we were really down. The problem with the engine was actually the gearbox and a small adjustment was all that was necessary to make it work.

It was useful having the boat on the south coast, and I used to stay on it when I was visiting South Coast customers Atlanta

Marine, Westerly, Marcon and various others. I was quite keen to move the Sea Wych on and a chap agreed to buy it subject to a visual inspection. He arrived at Wells with a trailer and to catch the tide as soon as he arrived we loaded the boat straight onto the trailer. The problem was that as soon as he started to pull the boat up the slipway we noticed the tyres had gone flat. I borrowed a foot pump and helped him pump up the tyres sort out his trailer, we finalised the deal and he gave me £1350 cash!

I went into the pub on the quay and ordered a round of drinks. When I pulled out the enormous roll of £10 notes I had just received for the sale of the boat, the pub went quiet then suddenly, they were all laughing.

CHAPTER TWELVE

The three-day week

In 1973 British industry was going through a rough time, with the National Union of Mineworkers working to rule and coal stocks dwindling. Prime Minister Edward Heath entered into negotiations with the NUM, to no avail. The militant trade unions seemed determined to bring industry and the Government to its knees. On 13th December 1973, to reduce electricity consumption and conserve coal stocks, the Heath Government announced measures including the three-day work order commonly called the Three Day Week, which was to come into force on 31st December. Commercial consumption of electricity was to be limited to three consecutive days each week. Heath's objective was business continuity and survival, and in an act of brinkmanship he called a general election in

February 1974 while the three-day week was underway, emphasizing the pay dispute, with the slogan "Who Governs Britain?"

The election resulted in the Conservative Party losing its majority, while the Labour Party, although it won the most seats, had no overall majority. Eventually Harold Wilson formed a minority government and called another election in October, where he won with an overall majority of three. The normal working week was restored on 8th March 1974.

The early part of 1974 was a struggle for us, as not only was I trying to build up the business, we now had the three-day week to contend with. We were fortunate to find another excellent Fabricator, Bill Cullum, who was able to drop straight into the work and was a great support for Brian. By now I had an efficient and hard-working crew and it was unfair to cut their wages by 20%. Although everyone had to comply with the power situation, I told the men that they could come in on the days without power and use hand tools such as hand hacksaws and files. Although in reality not much actual production was achieved on those days, the men would not have to suffer a big reduction in wages; several had mortgages to pay and families to feed.

The polishers needed continuous power, so there was nothing they could do as far as production was concerned. I had them cleaning the floors and doing some painting. We still needed to meet our production targets, but we all pulled together and the figures for the three months of the three-day week were remarkably good, with February being one of our highest ever months.

Jib reefing was taking off and I designed a bearing arrangement to enable it to be used on larger craft. I fitted it to the Kingfisher and tested various designs and bearing systems. At a Sea Wych owners' association dinner, one of the guests accused me of photographing his boat for our jib reefing brochure. This was absolute twaddle. He had made a jib reefer for himself with a slotted tube and fabricated reefing drum, probably after talking to John Sadler, and thought I had copied his design and photographed his boat. I couldn't convince him otherwise, and when he started going on about profiteering yacht equipment companies the conversation seemed pointless. If only he knew!

The Southampton Boat Show started in 1968 and was becoming established as a rival to the London Earls Court show. The Southampton show had the advantage of a deep water marina and was not limited in the size of boat it could accommodate. The early shows were a bit crude, with inadequate catering arrangements, and if the weather was wet the mud was awful. On one of the early shows the only catering was a small stall selling prawn cocktails!

I decided to exhibit the jib reefer at the show to see what level of business it would generate, and was amazed at the number of know-all types who tried to rubbish anything new. Some of the remarks were quite bizarre and some said "It'll never work". I had made up a small spar and rigged it up on a boat-shaped board to demonstrate the principle. As the sail was pulled out the furling line wound around the reefing drum and then by pulling the furling line the sail would be rolled up. Although this was only to demonstrate the principle and how it worked, some people seemed determined to break it by swinging on the sail or the furling line, making absolute asses of themselves.

At this time there were two main competitors doing jib furling. One was the South Coast Rod Rigging Company, which used a solid stainless rod for the spar. This rod also held up the mast and the system was more than double our price. It wasn't long before there were several copies of our system on the market, all using a copy of the extrusion I had designed! There was also the Colnebrook system, which was a furling system rather than a reefing system. This was also much more expensive. The beauty of the Cooney system was that it was a tube that rotated around the yacht forestay and was independent, whereas other systems rotated the actual forestay.

One of the exhibitors at the show was a catamaran designer called Pat Patterson. He was very interested in the jib reefer and wanted to fit it on his catamarans. I worked out that there was over 40% net profit in jib reefing spars, although the main business was stainless deck equipment, mainly on powerboats.

The business was going from strength to strength. Fairline were building bigger boats every year and Shetland production was increasing, these two companies being our largest customers. The Fairline 32 Phantom was launched in late 1974, while a Flybridge version was being developed, using the same hull, and work was under way on a new 40ft craft. We were now becoming known in the industry as a serious player, and we could undercut most of our competitors. I was running a very tight ship and was very "hands on" myself.

One morning a young Indian lad walked in looking for a part-time job. His family had just arrived in the UK from Uganda, having been thrown out by General Amin, who had decided to kick out all of the Asian people. He seemed very keen and Brian Kidd, the Works Manager, decided to take him on as a labourer. He could not TIG weld, but he could do most other things and was prepared to do anything asked of him. He said we should call him Singh as he was a Sikh, and as he was the only Indian we employed at that time it was not a problem. Although he was part time he was soon a valuable member of the team. He got on well with all of the other men and had a natural ability in the workshop. His main job was at the Corby steel works, threading steel pipes. When asked what he did he would say "I am a screwer", which caused much hilarity!

Some of the local people had complained about TV interference and we had the inspector round with detection devices, who ascertained that it was the Argon arc welding. We were able to fit suppressors to the equipment, which solved the problem. Everything seemed to be running fairly smoothly. All the factory occupants were fitting in, and an area that had seemed almost derelict was now a vibrant part of the local community. On the opposite corner to my office was a dress shop run by a Mrs Fisk, and her husband Peter, who was an accountant with a local company, used to come in for a chat from time to time. Our tenants Anglian Lamps seemed to be behaving themselves. Jim Plews had a new girlfriend who seemed to be embedding herself into the company. She was a very smart lady with a commanding presence, and Jim seemed besotted. He was occupying the ground and first floor areas of the factory and had sublet the top floor to RBW Automatic and Laser Engineering, a precision engineering company run by a Mr Joe Radley.

On Saturdays I used to work until about six o'clock and on the way home I would call in at the Old Friar pub for a couple of pints. It was here that I met Martin Smith. Martin was Managing Director of Battery Services, which had several electrical businesses in the Kettering area, and we got on very well. Martin was also ex-Merchant Navy but had been a deck officer, not an engineer. He was very interested in the boat and also in my business, which some people thought bizarre, being so far from the sea.

I decided to base the Kingfisher on our old mooring at Wells, and three of the other guys who had boats there agreed to help me crew the boat for the trip from Hayling Island. Ann drove us down to Hayling and we went out for a shake-down sail before setting off. Peter Morley was an excellent navigator, Keith Spain was very experienced and used to teach sailing and Glen Thomas was also a very competent sailor. We allowed a week for the trip, day sailing where possible, and it was nice to get to sea for a fairly long trip. There was no GPS or Decca Navigator available for yachts, but Peter Morley took over the navigation, with the rest of us running the ship.

The longest leg of the trip was from Lowestoft to Wells. Because of the weather it seemed we would miss the Wells tide, and as it was also getting dark I decided to anchor in Brancaster to await it. Peter, working on a series of running fixes, got us over the Brancaster bar and into the anchorage, where we dropped anchor, and the next morning we motored round to Wells. The Kingfisher, although a bit tatty, was the largest yacht in the harbour and there were a few remarks like "I suppose all the mooring fees will go up now bigger yachts are using the harbour!"

The Kingfisher had a draught of 4ft, which was quite deep for Wells, and sometimes on neap tides she only just lifted off, so we would go alongside the quay wall. The boat had twin keels, so she would sit on the sand nicely, the keels splayed out so at the bottom they were quite wide apart. The keels were also the fuel tanks and held 30 gallons each side. Both were leaking from the bottom seam and the boat manufacturers said the best way to fix them was to make a steel shoe and weld it over the bottom of the keel. As the fuel was petrol I thought this very dangerous, and decided to fill the keels with water.

I took Brian down to Wells to weld on the steel shoes, but as they filled up with water welding became impossible, so each shoe had to have a drain hole with a plug fitted to allow the water to drain out until welding was complete. The newer Kingfishers also had the keels extended with metal plates, so we brought *Agape* up to the latest keel specification.

VHF radios were just becoming widely available amongst private boats – commercial craft and fishing boats had been using them for some time – and we bought a Seavoice, an inexpensive radio produced for the mass market. Soon most of the boats at Wells had them. In the early days no one had had any training or operators' licences and some of the conversations were quite comical!

The electrics on the boat needed some work and rewiring, and Martin agreed to come down to Wells and do it for me. We chose a weekend which we hoped would be fine, and the weather was really good with hot sun and very little wind. We were tied up opposite the Golden Fleece pub on the quay, and as it was so hot we kept a regular supply of beer coming, in the end getting quite sloshed.

I wanted to fit a masthead light which was a combined tricolour navigation light and anchor light. I winched Martin up the mast in a bosun's chair. It wasn't a very good chair and was quite uncomfortable, but it was secure. The only problem was that when he came down he had no feeling in his legs and he complained that his balls were aching!

We planned some trips further afield the next year, a trip to Lowestoft and later over to Holland. We were quite friendly with Ken Campling and his wife Jenny, who was heavily pregnant. Sometimes we would sail together and drop anchor in Holkham Bay, waiting for the Wells tide. We would occasionally take a picnic ashore. Holkham Beach is massive and had been used as a location for several movies. I would take Ann and the kids ashore in the dinghy. Jenny, despite being pregnant, would often swim to the beach and back, and although she was a strong swimmer I was concerned for her. Ken was a navigator in the RAF and used to fly in V Bombers, but he seemed to get most weekends off to go boating.

Another boater was Norman Walton, who had a power boat

which he "sailed" with his son Stuart. The company Stuart worked for was Leslie Hartridge, a Volvo engine dealership, and he was able to get me a 25 HP Volvo diesel as a staff purchase. The petrol engine in *Agape* was becoming unreliable and I had decided it needed replacing. Down at the end of Wells Quay was Robin Golding, a shipwright who had quoted a good price to fit the new engine; the boat could lie alongside his wall while the work was carried out. Another Wells boater, Julien Tugwell, offered to pick up the engine from Hartridges and deliver it to Wells in his lorry. He refused to accept any payment for this, although I insisted that he should accept £10 to cover his expenses.

At the factory, with the bigger deck rails, we were becoming tight on space again, and I saw a piece of land for sale at the end of the Telford Way industrial estate. It measured about 0.7 acres and although it was a peculiar shape I estimated that it would be possible to build a factory of about 10,000 sq. ft., which would be ideal. I could sell or let my existing unit and with the three-storey factory next door fully let the rents would finance the building of the new factory. The site was being sold by the British Steel Corporation and I was keen to move the business onto an industrial estate and into a modern unit. I now had several power presses blanking out base plates for stanchion bases and the round discs for pulpit feet, and I planned to buy more presses to cut production times. Recruitment was a problem, as it was difficult to get people with the required skills and there was always an amount of training necessary.

CHAPTER THIRTEEN

Fire

It was Wednesday December 10th 1975, and I was looking forward to the Christmas break and the end of our financial year. At about 930 pm the phone rang, and Ann answered. "It's for you" she said, "Peter Fisk, something about the factory". I picked up the phone and Peter said "Kevin, I thought I had better ring. There's a slight fire at the factory and I thought you should know. The Fire Brigade are here and they seem to have it under control. I wondered if you were going to come in?"

When I arrived there were six fire engines and 40 firemen, and some with breathing apparatus were trying to enter the stairwells of the factory. Crowds of spectators were being kept at a distance by the police. Some of the Firemen were wearing white helmets, and these seemed to be in charge. One of them was the officer who had done the fire assessment just after Plews moved in, and he picked me out to get access to the adjoining areas.

Suddenly as I looked up at the factory, all the first floor windows shattered and flames burst through with a roaring noise, with smoke and debris billowing skywards. I felt weak at the knees and thought I would throw up, seeing my biggest asset going up in flames. The man in charge asked "Are there any gas bottles in there?"

I replied, "Not that I know of, but there are some next door."

I led some firemen into my factory unit, as this was a separate ground floor unit with just one connecting wall. It seemed reasonably unscathed apart from the smoke from the blazing inferno next door. There was no power, but the firemen had powerful torches and there was some light from the flames reflecting through the skylight. We needed to remove the oxygen and acetylene cylinders to a place of safety, and I showed the firemen how to hold the top and roll the cylinders. A series of loud reports, like rifle shots, rang out, but it was only the skylights shattering from the intense heat of the fire next door. I then realised that I was only wearing normal clothes, whereas the firemen were wearing protective clothing and helmets.

I disconnected all the argon cylinders and moved them out of the workshop, as by then the heat was becoming unbearable. There was nothing more I could do so I moved outside. By now the blaze seemed to be out of control. The firemen were directing their hoses through the windows, but the fire seemed to be getting worse. There were crashing noises from time to time and I imagined that these must be Joe Radley's machinery falling through the floors and crashing to the ground.

As I looked up there was thunderous crashing and roaring as the roof caved in, with flames and sparks searing into the sky. The watching crowd all went "Oooh!" and I thought bitterly "This isn't a bloody firework display!" I was in shock, not knowing what to do. Peter came over, seeing that I was distraught, and quietly said "You need a drink Kevin". I followed him into his house and he gave me a strong gin and tonic.

After talking to Peter and having a stiff drink I felt a bit better and went outside to see what was happening. By now a hydraulic pumping unit had arrived from Corby and it was able to attack the fire through the roof. At last the fire brigade seemed to be making some progress, and they seemed to be getting on top of the fire. There was nothing more I could do, so I decided to go home and return early next morning to try and sort out the aftermath.

The next morning the most urgent priority for me was to get our factory into production as soon as possible. All sorts of people wanted to see me from the police, fire service and local press. One group was from the loss adjusters working for Plews. One guy said "And who are you?"

I said "I'm Kevin Cooney."

"Oh" he said, "the son?"

"No, I'm the owner."

I was 31 at the time and looked a lot younger. I didn't realise at the time that I looked a bit young to be a property owner.

The fire made the front page of the local newspaper, the *Evening Telegraph*, and it was on the TV news. They had film of the fire with the flames roaring through the roof, but while I was there I didn't see a camera crew. The headline read "KETTERING'S WORST FIRE FOR YEARS" and the front page picture was of Jim. There were also pictures of the factory with flames coming through the windows and roof, and people pushing parked cars to safety. Jim Plews was around, but I didn't have much to say to him. He had appointed loss adjusters almost immediately and they were marching importantly around with clipboards, making lists of fire-damaged goods.

I appointed L. S. Harris Loss Adjusters to work for me, and it was soon apparent that I was woefully underinsured. I had bought the factory for £15,000 and it was insured for £30,000, which I thought would be adequate. The loss adjustors indicated that it should have been insured for at least £80,000, so 'average' would apply, which meant that whatever the claim I would only get 3/8 or 37. 5% of the claim. This came as a shock, especially when Plews' girlfriend told Ann and me in a meeting that they expected the factory put back as it was with oak panelling in the offices etc.

The factory had been solidly built with thick solid walls, and the floors were supported by massive concrete joists which were still intact. All of the staircases were constructed in solid concrete with toilet blocks at each floor, and these were also still intact. Most of the floors had burned away and the roof was gone, but the main structure had largely survived. On the plus side, my area of the factory only had superficial damage and could soon be back in production. We still had deadlines to meet and customers to look after, and the news of the fire would be round the industry within a few hours, so I couldn't afford for our customers to lose confidence.

Most important was to get the power back on and the place cleaned up. Much of the plant was smoke damaged or wet, but within a couple of days we were back in almost full production.

I had a phone call from David Wills of Fairline, who said that he was sorry to hear about the fire and could they do anything to help. I thanked him for his concern and explained that there was nothing they could do, but thanks anyway. I also assured him that we would soon be back in full production and would ensure that Fairline would not be held up for supplies of stainless steel parts. I then had a phone call from Sam Newington, Managing Director of Fairline, who said they would pay their account in full up to date and to let him know if I required any further help. Fairline were excellent payers anyway and always paid on 30 days, but it was reassuring to have their support.

There were a lot of unanswered questions. The cause of the fire was not clear, and the fire officers who came to see me couldn't tell where the fire had started or the cause. They were very interested in the paint dipping room with the sink full of paint, but surprisingly this room was undamaged, with the sink of paint intact. I think they thought it might be arson, but there was no evidence of this and with me being so under insured I was not a suspect.

It was rumoured that Anglian Lamps had a pay out from insurance of over £100,000. RBW laser claimed losses of £80,000, but my settlement from the insurance was a paltry £17, 850. The estimate to re-build the factory was around £60,000 and I thought I could possibly do a cheap job, but then to my horror I discovered that it was a listed building!

The most important task was to get a new roof to stop further deterioration of the property, so I contacted the council to see what I would be allowed to do and what materials would be acceptable. I needed planning permission, so I had to get plans drawn up and a planning application submitted.

The boating industry was booming and we were under a lot of pressure from customers. On 2nd January I went to the Earls Court Boat Show, where there was a stand with the Colnebrook reefing system exhibited. It had an extrusion that was a direct copy of our jib reefer, but it had some good points which I decided to incorporate into our design.

I went into the factory on 4th January and saw that we had sustained some storm damage. Apparently some of the locals wanted the place pulled down because it was dangerous, but everything appeared safe enough.

At the Boat Show all of our customers were selling boats and were optimistic for the coming year. On 7th January I wrote in my diary:

Hand polisher went up the spout today, now we have three machines all useless. I ordered another today so now we will have four. Looking forward to Boat Show once again tomorrow. Went to planning office today and met Mr Robinson who was very helpful even though I probably will have to put on a better roof than I had anticipated because the DOE have listed the property as being of particular architectural interest. I shall have to get planning consent to re-roof. He also said that planning consent would be allowed on the Telford Way site. I am very optimistic for the coming year. It's a great pity about the fire, there is so much work to do to get the place operational again and with us being so busy, time is too precious.

I took Bill down to the Boat Show and we sorted out designs for Ulstercraft and Atlanta Marine and visited all our customers. At the beginning of 1976, although we had the tragedy of the fire hanging over us, it was going to be a good year, and our factory area was soon up to full production. There was the land on Telford Way to be planned and the rebuilding of the Green Lane factory, so I had a few projects to concentrate on. There was a machinery dealer in Islip in a unit next to the bridge over the River Nene; the name of the place was Islip Mill. It was called Clifton Engineering and was run by an eccentric character called Mr Bell. I bought several pieces of plant from him, most of them well used.

He had several pet goats and when I first saw them I said "Is that a goat?" He said "No, It's a f****** Alsatian!" He used to try and get me to bend down to look at things, and the billy goat would butt me up the backside. I bought a press from him and had a long conversation with him as he was thinking of selling the property. He was asking £45,000, which seemed an enormous amount of money, but it would have been a good project for me, some of the appeal being the fact that it was a waterfront property and if Green Lane hadn't burnt down it would have been possible.

I was keeping up with my judo training and when work allowed I was training at the Kettering Premier Judo Club. I was trying to get Teri interested. There was a judo club for juniors in one of the schools where I used to take her and sometimes she would come with me to watch me train.

The specification of materials required for the roof on the factory was for tiles, but I had hoped for a cheaper alternative. It was most important to get the roof on and the place watertight. I could reinstate the factory for a lot less than the loss adjusters' estimates, but it would be a case of a substantial roof, new floors and walls painted. I decided to do the bare minimum. On Tuesday Jan 13th I wrote:

Spent some time trying to get the pulley off the press to enable me to take the flywheel and pulley for machining. Buckler Boats rang an order through for fittings and as usual wanted them immediately. I cannot understand why these companies do not order in plenty of time. Haven't yet received my free copy of Boat Magazine, which I believe was late going to print. We haven't yet received any orders from this advert, most of our enquiries coming from readers of PBO (Practical Boat Owner). I can't make up my mind at all whether or not to go all out for the site on Telford Way or Islip Mill. Jim Plews asked me yesterday if I objected to him reoccupying the two front bays of the Green Lane factory – these are the bays I fancy moving my machine shop into. I don't know whether he is trying to work a flanker or whether his request was genuine. The business really must pay its way this year, all income arriving from property must be made to work in other directions. Took the flywheel and pulley over to Covallen for machining and am looking forward to getting the press working. Should cut down production times no end. Shetland rang, have new job to quote on, will go over Thursday.

We were running quarter page advertisements for the jib reefer and fittings generally in *Practical Boat Owner*. The editor, Denny Desoutter, was very interested in me and the company and wanted to fit a jib reefer on his boat *Thankful*. He said he would like to visit and do an article on the company and the jib reefing system. I was keen for this to happen, as editorial can be better than advertising and it would raise our profile.

The two top employees in the firm were Brian Kidd, who was foreman, and Bill Cullum. Bill was after another 10p per hour even though last November he had agreed to hold his rate for 12 months. I was trying to keep the business profitable. All the jobs were timed and priced, but although we were profitable we were nowhere near 100% efficient. If I gave Bill a rise I would have to give the same to Brian, and so it goes on!

I gave in and eventually agreed the increase, but I was not very happy about it. I was beginning to tire of running the business with all the problems with employees and belligerent customers, and dreamed of moving down to the south coast.

At the end of January there was an announcement in the local press about a winding-up petition against Anglian Lamps. I was relieved and hoped that at last I would be seeing the back of them.

I used to try and visit Dad once a week. He seemed to be keeping fairly fit, although he was lonely and living alone. He liked to bet on the horses in a small way and was quite successful. Dad didn't drink, but he did like Mannequin cigars and used to sit watching the racing on the TV puffing away on a cigar with a cup of tea.

In February Plews came to see me regarding moving back into the factory. We were still in dispute over the rent and according to rumour they were having difficulty paying their employees.

Monday 1st March 1976: Delivered a load of fittings to Shetlands today and picked up an order for 400 more pulpits and 120 bow rollers. The requirement is 50 pulpits per week for the next 8 weeks. They also wanted re-quotes on the fittings for the 760 with a view to buying another 7 sets.

The 760 was a larger cruiser and was more luxurious than the volume Shetlands.

I had estimated that I could build the first phase of the new Telford Way factory for about £30,000, a low estimate. I took Tony Barlow, the bank manager, up to see the land, but he could give me no indication as to whether the bank would finance the project until I produced a detailed costing.

Friday 12th March: Had a long chat with the Titmuss rep. and the steel frame should work out to about £2 per sq. ft. I am really looking forward to this project and want to have the building up as soon as possible. Went over to see Sadler this afternoon, he does not think that I can build as quickly as I say but I hope to prove him wrong. It will be a pity if I have to sell part of this factory to finance the new one. I hate the idea of parting with any part of such a valuable asset. On Monday I shall try to get Plews evicted for failing to pay his insurance!

CHAPTER FOURTEEN

Stormy waters

The business was now doing really well, and we were steadily growing and taking on more employees. Yet the rest of UK industry was in the doldrums, unemployment was high and the Labour government and the unions seemed determined to turn Britain into something approaching a communist state. The economy was in decline, strikes were rampant and in the major industries record numbers of days were lost to strikes. Industry was suffering from over manning and restrictive practices brought on by the powerful unions. Inflation was running at a massive 27% and the Government's economic plans were in tatters.

The marine industry was doing remarkably well during this time. Most of the boatbuilding companies were privately owned non-union companies and they were efficiently operated.

Fairline, Princess and Sunseeker were all family-owned businesses and pleasure boating was an emerging market.

One morning I had a visit from two officials of the AEU union, asking if they could address the workforce and tell them of the benefits of trade union membership. I flatly refused and told them if they wanted to speak to the men they would have to do it out of working hours. I then asked them to leave. One of them said that if I didn't co-operate they could make things very difficult for me. I told them to bugger off and said that if they tried it I would close the place down and that would put 30 people on the dole!

I never heard any more from them. Anyone was free to join a union if they wanted to, but I wasn't prepared to have them interfering in my business. It was hard enough running a business anyway and my men earned above union rates.

Towards the end of March, Prime Minister Harold Wilson resigned, to be succeeded by James Callaghan. In April the Labour Government lost its parliamentary majority and continued to stagger from crisis to crisis. Margaret Thatcher was gaining popularity, but until someone was prepared to stand up to the Unions there was no hope for a recovery in the general economy. Fairline were well on with the development of the F40 and I was looking forward to the development. I had some ideas on the pulpit rail and hoped Fairline wouldn't want to do it on the cheap.

By now the work on *Agape* was complete, and I planned a shakedown trip round to Lowestoft.

Wednesday 12th May: Went down to the boat today. Martin Smith, Tom Piercy and I are sailing tomorrow to take her round to Lowestoft. Took her alongside quay to load gear and after getting her shipshape went ashore for a drink and a meal. Had a meal in Wilsons Restaurant got back fairly late and listened to weather forecast. Not much chance of sailing early morning.

13th May: Listened to 0633 forecast and decided not to put to sea. Eventually left early afternoon but went aground in Wells channel. Floated off early evening and cleared bar about 2000 hrs.

I had met Tom Piercy at the Poole Boat Show, the one and only show to be held at Poole, and the weather was dreadful. Tom had a stand next to mine and was an experienced sailor. He was keen to come sailing on what at that time was considered to be a big boat. Our trip round to Lowestoft was fairly uneventful. The main mistake was not sorting out a watch system, so we were all tired at the same time. The navigation aids were primitive, we had a compass, hand-bearing compass, charts and chart instruments and a primitive radio direction finder.

We arrived in Lowestoft at 1130 am and made fast to a Royal Norfolk and Suffolk Yacht Club mooring. The yacht club was quite posh, but we were made very welcome. We left the next day at about midday after a substantial lunch in one of the harbour restaurants. But as we sailed past the S. Caister, Martin became very sick and went to lie down. He was violently ill, probably something he had eaten, and Tom and I became concerned when he started vomiting blood. He turned in and was in his bunk when he became delirious. He was convinced that Tom and I had been bribed by his wife to poison him! At one point we thought we might have to restrain him, but after a time he fell asleep and remained in his bunk, mumbling, for the whole trip. We had headwinds most of the way with an unpleasant short swell, so we didn't make the Wells tide and anchored in Holkham Bay at 0200. Martin now was recovering and stood anchor watch while Tom and I got some sleep.

On 26th May I had an interim settlement from the insurance company and decided to hang on to it for a week or two. I was trying to get vacant possession of the factory but it was proving difficult.

Friday 4th June: Went to the bank today to sort out what to do with the settlement from the insurance company. I eventually decided to pay off the business overdraft and work in credit, saving myself 14% bank charges, and put the rest on deposit. I do not intend to rebuild the factory immediately, I want if possible to get rid of Anglian Lamps first and perhaps use the money towards building the new factory. I have paid a deposit on the land and that deal should go through within 8 weeks. I am really looking forward to building the new place. The workload shows no sign of let up and our turnover is averaging £10,000 per month. If we have a really good year this year it will be so encouraging. I think that the turnovers in the new place will have to start at about £250,000 per annum, consequently there will be one hell of a lot of organising to do. We interviewed some women today for the office.

Saturday 5th June: Jim Plews came in today and offered to take the factory off my hands for a nominal sum and allow me to occupy my part rent free for life. I think he must think I am slightly stupid. He said that if I don't sell to him I shall be made to put the factory back together exactly as it was, ie. renew oak panelling and repair lift etc. The point he does not realise is that I do not really have to spend any more money than I actually receive from the insurance company. The factory which is approx. 10,000 sq. ft. is at £5 per sq. ft. worth £50,000. Taking off £25,000 for repairs that would make the factory (Green Lane) worth £25,000 as it stands. Jim hopes to get the lot for nothing. Apparently they have changed their trading name, if the original company is in liquidation I can probably get them out.

Jack Stokes, the Managing Director of Shetland Boats, was a very clever and astute businessman. Every year he would invite boat dealers to stay at his house for a weekend and include some suppliers. He had a magnificent house about five minutes' drive from the Shetland factory, with a large indoor swimming pool in the grounds, and Ann and I were invited. There were several dealers present, including Max De Boon, the son of Ari De Boon, one of Shetland's Dutch distributors, several other dealers and all of Shetland's directors. There was a reception where the booze flowed freely and then we were taken out to dinner. I noticed that Jack Stokes didn't drink but was passing it round freely. Ann and I were sitting with Bernie Reinman at the dinner and had a pleasant time. We then went back to Jack's house and stayed over.

In the morning after a swim we had breakfast, which was served by John Stevens' wife. She was a very attractive girl, a bit like a young Barbara Windsor. We left just after lunch, arriving home about 1630, and there was then a mad rush to get everything packed up, as I was due to pick up Martin and drive down to Wells to load up the boat for a trip to Holland. We arrived at Wells at about 1930 and loaded *Agape* from the dinghy until the tide went out. Stowed gear and then went ashore for a couple of pints.

Saturday 7th August 1976: Cleared Wells fairway buoy at 0630 bound for Ijmuden. Had a fairly uneventful trip down the coast, getting over the initial queasiness fairly quickly. Went across the mid cross sand but it was not too bad and we left the mid cross sand buoy abeam 2010 hrs.

We were using a Walker Log, which was an impeller on the end of a long cord connected to a dial which recorded distance travelled. A line was then drawn on the navigation chart marking the compass course corrected for variation and deviation. The distance was marked on the chart every hour and on the end of the line was marked another line indicating the speed and the direction of the tidal stream. After allowing for leeway this should show the boat's position. Martin was very good at this, as he had been a deck officer in the Merchant Navy and I soon learned the method.

We also had a Seafix radio direction finder which would pick up signals from coast stations that were transmitted at certain fixed times throughout the day. The signals were in Morse Code and the method was to identify the signal, rotate the direction finder until the signal went quiet and then take the bearing with the compass in the top of the unit. On a small boat in a rough sea this proved quite difficult. The compass was often moving about so much it was difficult to get an accurate bearing. Martin thought this was quite funny, sitting in the middle of the North Sea on, a small boat, waving the RDF, soaking wet, waiting for a little tweet!

Although the RDF was new it didn't work that well. The contacts in the back of the unit were loose and we had to stuff a piece of breakfast sausage behind the battery to make it work!

Sunday 8th August: *Managing to hold slightly better than 120 compass when really the ideal course would be 100 compass. Sea and swell very heavy, we are having a rough passage and as soon as the watch changes the one off watch turns in. We will probably put into Scheveningen as we are being carried so far south.*

Monday 9th August: Arrived Scheveningen at 0100 hrs. very wet and tired, the cabin was awash. When we stepped ashore onto the fish quay to moor up it seemed peculiar because it seemed to be going up and down. Martin had just turned in at 0300 when the customs launch came up and told us to move down to the yacht harbour. We moved alongside a Victory 40, the skipper of which told us that he was leaving at 0600. We got up at 0600 and got the 0633 forecast. We gave a copy of our weather map to our neighbour, who was very pleased. We met the Harbour Master who directed us to another berth. Had a walk around Scheveningen but spent most of the day catching up on sleep. Rang Ann to tell her we had arrived.

Tuesday 10ᵗʰ August: Planned to leave Scheveningen about midday, got up and had a hearty breakfast. Martin hired a couple of bicycles and we cycled down to The Hague, did our shopping and arrived back on board about 1200. Departed Scheveningen 1300 and had a very pleasant sail down to Ijmuden, entering harbour about 1920. We'd called up the harbour central on the VHF and were told to use the small lock, but the gates were closed and we followed a number of other yachts into Norder Sluice. Cleared customs in the lock and were in the canal about 2020. Once in the canal we moored at a small yacht harbour near the steel works, had a meal and turned in.

Wednesday 11ᵗʰ August: Left mooring at 0910 and had a pleasant trip up the Nordsee Canal, clearing the swing bridge at 1100, moored up in Amsterdam 1145. As we were coming into Amsterdam we saw a Danish warship (destroyer type) and I told Martin to dip the ensign, little realising that there would be seven of them in line astern, so our flag was up and down like a Fiddlers elbow!

When our ensign was dipped I thought no one on the Danish ship had noticed, but then a whistle blew and we saw a sailor dashing aft, nearly tripping up in his haste to get to the flag staff aft to lower their flag! Dipping the ensign was a tradition whereby you lower your flag when passing another ship. They should then dip their ensign and as soon as their flag is lowered you then raise your own. It is a form of salutation rarely used these days and it was nice of the Danish Navy to reply to such a small yacht.

It was great to have arrived in Amsterdam, and we were looking forward to the trip through the IJsselmeer.

Thursday 12ᵗʰ August: Spent the day in Amsterdam doing little, weather very nice. Went ashore for a few pints and got into a conversation with some Dutch lads. One of them had a friendly disagreement with the barman, who promptly got out a hammer and nailed his tie to the bar.

The pub was called the Bell. This barman then produced a pair of scissors and cut off the tie. There were cut off ties hanging up all around the bar! There was a large bell on the bar and underneath the bell it had a plaque which read: "Whomsoever this bell shall sound for all within shall buy a round". It was funny to see some smart alecs walk up to the bar and thinking they were clever, ring the bell and then have to buy a round of drinks.

Martin and I loved Amsterdam and were amazed at the sights in the red light district with the girls in the shop windows and the sex shops with everything on display. There were "coffee shops" where the menu was for various types of drugs. Everything was on offer, although Martin and I were not into drugs – a few beers were enough for us!

Friday 13th August: Left berth in Amsterdam and motored down to the locks and through to the Ijsselmeer. Had a bad start to the day when we were caught in a gust of wind, the boat heeled and the pilot book, hatch cover and Martin's binoculars went overboard. We managed to retrieve the hatch and the book, the latter being ruined. We had a beautiful day's sail up to Hoorn, arriving about 1830. The harbourmaster very kindly allowed us to stay the one night for nothing. We went ashore and had a walk around the carnival. What remarkable people the Dutch are. I don't think I have been made so welcome anywhere in the world.

We left Hoorn and headed for Den Oeuver, where we had a berth in the enormous marina. In one of the bars we met a Brit who worked on one of the North Sea oil rigs. he told us about Danny's bar, where they were showing some very old films. We found the bar and there was a large screen set up showing old black and white silent films – Laurel and Hardy, the Keystone Cops, Marx Brothers and various others. There was an old lady playing a piano accompanying the films. It was remarkable –

she had the music just right, thrashing the keyboard furiously one minute and slowly and sadly as the film required.

The beer was flowing freely, and you didn't pay as you ordered but for what you'd had just before leaving. When it was our turn to pay the other people in the bar insisted on paying and would not let us pay anything.

We left Den Oeuver and headed up to Den Helder, tying up next to the naval base. Martin thought he would take a short cut to town by climbing up the pontoon and cutting through the base. As he started to climb onto the pontoon he suddenly realised he was looking down the barrel of a gun! The security guards took a dim view of him entering the base and sent him away with a flea in his ear.

Soon it was time to leave Holland. The navigation planning was done and we planned to leave around midday on the 15th August. The BBC shipping forecast promised a NE force 4 to 5, so we were looking forward to a brisk sail back after our pottering through the Ijsselmeer.

We cast off around midday and motored out into the cold North Sea, putting up the sails, a reefed main and a working jib, and as the afternoon wore on we prepared for a night at sea. I took the first watch and we soon got into the seagoing routine, checking the log on the hour and plotting the position on the chart allowing for tide and leeway. The chart soon started to adopt the zigzag pattern of our dead reckoning position lines.

The wind was increasing steadily and at the change of watch we put another reef in the mainsail. By now it was difficult to move around down below, so I have a routine whereby it's waterproof jacket off, trousers down over wellies, feet out of wellies and roll into bunk. When it was my turn for watch it was reverse procedure, the object being to get outside as soon as possible!

By now the wind was screaming through the rigging. The little boat was doing her best but she kept rounding up into wind. The mainsail needed another reef. To go out onto the deck was to get soaked by the waves sweeping across the decks, but it had to be done. The reef was put into the main and with storm jib set the boat settled down to a 4-knot beat towards the east coast.

It was pitch black and the wind was steadily increasing. Every now and then there would be a roaring, hissing sound, the boat would be picked up and then would be swamped by the foaming sea. We were both doing our DR positions and realised we were probably making far more leeway than we originally thought.

By now we were looking for the first signs of dawn. Nothing seems so bad in daylight, but it seemed to take forever to materialize. We thought we would start to see some lights or signs of the approaching coast, but as we stared into the blackness there was nothing, until suddenly there was a faint glow in the darkness that became a flashing light as we approached land, still many miles off. We checked our charts and our book of Admiralty light signals, took a bearing and realised that due to the storm we were 20 miles south of our DR position. We needed to go north. Although the wind was still howling it had veered slightly, so if we tightened everything in we could just make the course. I was disappointed that we needed to slog to windward to get back to Wells with the wind gusting at about 40 knots (full gale), but I was looking forward to fish and chips on the Quay.

As we headed along the coast we saw in the distance what looked like a submarine, and listening to the VHF radio traffic it seemed they had a tug alongside because of a problem. It gave us great pleasure to call on the VHF "Submarine No 49, this is the Yacht *Agape*, do you require assistance?" We got a very curt reply!

It was quite a slog up the coast. The Wells bar is only navigable two hours each side of high water, so we needed to be there about the right time, and I decided to put the engine on to increase our speed. The Wells bar buoy seemed to be fixed in a position just out of reach, but we gradually got there on the last of the ebb and cleared the bar with just 4 ft. under the keel. We tied up at the quay and one of the local fishermen came over. "Where have you come from?" he said. When I said "Den Helder" he said "You must be bloody mad going to sea in these conditions!"

CHAPTER FIFTEEN

A taste of flying

Although we were doing well, other companies were suffering. The whole country seemed to be in the grip of the unions, with new strikes being announced every day. There were piles of rubbish building up everywhere, frequent power cuts and post was not being delivered. Workers seemed to be walking out for the flimsiest of reasons, especially in the larger unionised companies with their restrictive practices. Britain was becoming the laughing stock of the world and was now regarded as the sick man of Europe. Luckily none of our customers were union dominated and were working efficiently without problems with labour relations. We were having to pick up our post from the sorting office in Kettering, and although this was inconvenient, at least we were receiving it.

On October 6th Bill Cullum handed in his notice, which was a bit of a blow. I knew there was a bit of rivalry between Brian and Bill and Brian was foreman, but I was sorry to see Bill leave.

Wednesday 6th October: Unfortunately Cullum is leaving on Friday, I don't know yet why. One theory is that he is starting his own business. I shall miss him but we will manage. The scaffolding is at last going up around Green Lane and the building work is to begin. I may just have enough money to reinstate. I am awaiting the plans on the Telford Way factory.

During the past year we had been in dispute with Anglian Lamps. I was keen to see the back of them and occupy the factory ourselves. They were occupying the two areas not affected by the fire and were paying no rent. In the lease there was no suspension of rent clause, and although I should have been covered by the insurance policy as they were still in occupation the insurance weren't interested. It seemed every few days there were letters going to and from our solicitors with all sorts of bizarre claims from both sides, but nothing much seemed to be happening. It was almost like the solicitors were playing a game of who could write the most letters which said least.

The reinstatement of the factory was beginning, the first priority being the roof. I was also looking for builders to price the new factory. Martin had recently moved into a very nice barn conversion. The builders who had done the work for him were Clipstone Builders of Geddington. The work was of a very high standard and Martin said Clipstones would build anything and had built factories in the past.

Peter Clipstone came in to see me. He looked just like a farm labourer in his working clothes and had a broad Kettering accent. "Hello m'duck" he said, "I've come to see yer about factory". One of the peculiarities of the Kettering accent was calling people 'm'duck'.

I got three quotes from building contractors, and the prices ranged from £45,000 to 105,000. I eventually awarded the job to Clipstones. I had long discussions with their site manager, Bill Swann, and decided I could work with him. To finance the project I had put my workshop on the market at £15,000, and it was sold almost too quickly. I was able to brick up all the connecting doors to the Green Lane factory to make the workshop a self-contained unit. I then needed the bank to fund the remaining £30,000.

Christmas came, the holiday I always liked best of all. The factory was closed and all our customers were also closed, so there would be no panics for parts they had forgotten to order. We always had Christmas Day at our house and my sister Anne, Tony and the boys, Ian and Michael, visited, together with my dad. Boxing Day we always went to Anne and Tony's. Sometimes Ann's mum and dad came also and we always saw Ann's brother Ron at some point over the festive period.

Each New Year Martin used to have a party, usually fancy dress, and everyone made an effort. Some of the costumes were quite exotic.

Monday 3rd January 1977: Normal Sunday at mother-in-law's, arrived home at about 1600 glad to be back to normal. Weather bitterly cold, must be the coldest winter for a year or two but luckily the snow seems to be holding off. This year should be very eventful, what with building a new factory, rebuilding Green Lane and expanding the business to sell into Holland and Germany. Also there will be the summer cruises in Agape. I think that at the end of the coming season I will perhaps put her on the market, I may try a motor boat next!

I had decided to buy some movie equipment so that I could film some of the sailing trips. There was quite a lot of movie equipment on the market, but I wanted to have sound. The set up I bought was a Chinon 805s zoom reflex and an 850 sound projector, together with a cartoon film for the kids. Unfortunately the sound didn't work, which was a great disappointment as I was so keen to see it working.

I started a Yachtmaster correspondence course in navigation and resolved to do two hours several times a week. We were up to capacity in our workshop and it was slowing production. With so much work coming in we were in danger of grinding to a halt. I would have liked to move into next door but we were still arguing with Anglian Lamps.

Friday 4th March: Went to the Telford site today and work has just begun on site clearance etc. It has been a long slog to get this far and to actually see men working on site. In the present factory we are so short of space that it is impossible to do jobs efficiently.

Tuesday 8th March: Golding rang today to say that Agape had broken free and was up on the marsh. I drove down and managed to get the main anchor out before the tide came in. As soon as she lifted off I slipped the engine into reverse and backed her off the marsh, pulled in some chain and she was free. I took my kedge out in the dinghy and dropped it. She then floated nicely to the two anchors, drying out at about 2300hrs. When she was dried out she sat within about 15ft. of the original mooring. In the morning I got up at 0600hrs. and attached Agape to her mooring, replacing the broken shackle with the shackle off the kedge. When she lifted off I tied the stern mooring on and then I went ashore and purchased some stout rope, a large thimble and assorted new shackles. The rope I put onto the stern mooring and replaced several shackles on the bow mooring. I left her hoping that she would now be secure, arriving home at about 1900hrs.

Fairline were well on with the development of the F40 and I was starting to design the rails, pulpit and ladders. The pulpit was the biggest we had so far attempted and it was difficult to fit it into the workshop. I decided to take it into the Green Lane factory on Saturday morning to bend it up, as no one from Anglian Lamps was usually around at weekends. As it was so big we ended up taking it out onto a flat roofed area on the first floor to set it out.

Saturday March 12th: Brian and I took some tube and the hand bender onto the first floor of Green Lane and started to manufacture the pulpit for the Fairline 40. This is going to be a really magnificent boat. After we knocked off at 1600hrs I took Ann and Janet up to Telford way to see the site.

The original project was for a factory of 3000sq. ft plus an office block, but this would have been far too small. I considered office space to be a waste of manufacturing area, so I changed things around and ended up with a 5000sq. ft. factory and no office. There was an area on the plan shown as a canteen area which I decided to use for office space. Although the site had been cleared and fencing erected, work on the actual factory had not started.

I had planned to split the existing factory into several units for disposal and already had my workshop up for sale to finance the new Telford Way project. As the new factory was so delayed and desperate for more space, I decided that the dispute with our tenants had gone on long enough and I was going to move into the factory anyway!

Monday 14th March: I have made a firm decision to move into the middle floor of Green Lane. The dispute with Anglian Lamps has now reached ridiculous proportions. This morning I organised the wiring and ordered another welder. I think I can probably put four more welders up there, to handle all of the small fabrication and welding jobs. I don't yet know how the politics of the move will develop, but no doubt something may develop tomorrow.

The move into the first floor didn't go down very well and

all sorts of threats and warnings were flying around, but I stuck to my guns, as I suspected Anglian Lamps couldn't last much longer. Sure enough, on 28th March a receiver was appointed and we entered into an arrangement with the company's guarantors.

Thursday 21st April: Work started on the new factory today, the only problem being that now I am repossessing Green Lane I don't need it. Also I think that we have almost outgrown the phase one 5000sq. ft. already.

Fairline asked me if we could produce fuel and water tanks. At that time with the plant we had we could not make them efficiently and would need an 8ft. guillotine and an 8ft. folder. I contacted Mick Webb, the machinery dealer we were using, and priced up the two machines we would need. The price came to about £15,000, and I would need finance to obtain them. I went back to Fairline and said that I could do their tanks, but in order to put in the plant they would have to agree to pay as soon as the invoice was received. They agreed in principle and I then quoted prices for the tanks. I negotiated with Dave Wills and they gave me the go ahead to buy the machines. I contacted Mick Webb, who arranged for him and me to view two machines in Norfolk.

I'd had a meeting with Sam Newington and Dave Wills the day before and sorted out the details of our agreement. Sam seemed quite keen as they were having problems with their existing supplier. Mick picked me up early one morning and we drove to Norfolk to the machinery stockist to look at some plant. I agreed to buy an 8ft Barnes guillotine and an 8ft Hydroform folder.

We were in the office doing the paperwork when the phone rang. "It's for you" they said. I was mystified – who on earth could it be? "No one knows I am here," I said.

It was Sam.

"Sam here Kevin, look we've had second thoughts about the tanks," he said. I was speechless. "Yes" he said, "I got the number from your office and thought I had better ring you before you go buying expensive plant!" I then spent quite a few minutes reasoning with him, eventually persuading him to let us go ahead with the deal!

Most of the designs for the tanks we took off the Naval Architect's drawings with any required modifications agreed by Fairline's engineers. Most of the tanks had two baffles dividing the tanks into three compartments. The baffles were welded in and had the corners removed to allow the fuel to find its own level. The tank design for the F40 was sent directly from Sam Newington and specified that the baffles were to be fully welded with just a 3/4" hole in the top of the baffle. I queried this, as I couldn't see how the tank could possibly work, but Sam was adamant that this was how the design should be. I then queried the design with Fairline's chief engineer and he said "If Sam said he wants it like that, do it like that".

We did the tank as requested. The boat when finished looked magnificent and I went down to Port Fairline at Birdham Pool, Chichester, to see it on the water. The agent, Brian Peters, was delighted with the boat and there was a lot of interest in the industry.

A few days later I called in at Fairline and the F40 line manager called me over and said "Have you heard about the 40 down at BA Peter's?"

"Why, what's happened?" I said.

"It ran out of fuel in mid Channel. Sam's furious."

The next morning in the post there was a letter from Sam. It said: "Dear Kevin, Are you absolutely bloody stupid? Producing a tank with just a small hole in the top of the baffle, it's obvious that it wouldn't work." The letter then went on and on about how stupid I must be.

I replied pointing out that I had queried the design and raised concerns both with him and his engineer and had been instructed to produce it that way. I also included a copy of Sam's original sketch. I then had a letter apologizing and telling me to point out in future to him any concerns I might have on any design issues. I had done this anyway, but in future I decided that I would refuse to make anything that I wasn't happy with.

Pat Patterson paid us a visit. He was planning a circumnavigation following the route that Sir Francis Drake took in 1577. Pat designed catamarans and was planning to do the trip in his Ocean Winds 33, which was a big brother to his successful Heavenly Twins. He was keen to fit one of our jib reefing systems for the trip. He was based in Plymouth, so it was quite a journey for him to come up to Kettering.

We discussed what was required and Pat ordered a jib reefer for the trip and was keen to fit them on the Heavenly Twins. he also invited me to go sailing with him down in Plymouth, which I was keen to do.

Sunday 8ᵗʰ May: Have been down to Agape this weekend. Drove down on Friday, got half way and had to turn back to pick up our movie camera. We managed to get some good shots of the launching, I hope they turn out OK. Poured with rain Saturday night but Sunday was very nice. The boat needs quite a bit of work before she goes to sea again. Went down in the Datsun truck and although it was crowded the children were very good. We had a surprise when we returned home, Brian Essam invited us to go for a weekend in Amsterdam. He will hire a light aircraft and fly it himself.

It turned out that one of Brian's mates, Stuart Luck, was a professional pilot and flew business jets for the Ford Motor Company. He was to be pilot and Brian, who had a private pilot's licence, would be co-pilot. Although the prospect seemed exciting I was not too keen. Flying was not one of the things I wanted to do and I told Ann to find an excuse not to go. I said "There's no way you are getting me up in one of those bloody things, they're not safe!"

Saturday 14th May: Flew to Amsterdam and landed at Schiphol just after 10 am. Stuart Luck was the pilot with Brian Essam as co-pilot, the plane was a Cherokee 6. A minibus picked us up from the plane and took us to customs etc. We took a bus to Central Station and booked our hotels from the info-kiosk. Unfortunately we were in two hotels, Stuart and Jane in one and Val, Brian and us in the other. We had lunch of sausage rolls and a pastry and then met up with Stuart and Jane and spent the afternoon meandering round Amsterdam. Towards evening it turned cold and wet and we all returned to Stuart's hotel for coffee. We went for a cruise round the canals in a boat and drank loads of wine, got pleasantly drunk and had a happy time. When we got off the boat Val and I rushed off across the road and fell flat on our faces between the tram lines. When we got up I was struck a glancing blow by a tram as it went past and I landed in the hedge. We eventually found a bar and cleaned ourselves up. We all returned to our hotels in a taxi.

On the canal cruise there was a party of Americans that had been diverted to Schiphol due to problems at their destination. They were a religious group on a pilgrimage to the Holy Land and they were teetotal. The canal cruise included cheese and wine, and as they didn't drink there was plenty of wine for us, and I don't like cheese anyway!

We had a pleasant couple of days in Amsterdam and were due to leave Sunday evening. We arrived back at the airport at about 6pm and ordered our duty free in the aircrew duty free shop. We took off at about 7pm, followed by a jumbo, and as the plane climbed, looking out we could see the tulip fields, a blaze of colour as far as the eye could see. Stuart allowed Brian to fly the plane back to Coventry, arriving at about 845 pm. I was quite impressed with the Cherokee 6. I really enjoyed the weekend and admired Stuart and Brian's flying abilities. I thought that I would like to learn to fly.

On Wednesday 25th I went with Brian to Sywell and he hired a plane and we went flying. It felt so exciting. Brian let me have a go at the controls and we flew over the house, but Ann didn't see us.

For some time Ann and I had been looking to move to a larger house. We were very interested in a large bungalow in Titchmarsh and if we could extend it, it would be ideal. Brian and Valerie had a large swimming pool in their back garden and we quite often went there for a swim and barbecue. I thought that perhaps we could construct a pool in the garden at the Titchmarsh house if the sale went through.

Monday 30th May: Drove to Kendal today. It is about 226 miles and I arrived back in Kettering at about 1600. Tomorrow Anglian Lamps are moving out of Green Lane (I hope). There may be some last minute aggro, and they are talking of taking locks and things with them. It has been a long struggle but I think I have eventually won! Let's see what tomorrow brings. We have decided on the Titchmarsh property, having found out that we can do the roof, and there is also room for a pool in the garden. Had the mortgage broker around this evening, so I think we will probably move in August. Pat Patterson rang and I am going down to see him in July.

Around this time a lot of people in the industry were buying sets of mouldings and kits to build their own boats. Most of the boatbuilders were offering kits ranging from a basic set of unfinished mouldings to a complete kit to finish a boat up to any stage of completion. We were advertising kits of stainless fittings and quite often I would visit customers to give advice and encouragement.

One company that specialised in boat mouldings, and probably the most successful, was Colvic Craft. They could supply everything from a 19ft motor- boat to a 50ft ocean going yacht. Quite a few boatbuilders based their boats on Colvic Mouldings, the main ones being Atlanta Marine and Oyster. We were supplying Colvic, but their main interest was selling their mouldings, which were of a very high quality. They only supplied our product as a service to their customers and mostly sent customers directly to us.

I decided to buy a set of mouldings for the UFO 34 cruiser racer, and went to see Colvic. They said I could have a 20% discount off list price if I became an agent. I thought I could possibly sell some mouldings, so I formed a company called Inshore Marine Ltd. Although I took a few half-page adverts in *Yachting Monthly* offering kits of parts and stainless fittings I never sold any!

There was a chap called Pat Cotton with a set of Colvic mouldings in Thrapston. His previous boat was a Sea Master 27ft power boat which he used to moor in Wells, and he wanted me to do the stainless fittings. The boat was a Colvic 28ft 6in Sea Rover and he was fitting it out on a plot of land behind his shop. I was watching the progress with interest, thinking that I might fit out the UFO 34 when it was delivered.

Anglian Lamps eventually left and I then had to finish off the reinstatement of the remaining areas of the factory. Allen Harris, the builder, had done most of the structural work, but there was a lot of glazing and decorating to do. We were already occupying the first floor, but when I went round and inspected the empty factory I found that in every toilet the toilet pans, cisterns, sinks and everything ceramic had been smashed. It looked as though someone had gone round with a hammer and smashed everything!

We soon took over the rest of the factory, and with the lift in operation it was not a problem moving parts around between the floors. The drivers that worked for BOC, the firm that supplied our argon, went on strike. We couldn't function without gas so it was a real threat to the business. The other main gas supplier wouldn't help. Their cylinders were a different size thread, so without a lot of modification they were not suitable. It seemed that whenever things were going well something would come up to throw a spanner into the works. It was eventually agreed that we could collect cylinders in our own truck at certain times.

Pat Patterson had invited me to go down to Plymouth for a sail in the Ocean Winds catamaran. I'd been looking forward to this and set out on a Friday morning for the trip to Millbrook where the boat was moored. Pat had a small boatyard with a dock and a slipway with several moorings and hard standing. The whole site covered several acres and was a former stone quarry. On the land he rented out plots for amateur boat builders.

We motored out of the river Tamar and round to Cawsand, where we anchored for the night. Pat produced a bottle of whisky and we had a convivial evening getting to know each other. He was a very experienced seaman, having competed in the Round Britain Race, and had sailed across the Atlantic doing delivery trips. He was due to depart on his circumnavigation "In the wake of Drake" in November. He had fitted a jib reefer, and as we sailed round to Looe we put it through its paces. The weather was perfect for sailing, but I had forgotten to pack my sailing shoes so Pat lent me a pair of wellies that belonged to his mate Bill.

I quite liked sailing on the catamaran, which didn't heel over like the monohulls I was used to sailing on, and the cat seemed much larger than 33ft due to the width (beam) of the hull. Another advantage of the catamaran was the shallow draft with the ability to dry out. I had a great weekend sailing and learned a lot about the characteristics of catamarans. Pat was a pleasure to be with, and he invited me down to sail the boat again before he set sail on his epic adventure.

Construction on the new factory was progressing, it seemed, at snail's pace, but this was probably due to my impatience to get the job finished. I'd ordered the set of UFO 34 boat mouldings and needed somewhere to put them during fit out. I had a concrete pad laid down by the builders at the factory, and had it made just big enough to accommodate the cradle I had made to fit the hull.

We were fully moved into Green Lane and were occupying the offices. We employed a mature part-time lady, Betty, and a younger woman, Jenny. Ann was in charge of finance and ran the office. We'd been supplying a company called Gilmax which produced the Hurley 22 sailing cruiser. They were in trouble and were not paying, so I asked them for a set of mouldings to settle the debt. I thought this would be better than losing everything, which would happen if they went into receivership. They agreed, so all I had to do now was to get the mouldings. I was using a debt collector called Andy Stubbs who had been successful with other bad debts and he seemed to think that this should work.

Work was still coming in and now that we had more space we were getting more efficient. I was looking forward to moving into the new Telford Way factory, which would give us more headroom for producing the larger rails. I had planned to do a trip to Holland similar to the last year's trip for the summer. On this year's trip, Ian, my nephew, was joining Martin and me for the trip and Ann was to join us in Amsterdam.

Saturday 30th July: Left Wells quay 0510, northerly wind.

Called Wells Coastguard on the VHF, but Gorleston answered. We told them of the timetable. We are all feeling very sick. I was first, followed by Ian, Martin was last. Approaching Lowestoft we all started to enjoy the trip. Ian went forward and lay dozing in the dinghy and Martin and I took some film. At 1830 the wind had died so we started the engine, arriving at Lowestoft 2040. Upon entering harbour the engine ceased to drive the prop. Upon inspection the shear pin had gone.

We arrived in Scheveningen on Monday 1ˢᵗ August. We had several problems with the engine shear pin, which kept failing although there was a flexible coupling that should have solved any shaft alignment problems.

Wednesday 3ʳᵈ August: We departed Scheveningen at 0825, clearing harbour about 0845. There was no wind, so motor was on. The mist closed in and we found ourselves in a sea fog, the visibility at times being only 20 yds. The fog eventually lifted, and at noon we were off Zandvoort. At 1330 we entered Ijmiuden harbour. Just as we were entering the lock the shear pin failed again! We managed to tie up at the pilot berth but we were told that we had to leave at once. We did however fix the pin, but it failed twice more before entering the lock. Entered lock 1545 cleared 1615 en route to Amsterdam. Engine shear pin failed 1640, tied up alongside main road to two lamp posts. Martin went ashore to try and buy a replacement bolt. He obtained two. Engine ready 1805 but needed further work and we eventually departed 1845. At 2000hrs approaching swing bridge, we moored in Amsterdam 2115.

On Friday 5ᵗʰ August a British yacht came into the next berth, a Maxi 9.5 skippered by Eric Thompson, the UK Pelle Petterson agent. Eric used to be the Managing Director of Offshore Yachts, one of our first marine customers. We were producing stainless steel for their Halcyon 27 sloop, but they went into receivership in 1974 or thereabouts. Eric and his crew came on board and had a few G&Ts. They invited us back to their boat the next day. Ian and I went to Central station to meet Ann, who was joining us for the rest of the trip. Whilst in Amsterdam Martin left the ship and was due to rejoin the ship in Enkhuisen or Den Helder for the trip back across the North Sea.

Sun 7th August: Left Amsterdam 1035 and entered Orangesluis, met a young German couple who were familiar with Kingfishers, having owned a 20+. They were in a Macwester 26. We cleared the lock and swing bridge and were into the IJsselmeer at 1300, sailed to Volendam arriving 1845 and moored alongside a large steel Dutch boat. Another British yacht arrived and the skipper, wife and little girl came aboard for a booze up. Ann made a curry for supper.

After Volendam we cruised in the Ijsselmeer, stopping at Hoorn, where we had to fit another shear pin in the drive shaft coupling. I drilled another hole and put an additional bolt through the coupling, hoping that would last until I could do a proper repair when we got back to Wells. At Hoorn there was a carnival with fairground rides and stalls selling all sorts of foods. Ian particularly liked the frites (chips). The weather was very hot and there was a happy carnival atmosphere. Ian went on several of the rides and we all had a great time, but all too soon it was time to leave and we motored to Enkhuisen, where we moored to the visitors' berth.

Ann and Ian decided to do some fishing and managed to catch 10 fish, rudd and roach, none of them suitable for eating! At Enkhuisen Martin rejoined us in the early hours of Saturday 13th. He'd arrived on the 9pm train and I had gone to the station to meet him, but we managed to miss each other so I returned to the boat. He was trudging round for hours looking for the boat. I had given him directions and the berth number and had put on the masthead light, but the Enkhuisen Marina is enormous. He arrived exhausted carrying a plastic bag containing some enormous bottles of duty-free gin, and although it was 2 am when he arrived we decided to have a couple before turning in!

We left Enkhuisen at noon the next day and motored to Andijk and then to Medemblik to pick up provisions, then on to Den Oeuver, clearing the locks and mooring up in Norderhaven, alongside a barge. We visited Maxi's bar again and had a few beers, but they were not showing the silent films this time! We left Den Oeuver but didn't call in at Den Helder. The trip across the North Sea was a bit rough, but having Ann on board made it a lot less taxing. Ann and Martin were sharing waterproofs, so at the change of watch Ann would struggle out of the waterproofs and Martin would struggle into them! This was no mean feat when beating into a north easterly gale. The wind was about a force 6 to 7 gusting 8 for most of the trip back and watching Ann and Martin's antics at the change of watch was quite amusing, but it only took 32 hours and we were back in Wells and tied up to the quay by 2000hrs.

The UFO 34 mouldings were due to be delivered and I had made up a spreader bar for the crane. This was a length of RSJ with a smaller length welded onto each end. This was necessary to stop the crane lifting slings pinching the hull. It had four large shackles for the slings and a central shackle for the crane hook. The lorry arrived with the hull and deck and the slings were attached to the boat and the crane hook fixed to the middle of the spreader. There was quite an audience with the builders working on the factory and some of my men starting to move things in. The mouldings were to be put into a wooden cradle that was on the concrete pad the builders had laid down. I had my movie camera to record the event and was quite excited at the prospect – the mouldings would look almost like a sculpture outside the front of the factory.

The crane started to lift the boat as I was filming. Higher and higher the boat went, until there was a loud crack and the spreader bar collapsed! Luckily it held together, and the boat was high enough not to hit the ground. The crane driver was able to lift the boat with the collapsed spreader bar into the cradle and surprisingly, there was no apparent damage. I had the whole episode on film. Although I was tempted to stop filming when the bar collapsed I was glad I didn't.

Agape was in a sorry state and I decided to bring her back to Kettering to tidy her up and put her up for sale. Dad rang to say that Cousin Mike and his wife Fran were going to be in the Isle of Wight for Christmas. They were in their yacht *Prion* and were attempting a circumnavigation. I had not seen Mike since I was a toddler and I barely remembered him. The family had emigrated to Canada in the 50s but had kept in touch with Dad. I suggested that they come to us for Christmas and arranged to pick them up from Southampton Red Funnel ferry terminal.

Thursday 29ᵗʰ December: Mike and Fran Cassidy came for Christmas, I picked them up in Southampton Christmas Eve at 1100hrs and we were back in Titchmarsh at 1400. Unfortunately the power cables were down due to the wind blowing a tree across them. Everyone mixed in extremely well with no personality problems at all. Worried that we would have no power the next day so Ann took the turkey to Val's to cook it. The power came on at 1900 and soon everyone cheered up. Mike and Fran liked the bungalow very much.

Christmas Day I cooked the breakfast and we had the usual exchanges of presents. Ann wasn't too pleased with the collarette I gave her but she can change it for something else. Mike took James to feed the horse and to look at the offending tree. It was a beautiful sunny day. My Dad and the Dewhursts seemed to fit in very well. Anne, Tony and family came for lunch. There were

14 in all and I could tell from the hum of chatter and laughter that everyone was enjoying themselves.

Monday was fairly quiet with Mike taking James for walks. Tuesday Ron, Kate and family came and we had a very happy day. Wednesday I took Fran and Mike round the factories and saw them off on the train at midday, feeling very sad they were leaving. This last year has been quite eventful. We have been busy at work, we had a few problems like the BOC strike but now the new factory is finished I can see a promising year ahead. I hope to obtain my PPL in May and am going to get really stuck in in the New Year. Up to now I have about 11 hours' experience. We have gone out a lot more this year largely due to our friendship with the Essams. We are now living at Titchmarsh and I like the village very much. Agape is now lying at the Factory and the UFO 34 mouldings are also there.

I was determined to do more flying this year and get my private pilot's licence. It was going to be a busy year with the move into the new factory and the new work coming in.

Thursday 5th January 1978 Left home at about 0815 and dropped the kids off at Angela's. Caught the 0926 to St. Pancras and arrived boat show about 1100. Visited Jeckells and a few other customers. We went to see the Cornish Crabber and Ann promptly fell in love with it. We went to the one afloat on the pool and although there was a floor show going on (Scottish dancing etc) we both had eyes only for the boat. I really would like to buy one of these and I think Ann feels the same. We could talk of nothing else on the way home, I think we may buy one.

The move to the new factory was scheduled to start, with the first phase going in on Wednesday 11th and phase 2 on Saturday 14th. I had been chasing Gilmax for the set of Signet 22 mouldings to cover their debt and Andy Stubbs had also been on the case. It was delivered on Wednesday 11th January, minus the stage 2 kit which should have been included, but at least I had something. if they went into receivership I would get nothing!

CHAPTER SIXTEEN

Trouble on and off the water

━━━➤✕◠━━━

We ordered a kit of parts to build our Cornish Crabber. The kit comes as a completed hull and all of the bulkheads and vertical partitions fitted. There is still a lot of work to do to complete the boat. At the new factory I'd had the floor laid ready for the second phase of the build. This provided a 2000 sq. ft. concrete pad and that's where I planned to complete the Crabber.

Now that we were into the New Year I was determined to do as much flying as possible and hoped to obtain my Private Pilot's Licence during the year. There were a lot of challenges, such as making production as efficient as possible in the new factory, refitting *Agape* and running two factories. We were still using part of Green Lane as a machine shop and that was where we were making the jib reefing systems. I was also planning on extending the Telford Way factory as soon as everything settled down after the move.

Friday 13th January 1978: Went flying today and after three circuits Paul Smith (the CFI) told me to land and go back to the threshold to practise the take-off from scratch, keeping the aircraft straighter with the rudder. However after I had done the pre take-off checks, Paul said he was sending me off on my own. He then called the tower and got out, having first warned me that I would probably notice a weight difference. During the take-off run the plane lifted off at about 60 knots and I had a wonderful feeling of relief that there was no one there to watch my every move. Visibility was so much better also with no one in the other seat. The circuit went according to plan and the landing was all right although the aeroplane seemed to float longer before touching down. The tower told me to clear to the next intersection and I did this. Taxi-ing back to the parking area I felt quite elated and when I got back into the office, Smithy said that I had done very well, but he always says that anyway!

I am not superstitious and had no problem doing my first solo on Friday 13th, but some of the others were horrified. Now I always look upon Friday 13th as "my lucky day". I had decided to give up drinking until I had passed all of the exams and been awarded my pilot's wings. My friends could not understand how I could go out to a dinner dance and not have a drink, but I found I could have a good time without getting plastered and after a time I used to enjoy being sober.

Thursday 19th January: Snowed like hell today, I expected something to make the move more difficult. A few bits and pieces were taken up there but nothing much. I asked the bank today for finance to put up another two bays and also an increase in the working limit from fifteen to seventeen and a half. Mr Sully (Bank Manager) said he thought that there would be no problem and that he would put it forward to Area Manager. When I returned from Telford Way later in the afternoon there was a message to ring the bank, but unfortunately it was too late. When I arrived home the children had built a snowman in the front garden.

The bank agreed to up the limit and to finance another two bays on the Telford Way factory. We were a lot more efficient in the new unit and I had employed several semi-skilled fabricators, hoping to train them up to the required standard. The store-man/buyer, Jim Knox, was ex-Navy and was good with customers. When exhibiting at boat shows Jim used to work on the stand and was a good salesman. Some of the other employees resented the fact that Jim got to go to boat shows, and to them it seemed as though I was giving him preferential treatment. There was an unpleasant undercurrent and some jealousy regarding wages. The more skilled fabricators were on a higher hourly rate than the lesser skilled, and this was a constant cause of argument.

They decided they needed a workers' representative and chose the machine shop chargehand, George Davis, who was in charge of manufacturing the jib reefing systems and the machine shop. The polishers were always on a good rate of pay due to the fact that it was a skilled job but very dirty. Their rate was slightly lower than the fabricators' rate but was made up with an extra amount we called "dirt money." Brian the foreman used to keep his eye on the situation but of course any increase in the rate would benefit him as well!

Ann and I had decided to start dancing lessons. There was a dancing school in Kettering run by Margo and Ivan Newman. Margo was a very attractive blonde and Ivan was dark-haired with almost a Latin appearance. At the first lesson there were about 85 people, of all ages, shapes and sizes. Margo and Ivan stood at the front of the class and as they called out the steps, slow slow, quick quick, slow slow, everyone marched around to the music. We then paired up with our partners and tried out the dance as Ivan and Margo went around correcting any wrong moves. Some of the class didn't have a clue and were getting themselves in a muddle, stopping and waiting for one of the teachers to sort them out. Week by week the numbers got less until there were about 10 couples that turned up regularly. I loved the dancing, having always been a dancer.

Wednesday 1st February: No flying today, it pissed down all day. Went to Wicksteeds Motor Club dinner and dance this evening. Met at Martin Smith's and went on from there. The meal was good, better than the last one and we all danced all night, Martin with everybody else's wife and Brian and me taking it in turns dancing with Pat (Martin's wife). We are all moved in at Telford Way and in production, last year we were only about 50% efficient. I am hoping for about 70% at least here.

The March wage increase was fast approaching, and although it was traditional to give a wage increase each year it depended on being able to get a price increase from our customers. This was looking unlikely as there seemed to be a slowing in the industry and although we were able to increase production due to extra capacity, customers were beginning to look closely at costs. I announced that the wage increase would be 6%. I thought that this was generous, but it wasn't well received. There was a lot of grumbling and moaning and George came to see me to ask for a larger increase. I was furious, although I kept calm and eventually agreed to an increase of 15p an hour and three extra days' holiday.

The factory extension should have been completed by the middle of March but was nowhere near ready. The concrete floor was there and the steelwork, but there was a hold up with the purlins that hold the roof sheeting.

The Cornish Crabber was delivered in March and I put it on the concrete base of the factory extension, thinking I could find time to work on it, but it seemed impossible with everything else going on.

Sunday April 2ⁿᵈ: I am 34 today and I don't feel any older. Ann bought me a gun, an English double twelve bore, and I was very pleased to get it.

The gun was a William Lee boxlock non-ejector, probably from the early 1900s. it was in very nice condition. Peter Clipstone, who was building the factory, owned the shoot at Kirby Hall, near Corby, and I became one of the guns.

Agape was up for sale and was at the factory. I had painted the hull topsides dark blue and the boat was in good condition. I was asking £10,000 and had a few people to look at it, and one of them made me a silly offer. He kept ringing me and in the end I agreed to let him have the boat for £7500, which was for the boat only and as it stood. He sent me a deposit of £400 And I arranged for a crane to lift the boat onto the purchaser's low loader.

The buyer arrived with his son. He had given me a hard time during the negotiations and was getting the boat at way below what I considered to be a fair price. He said he wanted to see the engine run and I told him that I couldn't run the engine with the boat out of the water as it was sea water cooled. In the end I rigged up a hose pipe so the engine could be started. Next he asked "Where's the fridge?" I reminded him that the deal was boat only, due to the low price. In the end I agreed to include the fridge. He then said "What about the dinghy?" and I said it was not included, but he started arguing so I agreed to include a dinghy. He then said "What about oars for the dinghy?" Once again I gave in and included a set of oars.

I then said "Look, now you have everything, what about payment?"

By this time I was getting quite annoyed with his whining, grabbing attitude. Then he said "I am not happy to pay the price, I think you should reduce it."

"I've done everything you've asked, now pay me the balance of the £7500," I told him.

He said, "I think you should reduce the price by another £500."

I was furious and told him, "I'm not going to sell it to you now even if you pay me the money". With that I stormed into the office, rang the crane company and cancelled. The 'buyers' obviously thought I was bluffing and were walking around smiling and laughing. I went out and told them I had cancelled the crane, but they didn't believe me. After a time they came into the office all smiles and father said, "Can we sort this out? Our low loader will be here soon." I said, "I am not selling the boat to you".

They then started to whine about not being able to trust human nature and making me out to be at fault. I said "It's you that welched on the deal and didn't complete. You should have done the deal as agreed instead of trying to get the price reduced".

"What about the £400 deposit?"

"I'm afraid that as you refused to pay the amount as agreed the deal is off and you lose the deposit" I said. He then started ranting and raving and demanding his deposit back. I knew Ann hadn't banked his cheque yet, but thought I would play him along a bit.

Betty and Jenny, the two office girls, were getting quite concerned at the commotion going on, and then a large low loader pulled into the yard. By now I was starting to enjoy myself, but I could see Ann wasn't too happy. The irate 'buyer' went marching out to talk to his lorry driver. I could see him waving his arms about and pointing to the office. I was chuckling to myself, and I think Betty and Jenny probably thought me slightly mad!

The man came back into the office almost in tears, and I started to feel sorry for him and agreed to let him use the phone to ring his bank to stop his cheque. After an awkward few minutes on the phone in the office with us all listening he stopped it.

I then handed him his cheque, which we had not paid in. He left without saying goodbye! On 1st May I had the Cornish Crabber trailed to the bungalow to finish it off. It went in the driveway in front of the garage and the garage served as a workshop. All the woodwork needed to be varnished to a very high standard and Ann did nearly all the varnishing. The method was to put on about four coats and then rub it down and put on a finishing coat. She worked very hard on this and as the boat approached completion the varnish work shone as well as, if not better than, a factory completed boat.

One of the last jobs was to paint the deck sheathing. The decks were marine ply sheeting sheathed with a non-slip polyester and I decided to finish the decks myself. I got in a dreadful state, plastered in paint, and in the end Ann had to take over. When the boat was finished it looked a picture and was probably one of the best finished Crabbers around. The finish on the painted hatch covers and the engine box cover was so good that people thought they were fibreglass!

All summer Ann and I worked exceptionally hard on the Crabber, but we took a break in June and went down to Cornwall to see Pat Patterson. Ann and the kids stayed in Cawsand in a boarding house and I stayed with Pat on *Sea Winds*. The weather was exceptionally hot and we all enjoyed the holiday. Teri and James spent most of the time in the sea or playing on the Beach. The name we decided on for the Crabber was *Meander*. Ann and I had worked so hard to complete the boat, so it was an abbreviation of "Me and Her".

Friday 11th August: We launched Meander today. Golding arrived at about 0800hrs. and drove off at 0900. The boat looked small as it disappeared round the bend and the litter and rubbish left behind were shocking. We left at 10.00 and arrived at Wells at about 12.30 and slid the boat down the slipway at about 13.15. I motored it off the trailer and anchored off waiting for Ann in the dinghy. Glen rowed over for a look at the boat and was impressed. We didn't quite make the mooring, going aground about 15 yards away. I put her on the mooring on the evening tide. The only discomfort with the Crabber is the way she leans over when aground.

I put the Green Lane factory on the market and it sold remarkably quickly. It was sold in two parts, the first for £8,250 and the second for £25,000. In view of the fact that I had previously sold a part of the factory for £15,000, the total price achieved for the factory was £48,350, not bad considering that I had only paid £15,000 for the whole site seven years ago!

I had the UFO 34 mouldings transported to Bedford to be fitted out at David Garrard's yard at Great Barford. I was far too busy to attempt it myself. The Telford Way factory wasn't finished until late June and the move caused all sorts of problems. Morale among the workforce became gradually worse until things came to a head and all the men walked out, that is all except Brian, Jim, Ray and Lou. It was all over money. One of the polishers found out that Jim the storeman was earning the same money. The men said they wanted more, or for Jim to only work 40hrs. I told them to get stuffed! They all stood out by the factory gate arguing amongst themselves shouting and carrying on. I then told Betty to collect up the men's clock cards and work out their wages and I would pay them all off.

They then realised what was happening and sent in a deputation to ask if they could come back to work. This was about 1130am and I said no, but they could start afresh after lunch at 1.30pm. This new tough attitude seemed to work wonders for discipline!

There was a lot of industrial unrest around, with the unions demanding ever bigger pay rises, although the government of James Callaghan was trying to keep rises under 5%. Ford Motor Company made a pay offer within the 5% guidelines. In response 15,000 Ford workers, mostly from the TGWU, began an unofficial strike on 22nd September, which became an official action on 5th October. Soon the number of people on strike rose to 57,000. During the strike, Vauxhall Motors employees accepted an 8.5% rise, and on 22nd November, Ford accepted 17%!

With all of the industrial unrest in industry generally it made workers think that it was OK to go on strike and disrupt companies. What they didn't seem to realise was that if they bankrupted the company they were working for they would all be out of a job. Although only a small company, we could not work under this constant threat and I made sure our employees knew this. Production was much more efficient in the new unit and we started to run out of work, so it was necessary to reduce overtime. The working hours were reduced to 6am to 6pm Monday to Thursday, 6am to 4pm Friday and 7am to 12 Saturday, closed Sunday. It was necessary to reduce the working week further in August and overtime was stopped except when necessary.

I was trying to do two flying lessons a week, weather permitting, and did my solo qualifying cross country in September.

14th September: Did my solo qualifying cross country today. I had a good flight to Cambridge but had difficulty seeing the runway and was high. However there was a good headwind and I got in all right with full flap. The trip from Cambridge to Leicester was uneventful although their radio was out, and I made a first class landing. I was so elated when I took off from Leicester that I called up Sywell from Market Harborough. I made a good landing at Sywell and was relieved to have the long cross country out of the way.

I had a lot of highs but also some low points during my training. One occasion was my first Flight Handling Test (FHT).

Thursday September 21st: Failed my FHT today, made a right mess up of it. It was a nice day but windy. The steep turns were rubbish and the practice forced landing shocking. I was trying to land from downwind and would never have made the field. Paul Smith was very good and put it down as revision. The worst part was walking back to the clubhouse and everyone asking how I had got on. I told Ann, but everyone else thinks it was cancelled due to the weather.

Tuesday 26th September: Did my FHT today and passed. I only expected to do a revision period, it was a real gusty day with the wind gusting up to 40 knots. The steep turns were passable and then we did stalling. We had to keep under flight level 3.0 due to the cloud base. The stalling exercise went off well and then Paul pulled the switch for the forced landing. The forced landing was exactly right (quote Paul Smith), so then we climbed out and headed back to Sywell. We did a normal rejoin and touch and go, then a precautionary circuit with 50 ft. inspection run, then a 500ft circuit and short field landing. As we took off again Paul said that if the next landing was satisfactory I had passed. Bit of an anti-climax, I felt so good but I am no better pilot today than yesterday. Nothing ever changes. During the debrief Paul Smith commented on how well I had flown the plane in the difficult conditions and said "No one could have flown it any better".

I bought Ann another car in October, an MG BGT. I think we paid a little bit too much for it but she really loves it. She has now started horse riding regularly and she goes playing squash once or twice a week. I won a cup for rifle shooting and also during October Ann and I were both awarded bronze medals for ballroom dancing. I never had an alcoholic drink all year and was pleased with myself for that.

Saturday 23rd December: I went shooting today, this being the last shoot of the current season. There have been 5 shoots up to now and on Boxing Day morning some of the lads are going round again. My first shot bagged a high woodcock. I only had one other good shot and downed a nice cock pheasant. I was very pleased to get the woodcock and everyone congratulated me. Apparently there have been a lot of woodcock about this year, which is a sign of a hard winter.

BB, the famous author, artist and naturalist, was a member of the Kirby Hall shoot and he often used to write of his exploits on our shoot days in his Shooting Times column. He was an accomplished artist and when some of the young beaters asked for an autograph he would do them a sketch of a countryside scene.

CHAPTER SEVENTEEN

Steady as she goes

1979 started as most years do, full of hope and optimism. On New Year's Eve it snowed heavily and we went to the village hop. Because of the shocking weather and the lateness of the hour our friends stayed at our house overnight. In the morning (New Year's Day) Ann and I walked in the snow-covered fields surrounding our garden and we discussed the coming months. The snow was crisp and the winter sun caused us to squint due to the reflections in the snow.

Going back to work was almost a pleasure as I drove down the industrial estate road, but this was short lived when I saw the shocking mess the gypsies were making all down the road. They had arrived shortly before Christmas, and although the road was private and gated they managed to get in and occupy a large area of land. British Steel, who owned the land, said we should close the gate at night, but every time anyone went to close the gate they were intimidated by a group of fierce-looking men. No one could walk past without being harassed by the gypsies and with their dogs snapping at their heels, it got to a point where no one could get past them safely. One of our office girls got quite upset and had to be picked up and driven through the chaos.

The factory owners down our end of the estate called a meeting with British Steel and the police. British Steel explained that they had applied to the court for an eviction notice, but the representative from the police said they had a Home Office directive telling them not to harass gypsies. When asked about the harassment of our employees by the gypsies we were told that there was nothing the police could do.

The weather was really cold and the whole of the country came to a standstill due to the snow and ice. The factory was cut off completely for one day. Most of the employees lost no time at all, although I did send them off early on a couple of occasions. On 22nd January, public sector unions held a 24-hour strike, the biggest individual day of strike action since 1926. Train drivers had already started a series of 24-hour strikes. The Royal College of Nursing asked for a 25% wage rise and the public sector unions were asking for a £60 per week minimum wage. There was a gravediggers' strike and unburied bodies were having to be stored in factory units!

During 1978, 9,306,000 days were lost in industrial disputes and in 1979, 29,474,000 days were lost. The winter of 1978-79 became known as the "Winter of Discontent" during which there were widespread strikes by public sector trade unions. While the strikes were largely over by February 1979, the Government's inability to contain the strikes earlier helped to bring about Margaret Thatcher's Conservative victory in the 1979 General Election.

Early in February we had a party at home. We invited about 50 people and most of them turned up. It was a happy occasion which broke up at about 5am. We had the usual selection of talkers, boozers, gropers and weepers and everyone thoroughly enjoyed themselves.

At one point we actually sold our Kingfisher (*Agape*), or thought we had. The purchaser sent us a £1500 deposit but then his daughter got pregnant and as he had to pay for a wedding he wanted to pull out of the deal. I sent him his deposit back and wished him well. He seemed such a genuine person and I felt sorry for him.

As the weather eased off I tried to work on the Cornish Crabber to get her ready for the coming sailing season. I purchased a Range Rover – I had originally fancied a Jaguar XJ6 but the Range Rover was much more practical, both as a working vehicle and an investment. One of our customers used to customise Range Rovers, so we did some reciprocal trading and ended up with new seats and carpets.

Our trading figures for 1978 came out during March, showing a good net profit. The turnover for the year was up 30% and the net profit was up by over 100%, which was quite remarkable considering the problems we'd encountered during the year. David Helsdown, a local businessman, came to see me. He had recently purchased a set of mouldings for a Colvic 38ft trawler yacht and wanted us to do the deck fittings. The boat was on a building site owned by his brother, a local builder, and the site had several fruit trees. Brian and I went over to do the job on site. We took a hydraulic bender to do the tight bends, but the long bends to fit the curvature of the side decks we bent around an apple tree!

I had decided to take a marina berth for the coming season and booked one at Woolverstone near Ipswich on the river Orwell. I towed *Meander* home to work on her and at last started to make some progress. I sold Ann's MG and my Alpine and bought Ann a Ford Capri from Nick, one of the flying instructors at Sywell who was leaving the UK to work overseas.

May: We launched Meander at Woolverstone Marina. Unfortunately she stuck on the slip and we had to wait until the flood tide to float her off. A chap we knew came over in his rubber dinghy and tried to tow us off using his oars. I put the engine into astern and he rowed like the clappers, but it didn't work and must have looked bloody peculiar. Brian and Val were down for the day and helped with the launching and rigging up. Another Crabber owner came over and introduced himself, there are three on the Marina including ours and I think ours is the best finished off. We set sail the next weekend rather nervous of the children's reaction. I was amazed, they loved it looking all around and asking intelligent questions. I don't know whether it is the year older or the change of cruising area, probably some of both. On 25th May we flew to Malta for an early holiday. It was a good holiday but we overate. We were self-catering and the T-bone steaks were so cheap! We hired a car and taught ourselves to sail board. The sun was hot, the sea was warm and we just did as we pleased.

July was a very busy month and there was a bit of unrest in the factory; everyone seemed fed up and lethargic and looking forward to the holidays. I decided to interview the men one by one to try to ascertain the reasons. The findings were quite surprising. Where I had thought falling living standards to be the problem it turned out that slack management, poor organisation and overcrowding were the main problems. I think perhaps a lot of this criticism was natural resentment of workers towards bosses, but in the main they were right. It ended up with me giving the middle management a talking to and an overall rise of 6p per hour to the men, which seemed to do the trick.

On 24th July it was Ann's birthday, and as a surprise I bought her 15 hours of flying lessons. One concern I had was that if we were flying as a family and anything happened to me, that would be the end of all of us. At Sywell they had what was called a 'survival training course' whereby if anything happened to the pilot the passenger could take over, fly the plane, follow a radio bearing and land the aircraft. I think Ann was surprised.

We broke up for our holiday on 27th July although I worked on the 28th and we planned to have a skeleton staff working during the holiday period. On the 28th we drove down to Woolverstone to start our holiday, spending the first few days at Wrabness, where we beached the boat to paint the bottom, doing one side each day. After leaving Wrabness we tried a trip round to Stone Point, but only stayed a few hours. The next day we tried the Deben and had a nice sail down, staying overnight by the Ramsholt Arms. we returned to Woolverstone late Sunday afternoon.

The next week we went to work. We had only had a skeleton staff working and on the Wednesday Ann and I took the afternoon off to go windsurfing at Peterborough. Thursday evening we went to our radio lecture. We went to the boat Friday afternoon and Saturday morning we set out once more for Wrabness, picking up the same mooring we had used previously. In the evening we went down to the Black Boy pub for a drink and got back on board about 2000 hrs. Ann put the kids to bed and then we had our evening meal of steak and fried potatoes.

The next morning we took the dinghy and outboard to a sandy part of the beach. As we ran it aground the propeller shear pin broke, so when it was time to go I rowed the dinghy while Ann and the children walked along the beach. It was a beautiful hot day. We cast off the mooring and ran back up the

Stour goose-winged, with the tide under us. When we turned the corner we were then fighting the tide and as the wind dropped off we started Thunderguts, our 7hp diesel.

With just having one office It was very crowded and we needed extra help as the company grew. I decided to buy a Portakabin office and ordered one with a reception area for the main switchboard and an office for me with my drawing board. We also started interviewing office girls.

Monday 13th August: Two new girls started today, Jayne and Rabinder, one of them a blonde and the other with black hair. Jayne is working in the main office and Rabinder with me in the Jackleg office. I wonder how long they will last? At least with two it's not too bad if one leaves.

Jayne was on accounts and pricing and was excellent mathematically, whereas Rabinder was good on reception and a very good typist. Although her family were Indian she wore normal clothes.

Saturday 25th August: Over the last few weeks things have run extremely smoothly in the works. Brian Kidd has been on holiday and Kevin and Geoff have taken an active part in running the show and done very well. Jim is now progressing the work and things seem to be working out. July was a record month. The turnover was £30,600 and I expect a year's turnover of about £300,000. I find this pretty remarkable when I think about it. In 1971 the turnover was £2,444 for the year and we made a loss of £710. I think now possibly the marine market may go sour, this would be a great shame if we had to lay men off because of it. I don't know what to expand into next year. Now we have finished with Luff spars perhaps I should be looking at furniture.

As I look around me I wonder if it was just luck that has made my money or something else. I have a knack for doing a good deal and I have done well out of my property deals and although I am wealthy compared to most people nothing has changed. I used to dream of having a big car and a yacht and now I have three yachts and a big motor car. I am not more content or happy just because of this, nothing ever changes, I am still the same person. I 've seemed to drift away from all my old friends because I have nothing in common with most of them. If I want something I usually have it. I intend to acquire an aeroplane next year. At the moment my leisure activities consist of sailing, windsurfing, rifle shooting, game shooting, ballroom dancing and flying. Why the hell am I writing all of this down, I don't know, is it perhaps that I can't talk to anyone about it? I'm going off sailing with Smithy next weekend, I can at least talk to him.

Thursday 30th August: A funny day today, I arrived at the office at 0830 and walked down to the end of the car park. It was a beautiful sunny morning with the smell of summer in the air and the birds singing as if rejoicing in the beauty of the day. A bobtailed rabbit scurried across in front of me and disappeared into the hedge, I never see the buggers when I have my gun with me!

There was the sound of bustling activity as I walked back towards the Factory. The men were all working away quite well and I wondered how long this apparent contentment would last. I managed to keep Rabinder busy today and I hope she is settling in to our lunatic way of going on. I took Ann to Sywell and found that both Robin aircraft were US, one with a busted engine and the other a split fuel tank. The engine on JN dropped a valve at 500ft. while Ian was taking off. He took off on runway 21 and managed to get back to land on runway 03, quite something!

The builders have been concreting all day and should soon have the floor to the extension complete. As soon as it is completed we can start to erect metal racks for storing the sheet.

Whilst doing the wages Betty found that Ann had made a mistake on Brian's money. On his holiday week she had given him £25 too much. It was decided to even it up this week in one lump. Brian was very cross indeed and had a long face all day, I wonder if he will stir the men up and cause any aggravation. Ann and I should be going dancing tonight.

Production was going really well and we were becoming well-established financially with another 3000 sq. ft. extension under construction alongside the main factory. I planned to use this area for pulpits, as boats were getting bigger and the men needed much more space to work in. I noticed that Fairline had stopped ordering some of the smaller items and when I investigated it turned out that one of their customers had started making small parts for his own boat and had copied some of our products and was selling them into Fairline. There was nothing I could do about this. The line manager who now did the buying thought it hilariously funny and made a point of saying how wonderful these other products were. The quality was on the whole quite poor, but it was not up to me to point this out.

On one occasion I noticed on the line making the Holiday 22 that the pulpits were not made by us and they had obviously been rectified. It appeared that the supporting leg had been welded on in the wrong place, sawn off and then welded on in the correct place. This was obvious from the distortion on the top rail and the obvious poor repair where the leg had originally been welded. Fairline would never have let us get away with such shoddy workmanship and I would never let any product out of the door if it was not up to standard.

In this instance I pointed out to the line manager the various faults and how amazed I was that he could accept such poor quality on a Fairline. The offending parts were all removed and sent back to the supplier and Cooney parts were then fitted. This happened from time to time, the problem being that I took it personally and would hate to see other suppliers' products on our customers' boats.

There was quite a lot of work coming in from other boatbuilders, but I had always considered Fairline to be my top customer and resented other fabricators getting in, especially if they were copying my ideas.

Saturday 1ˢᵗ September: Smithy arrived 0700 prompt, when I was still in the shower. We loaded the car, an enormous Citroen estate, and set off for Woolverstone. The day held promise, being slightly misty, and as we drove down Polopit young pheasants not yet wary of man stood by the roadside not moving until almost under the car wheels. We arrived at Woolverstone at about 0945 and left the marina berth at approx. 11. I put all sails up including the topsail. I had problems with this as the topping lift was the wrong side of the gaff, trapping the topsail halyard against the mainsail. I eventually sorted this out and soon we were sailing on a broad reach past Pin Mill. The river bends just past Pin Mill and to stay on the wind we had to tack. As we approached Harwich Harbour the wind was dead on the nose so we motored out to catch the tide up to the Deben entrance. It was a beautiful day with hot sun and a fresh sea breeze. When clear of Harwich Harbour we turned on to the wind and with the wind on the stbd. beam and the tide with us we started to make good progress. Martin was really captivated with the scene, the sun sparkling on the water, the ship with all sail set and the boat creaking and groaning as the wind stretched the sails.

By the time we entered the Deben we were on a run and we entered the river mouth at about 1400. I started to reduce sail soon after, getting the topsail off first. I asked Smithy to put her up into wind while I got the mainsail off her but he made a pig's arse of it and nearly put us aground. We eventually sorted it out and we continued to Ramsholt under jib and staysail. We picked up a mooring at Ramsholt and then had lunch, after which we had a snooze in the afternoon sun.

We decided to make our way up to the Tidemill yacht harbour at Woodbridge and unfurled our jib and staysail. As we approached Woodbridge, once or twice our centre plate scraped the bottom, telling us we were out of the deep water channel. There is no echo sounder on the boat so the centre plate comes in useful. The entrance to the Tidemill yacht harbour is very narrow and looks quite daunting, but we made it all right, tying up to the pontoon stern to, similar to continental marinas. By the time we sorted ourselves and the boat out it was 1800, at which time we went ashore, realised the pubs were open and had a couple of beers. I didn't really want to cook so we looked for a restaurant. The food seemed awfully expensive so we decided on a take-away Chinese meal. After eating on board we went ashore again, ending up in Sherlock's Wine Bar.

Sherlock's Wine bar was owned by Douglas Wilmer, a gifted actor who among his many roles played Sherlock Holmes in the 1965 BBC television series.

Sunday 2nd September: *We got up late and Smithy cooked breakfast. By about 1130 we had sorted out the boat and I went ashore to phone Ann and tell her I would not be home until Monday. We left Tidemill just after HW and set off for Ramsholt. We only put up sail for a short time and were soon motoring in light airs. As the evening progressed there were a lot of rain clouds about, which created a really beautiful sunset. I went below and started the meal while Smithy steered singing "Red Sails in the Sunset."*

As dusk approached we put on the navigation lights, I'd wanted to try them out and they looked very effective. It was quite dark as we approached Ramsholt and we picked up a mooring very close to the beach. I finished off the meal, steak, sweetcorn and sauté potatoes, which was eaten by about 2000 hrs. We rowed ashore at 2030 and went to the Ramsholt Arms where we stayed until 2245. I bought a bottle of gooseberry wine to take back and we sat out in the cool of the night listening to the sounds of the marsh. As I suspected, the mooring dried out, but luckily I was in the port forward berth and Martin was in the port berth in the main cabin, so I hardly noticed, but Martin had a rude awakening when the portable VHF set fell on him!

Monday 3rd September: I awoke to the smell of breakfast cooking and as I peered into the main cabin Martin thrust a mug of steaming tea into my hand with a cheery "Good morning Captain. We left the mooring as soon as the tide turned and managed to sail most of the way to the Deben entrance. The wind gradually increased in strength and was blowing straight down the coast. We tried a tack out to sea but made too much leeway and ended up motoring into wind and tide. It was blowing about a seven and it was hard work to make Harwich.

Courting my future wife Ann

Wedding day

Honeymoon

reman approaches the top of the factory as the flames light up the sky at Anglian Lamp:
Green Lane, Kettering.

Green Lane
Factory on fire

Sea Wych – first boat

Agape – preparing for launch after refit

Theresa (Teri) and James

Cherokee 140 – Isle of Wight

First
parachute
jump

Truck with full load

CHAPTER EIGHTEEN

Skydiver

As we ended 1979 work seemed to have levelled off, and there was not the constant struggle to keep up with demand. Although the Fairline work had come back to us, Shetland were slowing down and sourcing some of their supply elsewhere. This was annoying, because I had worked closely with Bernie Reinman on design and development, ensuring that their boat complied with maritime legislation and collision regulations. I felt the Southampton Boat Show should give some indication as to how the industry would perform next year.

Ann and I drove to Southampton on 16th September to set up the exhibition stand, which looked very good. The polishing on the products was exceptional, our polishers were improving and now I wasn't rejecting much at all. One of the products we were hoping to push was a self-stow bow roller, which used gravity and the anchor's own weight to deploy the anchor whereas some of the other designs used a complicated spring arrangement. The bow roller was designed to work with a Danforth-type anchor but we discovered that it worked equally well if not better with a Bruce-type anchor which due to its shape is difficult to stow.

A jib reefing customer, Judge King, had a problem with his luff spar, his boat was in Lymington and as I was staying in Southampton I agreed to meet him at the boat to see what the problem was.

Thursday 21ˢᵗ September: I went to Lymington to have a look at Judge King's jib reefer. I expected a frosty reception but he and his wife seemed quite friendly. I went out to the boat with them in their dinghy and inspected the spar. It wasn't quite right I suppose, although I couldn't find much wrong with it. I offered to have the system collected and reconditioned free of charge and this seemed to satisfy them both. They then invited me into the cabin for a drink. I had a couple of gin and tonics and then they took me ashore. I went for a drive round Lymington and stopped at a pub for a look at the menu. I had a drink and then decided to return to the hotel for dinner. As I walked in I saw Jim in the bar and we decided to change and then go to the Margherita restaurant. Our table was next to another with a small lattice screen between. On the next table were four people who became very chatty. I got quite friendly with the young woman next to me and eventually her boyfriend told me to f**k off. I didn't and stayed chatting to the young lady until about 0145.

The show was a success and there appeared to be a lot of business to be had from all of the enquiries that needed following up. It seemed unlikely that there would be a slack period this year and most of our customers seemed optimistic for the immediate future, although they were a little anxious as to what the Earls Court show in January might bring.

Friday 24th October: Rabinder *left today. I shall be pleased to see the back of her. At first I thought she would make a good secretary/personal assistant, but she became far too familiar, disrespectful, cheeky and lethargic. I have some girls coming for interviews tomorrow and I hope I make a better choice this time.*

The last few weeks have been quite busy, the factory extension is almost complete and I have been talked into allowing the large pulpit department to have it. We will be moving in within the next few days. Ann and I have obtained our radio licences and mine came in the post today. On the written paper I got 92% and Ann got 88%. Smithy (the CFI) was very pleased. Ann also went solo and has sorted out her landings quite well. I plan to do a trip to Sibson tomorrow and I hope to take Ann along.

Each Saturday if I was working I would call in at the Old Friar on the way home and meet up with Martin and one or two regulars for a drink and a chat. There was a group of fishermen that called in and it was a friendly crowd.

During my flying trips to Sibson I used to talk to the skydivers and enquired about parachuting courses. One Saturday evening I was talking to Martin in the pub and parachuting came up in the conversation. Martin said he wouldn't mind having a go and I thought it would be an exciting thing to do.

Monday 30th October: Fiona started with us today. I interviewed a lot of girls for the job, liking most of them. I felt that I wanted to employ every girl I spoke to - they were all on their best behaviour trying to give a good impression. I finally narrowed it down to two, Tracy and Fiona. Tracy seemed a steady friendly type but Fiona had a better telephone manner. In the end I tossed a coin and Fiona won. I was pleased in a way as she was the prettiest with long blonde hair and peaches and cream complexion. On Thursday I have a parachuting course booked.

In the pub on the Saturday I met up with our little group of regulars and during the conversation I said to Martin, "By the way, I've booked us on that parachuting course at Sibson". Martin, who was drinking his pint, suddenly choked, spluttered beer everywhere and said "You've done WHAT?"

"The parachuting, Martin" I said. "Don't you remember you said you would like to have a go?"

"I might have said that but there was need to go and bloody well book it!"

Thursday 1st November: Martin arrived about 0730 and we set out for Sibson not quite knowing what to expect. Ann is not very happy, I think she objects to me having time off work to go off enjoying myself! When we arrived we went up to the lecture room first and did some theory, we then went into the hangar to do some PLF training (parachute landing falls). During the day we did a mixture of lectures, PLFs and aircraft exit drills and towards the end I had a blinding headache. The training culminated in a jump in the Fan Trainer, which is a tower that lets you down gently. The day finished at about 1730. I rushed home and ate, showered and changed to arrive at the bank cocktail party at about 1915. I didn't know many people there so Ann and I chatted with the bank staff members until we left at about 2020. We then went to Wellingborough to the ballroom dancing classes. We did mainly cha-cha-cha, jive and rumba, arriving home at about 2330, and eventually got to sleep at about 0130.

Friday 2nd November: I peeped out through the curtains at about 0630, and it was a beautiful morning with the sun shining and hardly a cloud in the sky. Hell I thought, I shall probably have to make a parachute jump after all. Half way to

Sibson I remembered that I had not brought any clean underwear with me – apparently a lot of people pee themselves when they do their first jump. When we arrived at 0730 some people were already there all kitted out with parachutes and helmets. Our class had to do a few revision PLFs and then we were handed our parachutes. "Hotel Echo", the Islander was already warming up and the first "lift" were climbing in. I looked at Smithy and had a chuckle to myself, with his full face beard and helmet he looked a bit like a Viking. Everyone was chatting nervously, probably thinking as I was that we must be bloody mad to ever contemplate leaping out of aeroplanes.

The Islander took off and lumbered into the sky, in one way I wished I was on it because then it would soon be over, but then I was glad I wasn't. The wind direction indicator was dropped at 2,000 ft. to enable the jump master to ascertain the drift and the Islander came around and people started leaping out. As they descended one of the instructors passed remarks about people's canopy control and Smithy and I discussed different people's landing techniques. One person made a lousy descent, running downwind all the way and then landing with arms and legs at all angles, a wonder they never broke a leg.

When it came to our turn to go to the aeroplane I must admit I felt a bit weak kneed, but on the whole not too bad. The plane taxied to the end of the runway and turned. I was No. 3 with Smithy at No. 2. The engines roared into life and the Islander accelerated along the runway. It was a bit frightening taking off sitting next to an open door, but I held on tightly. The pilot throttled back and put down his flaps when we were approaching the dropping zone at 2,500ft. The jump master said "Feet out" and No 1 sat in the doorway, "Go!" and No 1 disappeared through the door shouting the numbers. We went round again and Smithy moved into the No 1 position. At this time I felt a bit limp all over. The pilot throttled back, flaps down and then it was Smithy's turn. "Feet out, Go!"

The jump master looked at me. "Feet out". I slid forward not wanting to look down, "Go!" I flopped out, shouting "One thousand, two thousand…" The falling sensation started to take my breath away, then there was a jerk and I was suspended just as I was about to say three thousand. I looked up and saw the parachute cords twisted, but otherwise the canopy appeared all right. I put my hands up and cleared the twist as I had been shown during training and rotated several times until it cleared. I put my hands on the toggles and tried steering the parachute. It seemed quite easy, and then I thought the ground must be getting close. I turned into wind (I thought) and put my legs together. The grass came into focus and I hit the deck with a wallop. My left foot hurt like hell and I also felt a bit shaken. I also felt a sense of achievement that brought tears to my eyes. I felt the same way as I did when Paul Smith told me I had passed my FHT!

I rolled over and jumped up, winding my parachute cords around my arms as we had been shown. After gathering up the parachute I started to walk back to the airfield, it seemed a hell of a long way. I saw Martin and No 1 walking together and tried to catch them up, but they were quite a long way in front and I didn't catch up until nearly at the parachute packing shed. I was dying to talk about it to someone.

We packed our chutes, or rather stood and watched a qualified packer doing them, handing them bits of break tie and rubber bands as necessary. Martin and I then went for a coffee, after which we went for our critique. The instructor said Martin's jump was perfect in every way and I was pleased for him. The man said that my aircraft exit was lousy, canopy control rubbish and my landing useless and downwind. Still, "you can't win em all" as they say. I also had to do some more training before I could do another Jump.

Martin was to go in the second lift No 8 and I thought I also had my name down for this. I went to the back of the hangar to do some more PLF and aircraft exit drill, I suppose this took about fifteen minutes. I then went to join No 8 lift, all kitted up in parachute etc, only to find that I was not booked into this one at all and I had to put my name down for No 11!

I saw Martin jump and he made a reasonable descent and landing. As I was waiting Sam Newington arrived for a flying lesson. I think he was surprised when he realised that I was a parachutist and even more surprised when I told him that I had a PPL. At long last it was my turn, the other six in the aeroplane were free fall and I was the only static line jumper. I was No 1 and as the plane took off a couple of the others gave me nods of encouragement. I was determined not to cock it up this time. It was a bit frightening sitting looking out of the door but I had my left foot jammed well in to stop me falling out when it banked round. The pilot throttled back, flaps down and then it was time to go. "Feet out", I sat on the edge and then it was "go!"

I felt as though I had made a reasonable exit and this time after the chute opened there were no twists. I immediately turned into wind and looked for the target area. It was behind me and the wind was light so I could hold (into wind) and land just downwind of the windsock. I felt a lot easier this time and got into the PLF position at about 500ft. My landing was heavy, hurting my right foot this time, but not too bad. I went back to the packing shed and after packing away my chute I went to find Smithy. I'd missed lunch but Smithy'd had two pints of beer and a cooked lunch and watched my jump!

I went to the office for my critique with slight concern but to my delight I had done everything right, or passable anyway. We left Sibson at about 1445 and Martin and I couldn't stop talking about our jumps and the parachuting we said we would have to do some more jumps. As we drove back I said to Martin "Ever tried hang-gliding?" "No I've never tried it." "Do you fancy having a go?" I said, "Yes" he said, "I wouldn't mind having a go". He then stood on the brakes, stopped the car turned and looked at me and said "NO I'M NOT BLOODY INTERESTED, DON'T YOU GO AND BLOODY WELL BOOK IT!"

We then had a laugh and he ran me back to work. I knew the lads knew where I'd been although it was supposed to be kept quiet, so I was determined not to limp. When I arrived home I enjoyed telling the family how clever I was, but Ann seemed a bit quiet, possibly even resentful. That evening Ann and I went to the Halloween dinner with Marilyn and Brian. We had a pleasant evening and eventually turned in at about 0230.

The marine industry seemed to be slowing down and a lot of companies were tightening up on their buying. Westerley Marine were buying stemhead rollers from us in batches of 50 and we had the production well organised and efficient. Brooklands Aviation, who produced the Dolphin power boats, were also buying bow rollers in batches of 50. We had redesigned the cast brass chrome plated items and were producing them in stainless steel. Our company was very good at producing small highly-polished stainless fabrications and we were able to produce them at very competitive prices. We had an enquiry for a stemhead roller similar to the Westerley design in batches of 50 and quoted a very keen price to secure the work. The company wrote back to us and said that it would be impossible to produce these items for that price and implied that we didn't have a clue. I was amazed at their attitude. We had been producing these types of products profitably for several years! I thought afterwards it may have been a ploy by a competitor to try and find out our prices, although if I had suspected this at the time I would probably have inflated the price to confuse them completely!

Friday 30th November: *Today I went to Fletchers to try a new pulpit. I think they will buy it and I hope they will be a very good customer in the New Year, we have some pretty good products for them. Tonight is the annual dinner and dance, there will be 44 people in the party and I hope it goes as well as last time. About four of the men are not taking their wives, I think they are probably going to have a go at Jane and her sister. This year has been good up until October but now the work has died off and this month will be the worst since August 78. One of the reasons for this is the move into the extension, cancellations of most of our Shetland boats work, Fletchers call off coming to an end and Fairline giving the Holiday stainless to another firm. The last of these is due to the foreman being vindictive, I sometimes wonder if he is like this with everyone or just with Cooney's.*

At the Christmas "do" most of the men took their wives or girlfriends, but four went on their own. Fiona and Jane from the office and Jane's sister went together as they were without partners. After the dinner we had a disco and it was embarrassing seeing the men dancing with the girls with their hands everywhere. I had organised a bus to take them back to Kettering and a lot of the men were plastered, some of them throwing up and being disgusting. There was also a fight on the bus and we had a complaint from the bus company. I decided after that not to do an organised dinner dance again!

With the slowdown in the industry and lack of new business coming in, the outlook was bleak, but a lot would depend on the Earls Court show in January.

CHAPTER NINETEEN

Down to earth

Bryan Essam had the use of a Cessna 150 owned by Cyril Dobson, a local engineer and inventor of the Oxford welder. Cyril lived in a large house in Islip. The aeroplane was kept on a field strip next to the river at Islip and in the winter the field would sometimes flood and the plane would be cut off from the landing strip. Bryan took me up a few times. It was a tidy little aeroplane in very good condition and he flew it quite often.

Wednesday January 2nd 1980: The Christmas break is now over and I wonder what the 80s have in store for us. I shall stop overtime today as work is scarce. I have not seen the order book so lean for years. There is a definite slump in the industry, I shall go to the Boat Show on Monday to try and find out what will happen over the next few months. New Year's Eve we and the Essams went to the Haycock at Wansford, it was a good night out although at £12.50 a head a bit expensive. The meal was a carvery and very nicely done with choice of starter and sweet. After the meal we danced until 0200, arriving home about 0300. Val and Bryan stayed at our house.

We got up at about 1000 and I cooked breakfast. After breakfast Bryan and I went to check the aeroplane in the Range Rover. The flood water had subsided from the airstrip but the plane was still cut off by the swollen dyke. I then drove to Woodford to pick up Ann from Val's house. We stayed for about half an hour and then drove to Bedford to look at the UFO. As we passed the Queen Victoria hotel in Rushden we noticed that they had a sale of sheepskin coats. I stopped and we went in and tried on a few. I eventually bought one for myself, but Ann could not find one that fitted. David had not done much on the UFO and was not there so we didn't stay long. We called in at Dad's and gave him my old overcoat!

Thursday January 3rd: Today I sold the Kingfisher, I hope it will be third time lucky. I agreed to let it go for £8,500. It is a gift at that price and I hope the chap completes the deal. Yesterday I stopped the overtime and there is unrest in the factory. In the gents' toilet someone has written on the wall, "Cooney you are a bastard." Before much longer I may show them just how much of a bastard I can be.

Most of the men realised that I had no choice but to stop overtime. Work seemed to have dried up, and although we had just enough to keep going there was no point in paying overtime rates for work we did not have. Within a few hours the offensive remarks had been cleaned off the wall and I got the impression that some of the employees were annoyed with the culprits.

I was working on the Kingfisher to get it ready for the new owner. I had removed the cylinder heads and was working on the engine. The Volvo MD2 had a problem in that it tended to bend the push rods that opened the valves.

Sunday January 6th: *Bryan rolled up this morning and asked me to help tow the aeroplane through the water and onto the airstrip. I arrived at the field at 1200 approx and we soon had the Cessna in tow. Val and Diana were in the Range Rover with me and as soon as we were clear of the water and mud Bryan taxied onto the runway and took off. I took the girls back to their vehicle and they went off to pick Bryan up at Sibson. I went home and busied myself with jobs around the house.*

Monday January 7th: *There were no orders in today and I think that if something doesn't turn up tomorrow I shall have to cut the workforce. It may be that will make the others pull up their socks, I don't know.*

I was extremely worried. Industry generally was slowing down and the marine industry was slow indeed. I knew that I would have to cut back on production and make some people redundant. I would try and keep on the better workers and get rid of the less skilled and the troublemakers. The turnover for 1979 was £299,471. The 1978 turnover was £251,751, an increase of nearly 20%, not as good as the previous year but still a healthy increase. I could not see there being a similar increase in 1980 and thought that we would be lucky to maintain 1979 levels of production. this would be a great shame when we had so far been so successful with increases year on year. Although Fairline were holding their own in the marketplace and we were doing most of their deck fittings, a lot of the big players were struggling to survive. Marcon Marine appointed receivers and Westerley, who had won the Queen's Award for Industry three times during the 70s, had to reduce their workforce from 700 to 250 due to reduced demand. All the sailing boat manufacturers were fighting for survival and sadly most of them were losing the battle. Inflation was rampant, and unemployment was increasing towards two million so it was difficult to be optimistic about the future.

Thursday January 10ᵗʰ: Had a meeting of chargehands this morning and decided to make five people redundant, among them Ray Gibson and Fiona, who was not at work today. I had the men in at about 930 and told them of the decision. There was no trouble or aggro and I felt sad, especially for Ray, who had been with us for about three years. I rang Fiona and then went round to see her. She was in bed with a cold but came down and Ann and I told her the bad news. I was glad her mother was there so I could assure her that there had been no misconduct on Fiona's part. I paid the men off at 1100 hrs. I paid them for the rest of the day and gave them all one week's pay in lieu of notice. I think it is better to do it this way and get back into production as soon as possible.

Tuesday January 15ᵗʰ: *I told Brian to give some of the men an hour's overtime this evening. There was a lot of bickering and eventually he weakened and allowed them all to come in. Morale improved dramatically and the works almost seemed "contented" once more. There are still a few sullen faces, chaps that used to smile and chat now turn away with stony faces.*

With the level of work coming in and the apparent downturn in most major industries I knew that I would probably have to cut the workforce further and perhaps shut one of the workshops. This would be a great pity, as I had built the company from nothing to one of the leading stainless suppliers in the marine industry and we were employing quite a few people, most of whom I had trained. Luckily we were in freehold premises with considerable equity and most of the plant was paid for.

Thursday January 31ˢᵗ: January seemed to sort out a thing or two. Cadle and Corley have now left and work has picked up. The turnover for January was £19,800 approx. which was about the same as Jan last year. It will be interesting to see how the pattern of work develops over the next year.

I went flying today, I had a check out with Ian Underwood and then had about an hour whizzing around on my own. I am still keen to own a plane but finances being what they are, I can't see much chance, the first priority being to get the UFO afloat. I can't see that happening for a month or two though.

Although in January things seemed to have settled down, work was still tight and there was no optimism in the industry. At the Boat Show orders for new boats were scarce and all the UK boatbuilders were laying men off.

I was still flying about once a month and was keen to purchase an aeroplane of my own. I fancied a Cessna 172 or a Cherokee, and there were a few on the market for around £8000 with a current C of A and not too many hours. I saw a 1965 Cherokee 140 advertised in *Pilot* magazine at an asking price of £8,900, which I thought a bit expensive. It was being advertised by LV Henderson Motor Co. Mr Henderson was Irish with a very strong Belfast accent. I rang him to discuss the aircraft, which was at Elstree, and arranged to travel to Elstree aerodrome to view it. Mr Henderson didn't turn up and when I rang him he apologised and said he'd got his dates mixed up but would be prepared to fly the plane to Sywell for me to view. The plane was very tidy and looked in good condition. The colour scheme was white, gold and black.

Tuesday March 18th: I tried an aeroplane today, it was a Cherokee, GAWPS. I was in the left hand seat and Paul Smith was in the right hand seat with Ann and another pilot in the rear seats. I did not fly it very well and was a bit disappointed with the experience. The plane checked out OK and although old is in very good condition. The asking price is £8,950 which seems slightly dear, but there is no VAT on the deal. There is another Cherokee at Sywell which is likely to be cheaper but it is not so well equipped. I am amazed how well the Cherokee carries the weight as it is supposed to be a 2+2 but carries 4 average people with 30 gallons of fuel.

I got Cyril, the flying club engineer, to check the engine and Paul Smith, the flying club CFI, to check the aeroplane generally. I was in a dilemma. The business was slowing down but I considered that as long as I kept my nerve, I thought that by tightening things up, reducing the workforce and getting more efficient we could survive.

With the reduced level of business I decided to close the side workshop and look for a tenant. This would save some of the rates and the rent would help cash flow. The Kingfisher was going at last. I eventually sold it for £9,500. Several of the prospective buyers had pulled out but I managed to achieve quite a good price eventually and the money would pay for the aeroplane.

I decided to employ a manager to run production, as it seemed to be getting on top of Brian. We interviewed several and finally decided on Hugh Gallacher, a highly-qualified engineer with a BSC honours degree. Brian was not very happy and didn't like Hugh, who he saw as a threat. Hugh was very professional and tried to be impartial, but there was an underlying atmosphere. I overheard a conversation between some of the men and one of them said "We'll soon get rid of that c***!"

Friday March 21st: *The Kingfisher went today, the crane arrived on time and everything was ready. Mr Porter arrived with his lorry and he looked worried to death. Hugh Gallagher came in today and he Ann and I went down to the Rising Sun for lunch. Mr Porter was just finishing off loading the boat and said "I quite understand, you just can't bear to see the boat go!" This afternoon I introduced Hugh to the middle management team and there were no grumbles or aggravation. This evening I offered Mr Henderson eight grand for his Cherokee and we eventually settled for eight thousand one hundred. I can't wait to get my hands on it, he may deliver Monday or Tuesday.*

We were still very friendly with Bryan and Valerie Essam. Bryan was quite enthusiastic about my purchase of GAWPS and looked forward to flying it with me.

Saturday 22nd March: *Judy Essam was married today. we arrived at the house at about 11 o'clock and had a drink. I left for the church at about 1145 and Ann stayed to do the video recording. It was a lovely day, everything went according to plan, the sun even came out for the photographs. The reception was at Wicksteed Park and was very pleasant, in fact I think it was one of the nicest weddings I have been to. After the wedding we went back to Val's, leaving at about 20hrs.*

Tuesday March 25th: Today we took delivery of GAWPS, but we nearly never made it. Just as PS was on finals to land, a crop duster (Pawnee) took off downwind, causing PS to take avoiding action. Mr Henderson persuaded me to let him keep the headset. The plane came in at about 1500 hrs. and after sorting out the paper work I ran Mr Henderson to the Peterborough railway station. Bryan Essam turned up and we decided to go for a whiz around. I handled it fairly well but mucked up the landing, it went with a bonk. I think the problem is that the Cherokee has a greater sink rate than the Robin and is heavier on the controls. This evening Brian and I took PS for a few circuits. I had studied the flight manual and was bringing her in at about 80 mph. I had just about got the hang of things and did a reasonable landing or two.

There was no available hanger space at Sywell, so I decided to base the plane at Sibson, where there was space but it wasn't very convenient. Quite often it would be necessary to move several planes out of the hangar to get to PS. I wanted to fly at every opportunity and took advantage of the long spring evenings, building up experience. I took Ann and the children up and they were quite proud of our aeroplane, and I noticed the envious looks from people. It's satisfying to have a nice car but there is nothing like the feeling of pride you get when climbing in and out of your own aeroplane!

Bryan liked the Cherokee and decided to look at one at Teesside, which is quite a way up north, so we decided to go in PS. We took off from Sibson at 1105 and flew up to Teesside. There were strong head winds and it took us 2hrs 15min., the longest trip I had done. When we arrived and looked at the plane it didn't look in as good condition as PS and was more expensive. We had lunch and took off for the return journey at 1540. The trip back only took 1hr. 20 min. as we then had a tailwind.

A trip to Skegness was planned for Easter Monday. Bryan and Val would fly in the Cessna and Ann, me and the children in the Cherokee. We were all looking forward to the trip, and the children were quite excited.

Monday April 7th: Today we all arrived at Sibson at about 11 o'clock and met Bryan and Val. The plan was to fly to Skegness for the day. We took off at 1125 and had a fairly uneventful trip to Skegness. We landed at 1210 on the short runway, but it was fairly level so I did not anticipate any problem getting off. We took a taxi into town and found a reasonable place to have lunch, and the children were exceptionally well behaved. After lunch we went to the funfair, Bryan Ann and James went on the big dipper and Val, Theresa and myself had a couple of goes on the Helter Skelter. I then took Theresa on the roundabout. We then all went on the ghost train, which wasn't very terrifying even for the children. After a walk we took a taxi back to Skegness airfield, and took off at 1500 hrs. We thought we would go and have a look at Wells, but the weather started to close in and as we headed back to Sibson it started to rain heavily and we landed in quite a storm. I was glad to be back.

After the Easter holiday when Theresa and James went back to school, James' teacher asked all of the children in his class what they had done during the holiday. When James told her that he had flown down to Skegness in his dad's aeroplane she didn't believe him and told him off for telling stories!

Sam Newington, MD of Fairline, also had an aeroplane which he kept at Sibson. It was a Fuji and was far more modern than my Cherokee. It had a variable-pitch propeller which needed to be serviced at regular intervals. On one occasion when his propeller was away for servicing I said to Sam "If you like you can fly my plane whilst yours is out of commission". He replied "What about insurance?" I said "That could be arranged" and he said "What year is the Cherokee?" When I said 1965, he laughed and said "Bloody hell Kevin, I suppose if it's been flying that long it should carry on a bit longer!"

I was a member of the Sywell Aero Club, and we would meet up at Sywell and then fly somewhere for lunch. Ken Plummer, Stuart Luck, Bryan Essam and Ann and I decided to fly to an airstrip at Keyston which was next to the Pheasant pub. The landing strip was quite short and as it was sloping we used to land facing uphill and take off downhill, provided the wind was light. As we were flying we could not have any alcoholic drink, but we had a good lunch, after which we went back to the airstrip and Ken Plummer took off and did some aerobatics. He had a Beagle Pup, which was aerobatic.

A club outing to Le Touquet in France was planned and I was looking forward to my first trip abroad flying my own plane.

Sunday April 30th: We arrived at Sywell at about 0830 and planned the trip. It was decided to clear customs at Southend due to the extremely high winds. We followed Stuart Luck and went in with very long finals. The landing was pretty lousy, but we walked away from it. We fuelled up and by the time we had cleared customs an hour had been lost. We took off and called up as we crossed the English coast and again when at mid-channel we then called Le Touquet. The landing at Le Touquet was slightly better than at Southend. We took a taxi into town and found a nice little restaurant for lunch, then wandered round Le Touquet. We returned to the airport at about 1600. We were the second plane to leave Southend but the first to land at Sywell. We unloaded the girls and immediately took off for Sibson. We got back at dusk and used the landing lights for the first time.

The village of Titchmarsh had been our home for about three years and we were well established in village life, mainly due to the children and their friends' parents. Both Teri and James had "best friends" and there were quite a few social events during the year. I used to go to the Wheatsheaf pub and I was quite friendly with Jim the landlord, who was also the chef. The food was very good. A few of the regulars had businesses and the conversations were sometimes bizarre.

Jim asked if I would take him up in the plane and I said that weather permitting I would take him for a whiz round on the next Saturday. The day dawned and it was misty with a slight drizzle. It just happened to be James' eighth birthday and his present was a dartboard. He was so pleased he threw his arms round me and gave me a big hug!

Jim turned up at 0945 and I took him to Sibson. We took off on runway 15, and it was misty with a slight drizzle and the visibility poor. I let Jim have a go on the controls as we flew over to Titchmarsh so that I could look over the village. He was interested to look at the pub from the air. We flew around the area for about an hour, with Jim flying the plane for some of the time, and after landing we went back to the pub. Jim was keen to tell the regulars of his exploits!

That afternoon Ann, the kids and I all went to Wellingborough swimming pool and splashed around for an hour. After arriving home I played cricket in the garden until James's birthday tea was prepared.

Monday May 12th: *I drove down to Southampton today. I am very concerned about the shortage of work. I called in at several firms, but work is scarce and at the moment I fear for the survival of the firm in its present form. The best response was from Trident Marine, where we may get in. I arrived back at the hotel at about 1700 hrs and had a tray of coffee brought up to the room. I lay on the bed to rest my eyes and nodded off for an hour. I washed and changed and went down to the bar at about 1845. I went to the Cowherds pub for a drink and the Berni Inn for dinner, finishing up back at the hotel watching a boring film on TV.*

With my concerns over the lack of new work, I had stopped overtime and made a few more men redundant. All the local firms were struggling. Hugh was trying to make the firm as efficient as possible with the available level of work and was introducing some unpopular measures. Stopping overtime and increasing efficiency to complete the available work within normal hours caused a lot of unrest. Some of the men were making jobs last longer just to be able to claim overtime.

In the UK economy, Inflation was running at 22% and the country was being blackmailed by powerful trade unions calling strikes for wage increases in inefficient industries. Efficiency was also suffering from the restrictive practices being brought in by unions. Mrs. Thatcher was determined to curb union power, and most of the population seemed to back her. The major industries, shipping, docks, steel, mining and the motor industry, were being strangled by militant trade unions and were losing market share because high wages were making them uncompetitive. All private companies need to make a profit or they do not survive, whereas public sector companies can be propped up with Government subsidies. Most of the nationalized industries, instead of existing to provide a service, end up as inefficient bodies run solely for the benefit of their employees.

In our company there was a problem between Brian and Hugh. As we were short of work all overtime was stopped and Brian wasn't very happy about this as he would be there a lot of the time with not much to do. Hugh was tightening up all round and Brian hated this, and there was quite a lot of bad feeling between the two, mainly on Brian's part.

Wednesday May 14th: *This morning I arrived at the office slightly after 0900. Sometime, after 11hrs. Brian Kidd came in and discussed his position. He claimed that I had no right to stop his overtime and that by doing so I had broken his contract of employment. He went on to say that I had three options: give him back the hours lost and pay him all hours lost so far, make him redundant, or he would take it to a tribunal. I listened and said little. Before doing anything or making any decisions I will take advice from solicitors. I wonder if stopping his overtime would constitute a breach of his contract. His overtime was stopped mainly because of the lack of work.*

It was a shame that the relationship was turning so bitter. Brian had been with me from very early on and we had shared both good times and bad. I considered that I had looked after him, but times and people change and perhaps it was time for him to move on.

I worked out how much redundancy money Brian would be due and together with accrued holiday pay and payment in lieu of notice it came to quite a large amount. I paid him all but £200, which I agreed to pay him as soon as I had enough money. Brian's wife Margaret came to the factory and stopped me at the factory gate. She was in a nasty mood and told me off, claiming that I had exploited them for years. I was a bit taken aback. I considered that I had always paid Brian a good rate for what he did.

Friday May 16ᵗʰ: Today I knocked off at 1300hrs. to go flying. This morning was a bit heavy and depressing, no work, the men unsettled, industry generally in a mess. It's not just us who are in trouble, most small businesses seem to be having problems and I think most of our competitors are in as bad a mess.

Jane said she wanted to leave. I was disappointed as I considered Jane to be completely reliable and loyal, and I eventually persuaded her to stay. By the time I had got the plane out of the hangar and checked it out, it was 1545. I went up for a couple of circuits, the runway was 07 and I did two good landings. I taxied to the apron and went to find Bryan, who was sorting out ZU (the Cessna). I let him take the left hand seat and we did 2 circuits with Brian landing, I then did one from the right hand seat just for practice and did a nice one. Bryan then left and I flew over to Sywell for a coffee.

The Brighton Boat Show was in May and I decided to fly down to Shoreham on 22ⁿᵈ and visit the show. I was talking to Sam Newington, who was flying down on the same day. We both took off in the morning and it took me about one and a half hours to fly down. I went round London to miss all of the London air traffic zone, but Sam, being a much more qualified pilot, went straight across London and arrived at Shoreham before me. We decided to share a taxi to the show and arranged to meet up when the show finished for a taxi back to Shoreham airfield. Fairline were exhibiting, but the feeling was that not much business was being done and most of the exhibitors were despondent.

Tuesday June 17ᵗʰ: Oh misery, misery, what a sorry state industry generally and Cooney Marine in particular are in. We have not one order on the books and not much chance of getting any. I don't know how long we can carry on. Brian Kidd has left, Jane left yesterday and Hugh is going at the end of the month together with some of the men. I have worked out that with seven men I need a turnover of about £12,000 per month to survive. Where will it come from? We have lost most of Fairline, all of Shetlands and have nothing to replace it. I've put the factory on the market in the hope that we can relocate to somewhere with less expenses and overheads.

I was fortunate that throughout my years of building up the business I had tried to build up a strong asset base. Consequently we were in a freehold factory and apart from a small bank loan on the factory and some HP on some of the machines we were "asset rich". When I bought the Green Lane factory an estate agent said to me, "Why buy premises when you can rent? You can then invest all of your money into the business!" This may have been good advice at the time, but I always felt happier with freehold premises and a strong asset base. If I had taken this advice my finances would have been in a sorry state.

I had decided to get out of the engineering business and try something different, a small hotel, pub, anything that did not involve manufacturing. I was training myself to TIG weld, the only process I was weak on as it was always easier to ask one of the welders to weld any small items I required. With the workforce gone I would then be able to produce things should any orders come in.

Tuesday July 3rd: I went over to see Sam Newington today to offer him our machinery and workforce to enable him to manufacture his own stainless. He seemed mildly interested. The figures worked out at approx. £25,000 for plant, £15,000 for goodwill and about £10,000 for stock. He said he would think about it and come over and have a look at us next Friday. He stressed that money was very tight.

It would have made a lot of sense for Fairline to take us on. The figures were negotiable, and at that time Fairline were buying products from other suppliers that we could have manufactured, saving them a lot of money.

Wednesday July 2nd: I went to the bank this afternoon to see if they would finance the rundown of the business. He (the bank manager) seemed slightly shocked that I was getting out, it must have seemed sudden. The accounts show that at 31st December the profit was healthy and the figures looked as though the future was rosy. I don't know whether he will play ball, we need £100,000 to sort things out. Everything is up for sale but in a depressed market situation I suppose everything will have to be cut price. My assets at the moment stand at £267,000, excluding my yacht under construction.

Friday July 4th: Sam came today to look around the factory. He brought Grant Walker with him (yes man). He waffled and whined for half an hour or so and Grant grunted and said yes at intervals, more to conform that he was still awake than to be constructive. I don't think he will take my offer. I have now sold the jack leg office and a welder and there has been a hot enquiry after the aeroplane, just my luck for that to be sold first. The bungalow is now sold subject to contract. Several more men have now gone and we are down to just seven.

Although a lot was happening I was managing to stay positive. My assets were far in excess of my liabilities and I planned to sell up and move on and try something different.

Ann and I were keen on windsurfing and weather permitting used to go to the Ferry Meadows sailing lakes on Wednesday evenings and the occasional Sunday afternoon.

Tuesday July 8th: The Cherokee seems to be quite sought after. Today a fellow wanted me to fly it down to Hurn to show it to him and offered to pay my expenses. I declined due to the weather and eventually he decided to fly down tomorrow to try the aeroplane out. Sam is discussing our takeover at a board meeting today, I wonder what the outcome will be.

Wed. July 9th: This morning I arrived at work quite early and quite excited. I would have an answer from Sam and possibly sell the aeroplane. I rang Sam at about 1030 and he told me to go over at 1200 to discuss things. I took Ann's car to Sywell and then Ann and I went to Oundle in the Range Rover. As we were going into Sam's office the receptionist asked if we would like coffee. I said "Yes please" and Sam's voice came through the door saying no, we couldn't have coffee as we wouldn't be there long enough. He then said that they didn't want to take us over because they couldn't afford it! I was rather surprised at his clumsy, rude manner.

We left Oundle and went to Sibson, where we cleaned the aeroplane and then flew it to Sywell ready for Mr Young to test fly it. Mr Young and party arrived at about 1930 and were immediately impressed with the aeroplane. They test flew it with Paul Smith and gave me a deposit cheque before leaving. What a day! Ann and I went to the bar to drown our sorrows before going home.

Friday July 25th: The last of the men left today. I was surprised that they all stayed until 500. A few of them went for a drink at lunchtime and they did not work particularly hard, but all in all the degree of co-operation was quite remarkable.

Just before lunch Ann and I gave Betty a small present. It was a gold chain and Betty was quite taken aback. She went round to say cheerio to the men but I went round to the back of the factory and sat in the sunshine, I hate farewells. After everyone had left I wandered round thinking of how it had been, the laughter and shouting, the noise, I could almost see everyone there. Brian Kidd smiling, Cadle singing, George wandering aimlessly about, Jim marching around and Ray at the packing bench. Despite the aggravation I think these have been happy years and I wonder if I will get as much out of my next venture.

CHAPTER TWENTY

Light at the end of the tunnel

⟫⟨

I was keen to move on, so Ann and I loaded up the car with the sailboard and the kids and we all set off to look at hotels, pubs and any business on the south coast and the Isle of Wight that did not involve manufacturing. We looked at the Gunfield Hotel at Dartmouth, which overlooked the harbour, and although a bit ramshackle it had potential. We also looked at several hotels on the IOW but were unable to make any serious offers until a buyer for the factory could be found.

During the morning of Friday July 29th the phone rang and it was Alan Mallows, the estate agent trying to sell the factory. He said there was a Mr Allison wanting to look at it. I realised that it was my old partner Geoff Allison. Throughout the 70s he had run his sheet metal business, working by himself, from our old rented premises in Grafton Street. He had now become involved with a chap who had a system for recycling plastic bottles and containers and Allison was fabricating the equipment. They needed larger premises and wanted to view my factory.

Whether this was genuine or Allison just wanted to gloat over my downfall I don't know. I think he was a bit surprised at the size of the units and the amount of plant contained in them. They came for a nose around, but did not make an offer and a short time after I heard that they had gone bust!

Sunday August 31st: This month we have spent some time away. At the beginning of the month we went looking for property etc. We went to look at Devon, Cornwall and the IOW. I think we will probably settle for the IOW. It has two airfields, plenty of coastline and the property seems reasonably priced. We have found a hotel that we would like to buy with water frontage and have offered £100,000 for it. We really can't do much until we sell at least part of the factory. We are still trading on a small scale, I am at work at the moment and I have a polisher in. Although we have only opened for about one week this month, with having a few part-timers in the turnover should cover overheads, bank charges etc. This evening Ann and I worked till about 530 and loaded the truck ready for Ann to do a delivery tomorrow morning. Had pheasant for dinner and watched the Onedin Line on the telly.

Monday Sept 1st: I feel a bit lethargic this morning, I don't know why, there is a fair amount of work to do and I have a couple of lads working. It's funny really, now they are on fixed price jobs the job times have come down by about 50%. If we were to continue the business, which we could do (I can make enough just to ride the storm), the lessons we have learned in the last few weeks would be invaluable. I think I could make as much money with about half the workforce. I would be happier if there was some positive movement on the sale of the factory, I think that if I am not careful, I will be stuck here for 12 months more.

I had some people around to look at the machinery we are selling off, they are apparently starting a business manufacturing stainless steel food machinery. They were very interested in me, and my products and today one of the directors rang me and asked if he could pop round to discuss a proposition. What it amounted to was this: I have an enormous factory and equipment to make stainless steel products but no work, whereas they have a product and a lot of work but no factory. Would I allow them, to make their products, in my factory, and pay me a rent of £250 per week, this to include the use of certain plant?

This proposal was very interesting and could have worked. I couldn't imagine strangers working in my factory and using my equipment, but I kept the talks open. The main product they wanted to produce was doughnut fryers. These were of a simple design, basically a shallow rectangular stainless tank with a heating element in the bottom. I had the sheet metal equipment to produce these and slightly altered the design to make the most economical use of standard sized stainless steel sheets. I made a prototype and they were delighted with the quality.

I was now becoming undecided. The factory was not selling and when I looked at all of the hotels, pubs and restaurants on offer I began to wonder why all these businesses were for sale. Orders were beginning to come in and I was employing some of the former employees on a system of piecework. All of the company jobs were priced at an hourly rate and each item had an allotted time. When the business was up and running every job was priced at materials plus labour, so I had a costed time for each job. When checking hours paid to employees against hours charged to customers we always seemed to be about 50% efficient. When I started paying the men on the basis of the time on the job suddenly the jobs were being done in half the allotted time, this was great for them as they could earn much more and great for me, going from 50% efficiency to over 100%.

Ann had been having flying lessons and was almost ready to take her FHT. I originally bought her a "survival course" which consisted of 15 hours flying and training to enable her to take over if anything happened to me and land the aeroplane. Ann enjoyed the training so much that she decided to carry on and complete the course to eventually obtain a PPL of her own.

The plane she did most of her training in was a Cessna 152, GBDBB, but tragically it crashed in May, killing the 17-year-old trainee pilot. We were both shocked upon returning from a weekends boating to see a picture of the crashed GBDBB on the front page of our local paper. Ann was both shocked and upset, as she knew the pilot and she'd spent several hours flying the plane. It was several weeks before I could persuade her to fly again.

Wednesday September 17th: Day off today, Ann and I went to Sywell and she did her FHT, scraping through with a partial pass. She is booked in tomorrow to finish everything off. When we left we went to the factory to sort out a few odds and open the post. We were there for about 20 minutes and left for Bedford at about 1230. On the way we bought some rolls and pasties and ate them in the car. We arrived at Dad's at 1345. He was fit and well and seemed happy enough. We went on to Garrard's to inspect the UFO. He seemed to have done a little bit and I am pushing for an October completion, I can't see much chance but can only hope.

The completion of the UFO seemed to be taking forever. David Garrard, although an extremely skilled shipwright, was very slow. He had been working on it since 1978 and the workmanship was first class, but I just wished he would get on with the job and finish it.

There was a wings party on Friday 19th. This is when all the newly-qualified pilots are awarded their wings. I was so proud of Ann when her name was called and she was presented with her wings. We had not told our friends, wanting to surprise them, and they were so happy for her.

Wed. September 24th: Ann took me flying today. I was very impressed with the confident way she handled the Cessna 152. She did everything right and I couldn't fault her general flying. She let me have a little go at the controls, the first time I have flown since selling Papa Sierra. After leaving Sywell we drove to Bedford to have lunch with Father. He was in good spirits and we left at about 1415 to see the UFO. I was surprised to find that that Garrard actually had someone working on it, the chap was putting up bearers for the headlining panels and most of the woodwork was covered in newspaper and masking tape. I can't see the boat being ready for launching this year, although David seems to think that the end of October should see it finished.

As I was employing some part-time workers I was opening the factory at weekends and having Wednesdays off. This seemed to work quite well, as I was working on the tools myself with a few part time workers. Sometimes Ann would help out, and I would have her working presses, drilling and simple lathe work. I was doing all of the polishing, and was quite often covered in polishing compound and with a black face. It was amusing to see the reaction of representatives from suppliers when confronted with this apparition who was the boss of the company! They would look at me with distaste and talk down to me. Sometimes I would play them along and if I was busy or took a dislike to anyone I would just say to them "Sorry, the boss isn't here today!"

Thursday September 25th: I worked from 0800 to about 2030 today. I don't know if all this grafting is getting us far, we seem to be selling a lot of fittings but I don't feel very content. I feel I would like to shake off this millstone the business has become and do something different. The only problem is that whatever I do, after a time it becomes boring and I want out of that too. Flying still excites me but probably only because I don't do much of it.

I hadn't flown since I'd sold the Cherokee. I had been up with Ann a few times in the flying club Cessna but decided to book some flying for myself in October. I had a check out flight in G-BHHG on 1st October and booked a few hours' flying.

Tuesday October 7th: There was a dreadful storm in the night and when we got up this morning some of the back guttering was hanging loose. I repaired it and cleared the gutter out as it was full of moss. I've been very busy today, work seems to be building up and I may soon have to employ someone. There are some interesting leads and I may reflate the business if things start to improve. The food machinery man came in today, it looks as though I shall end up making their machines for them. I don't know what to do, one half of me wants to pack it in whilst the other half wants to make a go of the business. Peter Cullum (Bill's brother) the polisher has just arrived (1748) and he will stay till about 2000.

One of the problems with closing down a business is keeping the creditors at bay. I had every intention of paying everyone, not on the strict 30-day terms that our suppliers had been used to but I would never welsh on a debt. When I realised that we were losing a lot of business I talked to the bank and they agreed to stand by me. I had to keep them informed of progress and provide regular cash flow forecasts. I contacted all of our suppliers and told them the of the situation. They were understanding and said that as long as I kept paying off the debt they were prepared to work with me.

Tuesday October 28th: *Yesterday I sold the Range Rover. I had to drop the price to £3000 but it is a relief to turn it over. I heard today that my spare land is now definitely sold. All in all things are not looking too bad. The design on the doughnut fryer is now sorted and I hope to shift about 10 machines next month. I have managed to find someone to do the Fairline 40 stainless who is a very good welder and can do the job comfortably. There is very little interest in the factory, which is a pity because I shall probably miss the Lisle Court Hotel. I worked until 2130hrs. last night, the stainless fittings business is really picking up especially Fairline Boats.*

I was trying to do as much flying as possible to keep my licence current, and also I loved the feeling of freedom that it gave. As soon as I arrived at the airfield my worries evaporated and all I had to think about was checking out the aircraft and flying it. Both Ann and I were flying the Cessna 152 Hotel Golf, not together, as we both liked flying on our own. We would have liked to buy another plane but finances were very tight so we were making do with the flying club plane.

We were now getting busier and I had to work a lot of hours and employ more people. Bill Cullum was now working for me again but only part time. He was a lecturer at the local college and he could manufacture a Fairline 40 pulpit (bow rail) in 7 hours – the time on the job was 30 hours!

I still had a dream of selling up and moving to the coast and there was a very nice hotel that I would have liked to buy on the Isle of Wight, but as the engineering business improved this dream always seemed to be just out of reach.

Wednesday November 12th: *It is now 1817hrs. I have three*

men working besides myself and really we seem to be surviving the depression quite well. We are a bit behind on the doughnut machines. Four of them should be going out today but I think It will be Monday before anything goes out of the door. Marine work seems to be holding steady, we are still doing a fair amount for Fairline, who appear to be keeping their heads above water Ann was working on the press most of today and I have been doing all sorts of different jobs. I have just finished brazing some pickup pipes for Fairline. Tomorrow is our day off, Ann is taking mother shopping and I am going flying at 1000h and then on to Father's for lunch. I shall visit Garrard to check the progress of the UFO during the afternoon.

I had hoped to launch the UFO in 1980, but it was not to be. It was a mistake to give the job to David Garrard, as with all of his other work he was not able to spend the time necessary to complete the boat in a reasonable time.

Tuesday November 18th: *I am getting a bit fed up with things at the moment. The fryers are moving a lot slower than I had hoped. I went down to Matlock and Brown (the customer) today to see the setup. They had a couple of our machines in the place but did not do any actual frying. John Preston, one of the Directors of Autobake, apparently spent quite a time in the Mediterranean and has charts that he will let me peruse. We are working this Thursday afternoon, I think it a mistake but we need to get a Fairline 40 pulpit out this month to keep Fairline happy and to help our cash flow. The first batch of frying machines are nearly finished, the largest task being the final finishing of the inner kettle. I am having a demonstration of a hand finisher this week and I hope this will speed things up.*

Ann and I had decided to do an aerobatics course, mainly because this seemed like an exciting thing to do but also to improve our general flying. At that time Sywell Aero Club had two Beagle Pup aircraft that were cleared for aerobatics. Ann and I had flown these whilst doing stalling and spinning during our PPL training. Aerobatic training was practised at 5000 ft to enable the pilot to recover (regain control if anything goes wrong) by the time 3000ft was reached. As I climbed to 5000 ft it was a glorious day with a slight heat haze over the Pitsford reservoir. The safety checks, ensure harness is tight, steep turn to the left and then one to the right to ensure all is clear. The barrel roll was the first exercise – dive the aircraft to 130 knots, pull back on the stick and roll the aircraft. We then did a loop and a stall turn. The Beagle Pup was fairly low powered, so it was necessary to dive the plane to achieve the speed for the manoeuvre.

Thursday December 4th: Went flying today with Paul Smith. We took off at about 1020 and climbed out over Pitsford lake to about 4000 ft on the QFE. Paul asked me to demonstrate a roll. I did one to the left and one to the right and then Paul demonstrated a loop. I did a loop and it was reasonable. We spent some time doing loops and rolls and to finish Paul did a stall turn. This manoeuvre is probably the more difficult and we did not have time for me to practise one. I thought aerobatics would be much more terrifying than they are, although Paul is very good and probably if done with one of the "cowboy element" aerobatics could be awful. On our return to the field, while downwind, Paul pulled the switch and we did a practice forced landing.

Quite often Ann and I would go to Sywell together and one of us would go off with Paul in the Beagle Pup doing aerobatic training whilst the other went for a fly around in the Cessna 152. Orders were flooding in and the system of working weekends and having Thursday off was fine, but with pressure of work quite often it was not possible to have a day off in the week and some weeks I had to work every day, sometimes late into the evening.

Wednesday December 10th: Well here we are, nearly Christmas again. I worked until 2100hrs last night. I have now employed Singh on a full-time basis and he appears to be quite skilled. I could do with some time off.

Sunday December 14th: I worked today from 0830 until 1730. Bill completed a Fairline 40 Pulpit and did some work on a washing trough. Due to EEC regulations most food processing establishments have to provide additional washing facilities and the end result is that we are getting more work. It's pouring with rain and Ann hasn't arrived yet, she comes in some Sundays to give me some moral support and to catch up on odd jobs.

As the year drew to a close I thought of the momentous events of the last twelve months. The business had gone from a successful and profitable enterprise employing 30 people and established as the leading independent manufacturer of stainless yacht fittings to nothing. I was so sad to see the empty factory when everyone had gone. I couldn't bear to say goodbye to everyone and went round to the back of the factory until they had all left.

I was really keen to do something different and had the factory sold, I would probably have bought a hotel, perhaps on the Isle of Wight. I had bought and sold an aeroplane and in the short time that I had owned GAWPS I had flown 55 hours. this was the cheapest flying I had ever done.

However, the business was starting to take off again, and I was beginning to become enthusiastic about the prospects for the future. The most important lesson I had learned was to pay the men for what they produced rather than just for being there. The piecework system I had introduced was in my opinion the best system possible for a production workshop. The main advantages were that the work was always done within the costed time and the person doing it could make a lot more money. Most of the jobs were being done in "double time", which meant that not only was the employee making more money, we were able to progress a lot more work. The danger with this system of working is that quality will suffer because jobs are being rushed through to earn maximum wages. However the ruling was that the men had to do their own rectification and this time was not paid. There were a few grey areas, and sometimes I would give a few extra hours, but generally the system worked very well.

It also minimizes the problems of supervision – if a person isn't working, they are not being paid. We didn't have "tea breaks" as such. I said that they could stop for a break any time they wanted, as it wasn't costing me any lost production.

Wednesday December 24th: We worked until about 1230 today, and as the men knocked off I gave them their bottles of booze and wished them Merry Christmas. The Cullums I gave a half bottle of Scotch, Singh a bottle of red wine and John I gave a full bottle of Bell's whisky. I then had lunch at the factory. Ann had a mushroom omelette and I had a mixed grill. The trouble with Chinese takeaways is the lousy chips. I then sent Ann home while I wrapped James's billiard table and her presents. I left Kettering at about 1400 hrs. and drove to Bedford in the truck to pick up Dad. He wouldn't wear the new coat I bought him, in case the truck made it dirty, I don't blame him really. With Dad's case and bags of presents etc. it was quite a squeeze in the cab of the truck.

During the evening Ann's mum and dad came over and I stuffed the turkey and cooked the enormous leg of pork. I drank quite a lot of gin and turned in about 0100.

CHAPTER TWENTY ONE

A year of indecision

⊃✕⊂

It was now clear that Cooney Marine would survive if I wanted it to, although I still dreamed of moving to the coast and trying a completely different business venture. There were a lot of orders coming in daily, but because of the way of working and the piecework system, we were able to keep customers happy and if we looked like falling behind with production we could work a few more hours or employ some former employees on a part time basis.

Friday February 6th 1981: The year so far has been quite reasonable. in January the firm turned over about £12,000, which is quite remarkable when you consider that we only have two full-time employees and a few part time. On Friday (3rd. Feb.) I went flying at Sywell, with Paul Smith to practice aerobatics. I was pleased with my loop and roll, but I still have a problem with the stall turn. I did a superb landing but although we did our aeros near the factory, Ann didn't see us. Yesterday it was Ann's turn for aeros, but she wasn't very well so I took her up in the Pup for a fly around. We then went to Bedford to see Father and then on to the UFO. There wasn't much sign of progress and I was disappointed, I can't see it being ready for the early spring, there is so much to do.

Tuesday February 10th: I paid Garrard a surprise visit today. No one was working on the boat. I get so fed up, week after week I have been going over there and the progress is pathetic. I have now told him that unless he gets his finger out and makes significant progress over the next couple of weeks I shall take the boat away and finish it myself. This would not be a very practical idea, but I am determined to do it. The boat would fit into the bottom workshop quite well, the problem being getting in and out as the height would be about 11ft. to deck level. The main advantage would be that it would be under cover so I could work on it regardless of weather. Ann is concerned that the general finish would suffer, but I don't think it would turn out too bad. at least the engineering could be checked out by me. What I should have done is to fit a pre-prepared wooden kit into the boat, that would have made it a fairly easy task and it would now be on the water.

Colvic Craft, the company that produced the fibre glass mouldings for the UFO range, had several companies using them as a basis for their products. They had a range of craft from 19 to 50 feet and they supplied the DIY boat-builders as well as the trade. At this time in the industry the home-build market was big business and there were numerous people building large boats in their back gardens. It was good business for us and I used to like visiting customers to advise them. Nearly all the major boat-builders would sell anything from just a bare hull to a complete kit of parts to finish a boat. The downside of this was that some of the home builds were of very poor quality, although some were excellent. Colvic UFOs were being fitted out by several boat-builders. Oyster Marine, were fitting out UFO 34s with a slightly different interior layout, although I was going for the standard layout. Some of our customers who had finished their boats and were sailing them would come in and tell stories of trips they had done and I would be quite envious hearing of their exploits whilst my boat was still ashore being finished off.

Wednesday February 25th: I am looking forward to my day off tomorrow. I have been giving Garrard a few surprise visits over the last week or two and I don't think he likes being pressured. I called in Monday and surprise surprise, he had a new chap that had started and there were two of them working on the boat.

On Monday I did something I have not done for some time. I called on a few old customers going as far as north Norfolk and ending up back at Garrards. I arrived home early and cooked dinner for Ann, who was still at work, so when she arrived home at about 1915 hrs. she was quite surprised. That evening I called in to see Gene Godden (gunsmith) to have my game gun done up and to ask his advice on filling in my firearm certificate renewal and variation. This morning we went to see Spavings (accountant) at Rushden. It now looks like we may be operating Cooney Marine in some way shape or form for at least another year. I still intend to move to the coast as soon as I can sell the factory. I had a builder in today to give me a price for extending the bungalow.

Kate, Ann's sister-in-law, found out that she was pregnant. Ron, Ann's brother was 42 and I think it was a shock for him as his existing son and daughter were now teenagers.

On Friday night there was another wings party and Ann

and I went along with Val and Bryan and some of our flying buddies. The booze was flowing freely and I was sitting next to one of the Sywell flying instructors. During the conversation I happened to mention Ron, who was also a pilot but on gliders. I said to this guy, "My brother-in-law, silly bugger, 42 years old with grown-up children and he's put his missus in the pudding club". He looked at me with a smile and said, "I know what you mean mate". He pointed to the swollen tummy of his wife sitting next to him and said, "I'm a silly bugger too!"

It was around this time I decided to take up karate. I was 37 and decided that if I didn't do it soon I would be too old, so I Joined the Kettering Shotokan Karate Club. The training was very hard and once a month Mr Asano, a Japanese master, would visit to train us. I was able to keep up with the training, and martial arts as was practised in that club enabled me to attain a good level of fitness.

Saturday 7th March: On Thursday we couldn't fly due to the weather. We had a tidy up of the house until Pat the cleaning lady arrived and then we drove to Bedford. We took Dad some Kentucky Fried Chicken and he seemed in good spirits. The fish and chips from round the corner seem to be a bit greasy and undercooked so we have not had them for a week or two. We left Dad's at about 1415 and drove to Gt. Barford to see the boat. There were two men working in her and progress seems to be quite good, I shall now possibly let him finish it off providing progress continues. We left fairly early as Ann's mother and father were not babysitting because they had flu. At dancing we are doing the slow foxtrot. It hasn't clicked yet and I think it will probably take a few more weeks' practice.

Today I changed all of the calendars, most of them were still on January. I don't think I like the March girls very much. One of them has a big fat arse and pendulous tits, another looks startled and another is wearing a mackintosh hood and only her face is showing. I have four men working today, we have enough work to survive but I don't think we will be breaking any records this month for turnover. It almost seems to be slowing down again, which is surprising for the time of the year. I think the Budget is next week, it is rumoured that there will be a 2-3% reduction in the MLR, I can't see it happening but if it does it may cause a mini boom.

We have now received the new reefing spar leaflets, I think it possible that we may sell a lot more and Ann is planning a mailing shot. It is a very good product and I don't know what to do with it when we wind up. This is also true of the whole business. We have good products and are now producing them profitably, it will be a shame to throw it all away. We have booked a few days' holiday at Easter on the Isle of Wight I suppose this will start the old wanderlust going.

The Budget was controversial. Margaret Thatcher and her Chancellor, Sir Geoffrey Howe, were determined to cut borrowing and introduced measures to this end. Many of their policies were unpopular but as Thatcher said in her October 1980 conference speech, "The lady is not for turning!"

Unemployment was at an all-time high, mainly through the major industries becoming uncompetitive due to excessive wage demands and restrictive union practices.

Saturday 4th April: Last Wednesday I went to a karate club. I started to try to regain fitness and I hope it proves interesting enough for me to become enthusiastic about it. The instructor was very good but I was surprised how unfit some of the people were. Even the young ones seemed to be making heavy weather of the exercises. On Thursday we visited Dad, he was very poorly and anxious and I am a bit concerned for him. He was shaking quite badly. We took him to Gt. Barford with us and then took him shopping, and when we left he seemed a lot better. After leaving Bedford we went to Sywell and I took Ann up in the Pup to do some aeros. We climbed to 5000ft. in reasonable visibility over Pitsford reservoir. I started with a barrel roll and then did a couple of loops. We only saw one other aircraft at that level several miles away. There was a haze layer between about 1500 and 2500 ft. so at 5000 we had quite good in-flight visibility and we couldn't see the ground.

I tried some stall turns. I dived the aircraft to reach 120 knots and then pulled up. As the speed dropped to 110 I applied full power, pulling the aircraft up until it was vertical, held vertical for a second then full left rudder, as the nose cut the horizon powered off. As it dropped vertical check straight with rudder and I eased out of the dive. On the second one the airplane went over on its back but the third was OK. I climbed back up to 5000ft. and handed over to Ann to do a roll. It is more difficult from the right hand seat and when she dived the airplane she was left wing low – the roll wasn't too bad though. As we were non radio, I did a standard 2000ft rejoin and the landing was good enough.

When we arrived home Ann's mum and dad had cut the lawn and there was the smell of fresh cut grass in the air. The garden looked neat and tidy with the daffodils nodding their heads in the evening breeze. At dancing Clare, one of the young helpers was not wearing a bra and her pert breasts stood out proudly against the fabric of her dress. She is a pretty young thing with a super personality.

Thursday was also my birthday. The children brought their presents in and got into bed with us. James bought me a shooting magazine and Theresa bought me a book, I had a wallet from Ann. I am at work at the moment, I only have three men working and there is not much work in. Last month was a very good month for turnover and the overall position seems to be improving fairly rapidly.

The end of year figures for 1980 showed a loss of £17,612.

This could have been much worse if we hadn't taken the measures we had. Laying off the workforce and selling assets such as the land on Telford Way, the aeroplane and unnecessary vehicles had definitely helped. In 1979 the profit for the year was £18,518, which worked out to 6% of turnover, but in 1978 the profit was £27,598, or 11% of turnover. The main reason for this drop in profit percentage was low productivity as the turnover for 1979 was about £50,000 up on the previous year. The fixed assets for the business at 31st December 1980 showed a healthy surplus of £119,540, which although £19,000 less than the previous year was still a healthy balance. We'd had to produce a cash flow forecast for the bank to ensure their continued support and although largely guess work this was to prove close to expectations.

The UFO 34 was nowhere near finishing, and I could see that it was unlikely to be finished in time for the 1981 season. Cash flow was improving month by month and with our efficient way of working as long as there was enough work coming in we would survive. The advantage we had was that Ann and I were doing a lot of the production ourselves, keeping wage costs down to the minimum. Any people we employed were only paid for what they produced.

Tuesday May 18th: Last weekend Ann and I flew to Spain to inspect some property. We went on one of the "cheap" inspection flights that are often advertised in yachting journals. We arrived at Barcelona at about 3pm Friday and then had a 2-hour journey by taxi to Ampuriabrava and we stayed in Rosas at a very pleasant hotel. There was another couple with us, Pete and Lyn, and a representative of Residamar flew out with us. During the weekend we looked at lots of apartments, villas and town houses both on the waterfront and off. The development at Ampuriabrava is very nice, canals have been dug out about 80ft. wide and a large proportion of the properties have moorings for boats.

We eventually found a nice small house that we would like to buy. The biggest problem as far as I can see is whether we could take more time off safe in the knowledge that everything here was operating satisfactorily. The other thing I wonder about is whether I could use the house and the UFO to full advantage. I can afford to buy the house, but only if everything here works well enough to pay for it.

13th June 1981 I think this year will be remembered as the year of indecision. We are waiting for the bank to give us the OK on the house in Spain and I think we may not wish to go ahead now. Ann is worrying herself silly thinking that perhaps we can't afford it after all! I really don't know what to do. There is also a chance that the UFO will not be finished in time for our August break. The cash flow is holding up but we are a bit tight all the time. Overheads are very high due to the size of the place. We are working more efficiently than ever before, but the bank charges are killing us off. We are having difficulty reducing the overdraft, which is running at about £50,000. I think what I would like to do is find a better house in the UK possibly with an acre or two and buy a small apartment at Ampuriabrava to see how things go. All of these plans are hypothetical at the present time as the bank may turn us down.

15th June: *The bank wouldn't play ball with our schemes to have a place in Spain. I just rang and spoke to Mr Hill (bank manager). He said he was sorry and the reasons were that we were not contributing enough, they couldn't keep an eye on it, and they think that after last year a time of consolidation is necessary.*

23rd *July: At the end of June we did a stocktake, as we intended to do some accurate half-yearly accounts. When the figures were produced we saw that the situation was better than we imagined. The net profit was 21% and on the half year's working we were showing a profit of £13,000!*

It now looks fairly certain that the UFO won't be ready for our holiday so we have booked 2 weeks' self-catering at a Ladbrokes holiday camp. We are taking My dad with us to give him a break, he seems to be looking forward to it. We have rigged the Gh 14 Dinghy with a 35hp. outboard and we will be taking that along with us. With the sailboard on top of the car, five of us in it and the dinghy behind we will be carrying quite a load.

We have found a tenant for our other workshop. We moved out during the latter part of June and they moved in early July. The rent is £4,800 per year plus rates and insurance etc. On the 11th July we went out to dinner with Val and Bryan, and when we returned we found our house had been burgled. Luckily there was very little missing and I hope I can claim on my insurance. We have now sold our house and are hoping to purchase a farmhouse in Ringstead. The house is in reasonable condition and has 2.5 acres of land with an option to purchase additional land if required. The purchase price is £54,000, which is a lot of money. We have postponed plans to move to the coast for the time being.

The decision to abandon our plans to move to the coast crept up on us as business gradually improved. It was starting to make money again and it was becoming less of struggle to survive. I was still doing all of the engineering work. I could set up the capstan lathe and turn out nylon rollers in seconds. I did all of the regrinding of press tools and manufactured some also, although I did have some press tools made by a company in Bedford.

Our creditors were now being paid on time. I had always tried to pay people on 30-day terms and we were now getting back to this method of payment. One of the steel representatives, who was also a director of the company, complimented me on my efforts resulting in the survival of the business. He said he thought an older man couldn't have done it! Ann had the faith in me and together we worked through the bad times.

27th August: *We had a nice holiday in Wales, the weather was good and both Ann and I suffered slight sunburn. We used the boat most days, and did quite a bit of fishing. We tried water skiing but failed miserably. The only one in the family who was successful was James, who got up first or second pull and was quite good. Theresa was also successful but not as good as James.*

On the last day but one we got our car stuck in the sand and Ann burnt the clutch out. The AA towed us into a garage in Swansea and I spent the last day of the holiday hanging around waiting for it to be mended. The holiday really did Dad some good, he got very brown and at the end of the holiday looked 10 years younger.

Last weekend we went down to see Pat Patterson, we didn't arrive until about 2100hrs. We stayed in his house on the first night and got up at about 0800 Saturday morning. We eventually left the mooring at about 1030 and motored into Plymouth harbour en route to Mevagissey. an uneventful trip down in warm sun with a 3 to 4 knot breeze and little swell. Saturday evening the three of us went ashore in Mevagissey and had a few drinks, returned to the ship and I cooked dinner. We turned in at about 1200 but were then rudely awakened at 0730 Sunday morning as the fishing boat we were lying alongside was putting to sea.

As we sailed, Ann put some sausages in the frying pan and at about 0930 we were becalmed, so we downed sails and all went below for breakfast. After breakfast we decided to lunch in Polperro. We tied up to a buoy in the bay and rowed ashore for lunch, drank several pints and then returned to the ship. Patterson decided to go for a swim and took all of his clothes off except underpants and then holding his nose, leapt over the side. Ann and I put on our costumes and did likewise. The only problem Patterson had was that his pants were of the shorts type and every time he climbed the boarding ladder his prick fell out!

We set sail from Polperro and I went below to cook lunch. I chopped half a pound of bacon into squares, fried it with onions tomatoes and potatoes, then beat three eggs and poured it over, finishing it off under the grill. It was very good. Patterson then went on the whisky and turned in at about 1600. I brought the ship round into Plymouth and anchored off Cawsand. We stayed the night in Cawsand and returned to Millbrook Monday morning.

I was still doing a lot of the polishing myself. The job requires a lot of skill and is a very dirty job. I was finding it difficult to train anyone to do it because I was so busy on other things. Although it paid very well and on piecework a polisher could earn a lot of money, it was difficult to find someone with the skill and intelligence to do it, who didn't mind getting dirty. Most of our product was now being fitted on high-end luxury motor yachts, so the finish had to be blemish free. A lot of people didn't realise that the material was stainless steel and thought it was chrome plated. Quite often I would work late into the evening polishing parts for the next morning's delivery.

22nd September: *The person who was going to buy our house has now backed out and although there is another couple that say they want it the prospect of our acquisition of Middlefield Farm is suddenly in doubt. I have another employee starting on Monday, we are getting behind with Fairline and I don't like it. I would hate to lose any business. On paper we seem to be doing nicely but I am not too pleased with the way things are progressing. We need more staff, more work and a more secure order book. I am going to polish some deck rails now to clear an overdue order and I shall deliver them tomorrow morning.*

Another problem was the buying departments of some customers. A lot of the boat-builders had expanded their production and the buyers were a bit out of their depth. Quite often they would ring up to chase an order that we had never received. In most cases they had forgotten to order parts and then blamed us for non-delivery. Sometimes the comment was "Well you should know what we need anyway", although we were not allowed to supply anything without a purchase order. Once when we were "behind" with fittings that had not been ordered I pointed this out and had a very short and sharp letter from Sam Newington saying, "Kevin, I expect you to supply us with our stainless steel requirements without question!"

I always tried to do just that and would work day and night to keep customers supplied on time. Sometimes there would be a panic and we would work all hours to deliver some part or other, only to see it in the stores unfitted a week later. It got to the stage where I would go round to the different production lines and liaise with the line manager and the fitters working on the boats.

Another problem was the fitters. Sometimes they would fit a part in the wrong place and complain that it did not fit. Where possible I would help out and alter things to save the guy from being disciplined. I was doing all of the design work on the Fairline stainless parts and a lot of my parts were being copied by other boat-builders. I didn't really mind, but Fairline were not too happy that their parts were being copied. The strange thing was they were copying the good designs as well as the not so good, and it was amusing to see at boat shows new design boats with old design deck fittings that Fairline had already stopped using.

6th October: The weather today has been reasonably seasonal, it started cold and misty then the sun came through and it was fine for a few hours, quite warm in fact. This afternoon it clouded over and turned to rain. I went to Fairline first thing to sort out some special fittings for the Fairline 40. Last Thursday I went to Christchurch with Martin Smith to look at a catamaran. He decided he would like it and his wife Pat seems quite enthusiastic, which is amazing because she can't stand water or small boats. He made an offer and is now waiting for the owner to make a decision.

The catamaran was a Catalac 9 metre and it was on brokerage with Tom Lac Catamarans and was in reasonable condition. We went out for a demo and Martin was impressed with the handling of the boat. It had been manufactured by Westfield Engineering who built the Kingfisher range, so we knew it was well built.

We went into the office to discuss the boat with Tom. He and his wife Mary ran the company that marketed the Catalac range. Martin decided not to have a survey and asked Tom if he would look the boat over and check for any major problems. The asking price was £15,000 and I advised Martin to make an offer of £12,500. As we drove back Martin was excited, and planning voyages and adventures far and wide!

Earlier in the year one of our customers, Lytton Boatbuilding, had gone into receivership and as I had seen it coming and had not wanted to lose all of the £4,500 they owed I managed to obtain a set of boat mouldings to approximately the same value. The boat was a Discovery 850 power cruiser and I thought I might fit it out myself. Where I was going to find the time heaven only knows! It had been sitting on our car park for months and I eventually found a buyer. I had to let it go for a lot less than the book value, but it was better than losing everything. David Garrard had agreed to lend me his crane-lifting slings.

8th October 1981: I went to Fairline this morning to modify some side rails that needed springing out. I returned home at about 0945 and then we went to Bedford to see the UFO. Although the boat is nearly finished it seems to be taking an age to finish off the last few odds and ends. David wasn't there so we went on to Dad's for lunch. I got fish and chips from the shop round the corner, we normally have Kentucky Fried Chicken but the shop is the other side of town so I didn't bother.

We left Dad's at about 1330 and went back to Barford to see Garrard. He had just returned with the berth cushions, which we put into the boat. Now it is all varnished out and with the cushions in, the boat looks quite nice. I am looking forward to the day we launch her, the building of the yacht seems to have taken ages and I can't help feeling that when she is launched I will be slightly disappointed that there is no new boat to look forward to. I shall have to get another project on the go.

We left Bedford and headed for Sywell. When we got to Bromham I realised that I had not collected the lifting slings. The Discovery 850 (boat mouldings) are being collected tomorrow so we returned to Garrard's and I phoned the flying school to cancel our 1600 booking. We went to dancing and were doing the slow foxtrot and rumba, we also did a new step in the cha cha.

10th October: Saturday morning again. The Lytton (27 ft. cruiser mouldings) went yesterday. It took about 4 hours to load, it was pouring with rain and blowing a gale. I borrowed Roger Humphries' fork lift and used in conjunction with our two-ton gantry it made the job a lot easier. I've had a shocking backache since yesterday morning and humping and heaving the boat around didn't help matters. On the way home I popped into the

Wheatsheaf to unwind and ease the pain with a couple of pints. I met Neil Drage in there, who wants to buy our house. He assured me that he still wants it, and I am hoping to get moved into Middlefield by the end of November.

Today I don't feel much like work. The backache only hurts when I move. I have a few men in this morning and Mum-in law-and Ed are doing the wrapping up. In the night the wind was so strong that it blew the gantry over. Luckily I still have the forklift here to right it. I shall go home early if possible and perhaps not come into work tomorrow. There is a lot to do but I think it is about time I had a Sunday at home, I haven't had a Sunday off for about 6 weeks.

20th October: Went to Martin Smith's on Saturday night and had a super meal of game pudding. Pat really is a super cook. We watched films for the rest of the evening. Last night I took James to karate, I think it was probably the hardest session yet. The gypsies are trying to move in again, I wonder if they will succeed. We are locking gates and things but as they are above the law it seems they are able to do as they please, anyone opposing them is in the wrong.

Around our factory there was a considerable amount of undeveloped land owned by British Steel and although it was fenced off and gated, any weakness, was exploited by the travellers and once moved in it was difficult to move them on. On our site, although there was a secure fence and gates were always locked, nothing could be left outside or it would be stolen. Every morning one of the men would walk round the perimeter of the site to inspect the fence for breaches. One pick-up truck was stolen and another broken into and the steering lock smashed and radio stolen. The factory was broken into on several occasions and a large quantity of stainless steel, part finished product stolen, as well as finished items ready for dispatch. The thieves would only get a few hundred pounds in scrap value but the cost to us was enormous with the disruption caused. We were insured, but the insurance barely covered the cost of materials lost. Our insurance company gave us an ultimatum: get an alarm system fitted connected to the police station or you are not covered!

31st October: *We won the gypsy battle. On the morning of 21st October British Steel moved in with a bulldozer and dragged them off. It was a smart operation and everyone is pleased that we never had them for the winter again. Tonight we are going to the Sywell Aero Club booze up, I am quite looking forward to it. It is 1630 and I am at work, we will be knocking off soon.*

The sale of our house is once again held up, someone has backed out down the chain. The owner of Middlefield is pushing for an exchange of contracts, so there is a chance that the whole thing will fall through. This month the turnover will be reasonable but not excessive. Each month I think the work will not hold up, but we seem to survive. I haven't got much in for November but I may be able to deliver some doughnut machines to boost it up.

The UFO is all but finished, the woodwork is first class and the velvet cushions look superb. I am looking forward to an early season next year. I still have not let the 3000 ft. unit, I think perhaps I will find something to do in there myself. Martin Smith's offer has been accepted and he is very enthusiastic, they are going to stay down on the boat this weekend and take her for a sail tomorrow. They invited Ann and me down for a sail but it is a long way to go for 1 day and I feel knackered and could do with a day at home.

21st November: *Quite an interesting month so far. On the 7th. we had the first shoot of the year. On the first stand I did not see any birds at all and I don't think anyone shot anything. My next position was down in the hollow near the ash tree. Just* as I was taking up my position a cock pheasant flew over quite high. I was having a pee at the time and raised my gun and shot the pheasant with my winkle out. It was a good shot and the pheasant was dead. I shot three more from this position, although one was claimed by another gun and as I had done so well, I did not press the point.

We next went down to the long wood where I took up position. My first shot took a high bird and that was all I bagged all day, however if I include the one I found dead in the road on the way in, in all that makes six birds, quite a good bag. I am going again tomorrow, I wonder if I shall be so lucky.

Yesterday evening was the Karate Club competition. I went in for it and my opponent was a green belt. I had a good fight and think I should have won. It went the distance (2 minutes) and no one had scored, so we fought for an extra 30 seconds. My opponent scored with a kick to the stomach, in actual fact he missed but was awarded the point. I really enjoyed myself and felt great afterwards even though I lost.

Tuesday December 8th: It snowed last night, the first snow of the year for us, and it has been freezing hard all day. This morning I did a trip to Fairline to check a few dimensions on the new Fairline 36. I then had to take some radar masts to Corby for stove enamelling. When passing through Weldon I decided to call in at Kirby Hall for a walk round the shoot to try to ascertain what has happened to all the pheasants. The last two shoots have been pathetic, hardly any birds at all. As I walked through the pen my foot caught in something, a bloody snare! I think the Pheasants have all been poached and several of us have suspicions about who is having them.

It is now 1808 and I am thinking of knocking off soon. Singh is working away steadily but somehow this week's production has not seemed to flow as well as usual. It will soon be Christmas. Last Thursday James and I did our karate *grading, both passing. Last night Ann and I went dancing in Wellingborough so that I could have a dance with Clare prior to the medal test on Saturday. It was a very good evening and we really enjoyed it. It's not the same on Wednesday at Kettering, there is a far better atmosphere on Monday night. Ann wants me to give up Monday night Karate but I really enjoy that also.*

24th December: Christmas Eve again, it is 1135, all the shopping is done and money made up for the men. I went to Fairline this morning to hand out a few bottles of good cheer. We will work until about 1300 hrs. and then I shall close up the factory and go to Bedford to collect Father.

Last night we went round to Val's to give them the presents etc. We expected to go out with them for a meal, but Bryan has been ill and unable to go out. We left Val's at about 2100hrs and went home to check the children. They were OK. so we popped down the Wheatsheaf for a bar snack. Stephen Smith from Swindalls rang to say he is expecting an offer of £145,000 for the factory. If the offer is firm I shall probably accept. The weather is slightly milder today although the fields are still snow covered. Ann bought me a beautiful rifle for Christmas and I have bought her a few presents. This year has been fairly successful, we have kept our heads above water and are hoping for a better year next year.

I collected Dad early and we had a pleasant evening. I was busy preparing the turkey and I plucked a brace of pheasants as I won't have much time during Christmas Day. We went down to Watts' shop raffle and the children won three prizes, much to our amazement and their glee.

Boxing Day: I got up at about 0730 and had a quick breakfast, I left the house at about 0835 and arrived at Kirby Hall at about 0910. It was bitterly cold with the ground covered in frozen snow and ice sometimes up to 9" deep. On the first drive I bagged a nice hen pheasant with my second barrel. There was quite a bit of shooting and I was surprised, thinking that the birds had all disappeared. We had a good morning's shooting, the bag being 17 pheasants, two partridges and a rabbit. It was almost unbelievable considering the poor shooting up to now.

27ᵗʰ December: It snowed quite heavily during the night and it was touch and go whether to go to Ron's for the day. I eventually decided to risk it. We picked up Mother-in-Law but Father-in-Law was in bed with the flu. We arrived at Ron's at about 1345 and had a reasonable day. Kate did a wonderful lunch and Ron gave me some very large brandies after. We left about 2100 hrs. and had a lousy journey home in the snow.

1981 was an interesting year. The business had sorted itself out and with a lot of hard work and effort it could continue to be profitable and successful. The number of employees was steadily increasing and work was holding up so much so that I was tempted to take the factory off the market.

Over the New Year period we were off to Crete for some winter sun. I needed a holiday "away from it all."

1ˢᵗ January 1982 I felt awful and wished I hadn't drunk so much, after this holiday I shall give up drinking for a few months. Now '81 is out of the way I wonder what is in store for us. I shall certainly sell the factory if I can get enough for it, which will take a lot of pressure off the cash flow. Repayments and interest are running at over £22,000 per year, which is keeping us sailing very close to the wind! I shall be most interested to see the end of the year figures, they will probably be reasonable as we have kept our heads above water and lived well.

I will try to change vehicles this year, we could do with at least one good car. I am looking forward to the spring and launching the boat. I would love to take it to the Med. but do not have the time. There is no one who could take over for long enough for us both to go. I am looking forward to some more flying, I haven't done any for weeks.

In February 1982 Laker Airways went bankrupt. The Laker Skytrain was one of the first "no frills" airlines and since 1977 it had operated a daily transatlantic walk on, walk off service that did not require advance reservations and worked on a first come, first served basis.

On February 20th Macmillan and Khrushchev met for peace talks. This was at the height of the Cold War and was seen as an important development. On the same day Ireland, for the first time, allowed the sale of contraceptives.

After months of false alarms, we had agreed on a house. The farmhouse didn't work out, but then the Titchmarsh property sale went through and we had to find somewhere quickly. We were moving to a house in Warkton Lane in Kettering, considered to be the desirable end of town. It only had two bedrooms but another could be added by incorporating the very large upstairs landing, and I planned to extend the house into a four-bed by building over the garage.

The accounts for 1981 showed a net profit of £16,500, which was disappointing, as I had expected at least £20,000. There was a lot of pressure to keep prices down, but we were as competitive as anyone. With the production on piecework I don't think anyone could beat us on production times, and I estimated that we were 10 to 15% cheaper than our competitors. I was, however able to obtain a 7% price increase. I also planned to produce some more accounts at the end of June to ensure that we were on the right track.

The move to Warkton Lane took place on 9th March. There was a lot of work to do and we had a kitchen fitter/carpenter fitting out the kitchen and utility room. I planned to keep all of my guns in a purpose-built gun safe in the utility room, which was being built. I had ordered a steel door from H B Humphries, a fabricator on Telford Way.

Then Dennis the kitchen fitter rang me to say that when he returned from a visit to the builder's merchant he had called the police after noticing a gun propped up against a tree in my garden and one of the kitchen windows broken. When I arrived home two police cars were in the drive and a van with a dog unit. When I checked, my William Lee 12-bore shotgun and Finnish Lion .22 rifle were missing and a .410 shotgun was propped against a tree in the garden. The thieves had been through the house and taken most of Anne's jewellery and lots of other things. I rushed upstairs to where I had hidden my handguns and thankfully they were still there. At that time I owned a .22 Smith and Wesson semi-auto pistol, A Smith and Wesson .44 Magnum revolver, a Smith and Wesson mod 10 .38 Special revolver and a Beretta 9mm semi-auto pistol.

Dennis the kitchen fitter was apologetic, but it wasn't his fault, he had locked the house and was only gone for a short time to pick up supplies from a builder's merchant. The biggest loss for me was the shotgun, as it was my game gun and I always did well with it on shoots.

2nd April: I am 38 today and I don't feel any older. This year so far has gone quite well. Cash flow is reasonable and we moved house to Warkton Lane on 9th March. Fairline have started to buy fittings from another supplier, but as there is a lot of private work about we have not suffered much as yet. Their production has increased on all lines, so we are still very busy from them. The product they are buying from the other supplier is of very poor quality and we would not be able to get away with the rough finish and poor workmanship.

CHAPTER TWENTY TWO

War and peace

On April 2nd Argentine forces invaded the Falkland Islands, entering the capital, Port Stanley, early in the morning. The garrison of Royal Marines was outnumbered and outgunned, and after some brief skirmishes governor Sir Rex Hunt ordered them to lay down their arms. Other British territories including South Georgia were also seized. Mrs Thatcher ordered a task force of over 100 ships led by the aircraft carriers HMS *Hermes* and HMS *Invincible* to set sail for the South Atlantic and retake the islands.

I decided to call the new boat *Target* after our monthly production target and applied to the British Ships Registry at Harwich for the name. Unfortunately that name was not available and I had to submit alternatives. The name finally allowed was *Blue Target*, and with the blue stripes down the hull and the name in blue the boat looked stunning.

23rd April: *The UFO is now nearly complete, all that is now left to do is a little bit of plumbing and a general clean up. The joinery is first class and I think everything has been done properly, although I want to check out the engine installation. It will be nice to have it on the water. I don't think we will do any really long trips for a month or two, there are bound to be teething troubles. This month we have been under a lot of pressure from the trade and general public, but we are now just about on top. I don't know whether this is a good thing. Business still seems to be very hand to mouth, but we are paying everybody and doing all right out of it.*

We are in the process of furnishing the house. We have bought some reproduction furniture and are looking for a few antique odds and ends. we already have a balloon-back Victorian chair and a kidney back chair. I would like to get hold of a button back chair and a heavy coffee table. The children have settled in well to the new routine although Theresa has not yet found a friend.

On 25th April, South Georgia was retaken, by Royal Marines following a bombardment by Royal Navy ships. Prime Minister Margaret Thatcher told the nation to rejoice at the news. On 1st May a Vulcan bomber, after an 8000-mile round trip from Ascension Island, successfully attacked the runway on Stanley airfield. The next day, the Argentine Cruiser *General Belgrano* was sunk by the Royal Navy submarine *Conqueror*.

8th May: Last Wednesday Ann and I went flying. I had a check with Brian McCann in the 121 and then took Ann up, as I wanted to see the new house from the air. With the screen of trees around the house it was difficult to see much from the air, and I didn't want to get too low over Kettering. Since the start of the war between Britain and Argentina the news has been dominated by every detail. I now only have the television on at news time, none of the other programmes are as interesting as this real-life drama. The Argies are certainly in the wrong and I have the utmost respect for the Government for taking a positive line.

HMS Sheffield has been crippled and may have to be scuttled. This would be a great shame. I think everything should be done to salvage her. I wonder what they will do next. Their economy is bankrupt and most of the world is supporting the British cause.

The UFO should be launched next week. I shall be surprised if it is ready but will look forward to it. Apparently Ken and Jenny will be on the next pontoon in their Snapdragon. It will be super to see them again, we had some good times when at Wells.

16th May: The Task force bombed the Falklands again this morning and yesterday Marines did a daring raid on one of the Argie airfields, destroyed eleven aircraft on the ground and blew up an ammunition dump. Apparently there were no British casualties. I wonder when Mrs Thatcher will give the order to invade. There is of course a chance that there will be a diplomatic settlement. I think this would be a big mistake by the Government. In my opinion we should kick out the Argies and offer the USA an airbase on the islands, also keep a compact fighting force of our own down there, this way we could monitor our interests in the Antarctic where there could soon be problems. The Argies could then be told that any attack on the Falkland Islands would incur a massive retaliation against the Argentine mainland.

We had Val and Bryan for dinner, sorry to dinner, last night and had a pleasant evening. Yesterday Ann and I went looking for some dining chairs, and found some beautiful Regency style chairs in a shop in Wellingborough. We did a deal for 4 chairs and 2 carvers. The chairs really look nice with the new table. I shall now probably furnish the dining room in the Regency style. The UFO should be finished on Tuesday and ready for launching on Thursday, I shall go over Tuesday and make up the guardrail wires. I shall also give the boat a final inspection before it leaves Great Barford.

This afternoon we are taking the children to Val and Bryan's pool. We are taking Theresa and James's new friends with us. It should be a pleasant interlude, we will have dinner when we get back at about 1730 I suppose.

Anticipation was at an all-time high as the launching day for our beautiful yacht approached. Ann and I could think of little else; it was almost like waiting for a new baby, and a new delay seemed to occur every time our hopes were raised. Receiving the final bill was a shock to the system, as it was far higher than I expected. I had closely watched costs and had an idea what the final figure was likely to be but my estimate was hopelessly wrong!

5th June: Today we went to see Garrard regarding his final account. Whilst we expected to pay another four thousand pounds, the eventual bill came out at over nine. Ann was furious and hardly said a word. We both thought he must be robbing us. We had managed to scrape some cash together and could just about manage six. Saturday evening we went to a barbecue at Mick Webb's farmhouse. It was a super evening but the thought of Garrard's bill hung over us like a black cloud.

Money was fairly tight and I thought I'd budgeted adequate funds to pay the final account. I didn't want to do anything to delay the launch of the boat. so I decided to try to negotiate with Garrard to leave some of the equipment off the boat, get it launched and then take the items that had been left off at a later date when my finances improved. He was not very happy about this, which was understandable, but I was anxious to get the boat on the water after it had taken so long to complete.

Monday 7th June: *We went into work and sorted things out and then left for Bedford. On arrival we found the boat just about complete and went in to do battle. By the time I had finished we had reduced the bill by about £800, more than I had hoped. I then confronted him with the errors in addition and reduced it by a further £500, the total now reduced to £7,700. I then reduced it even further by leaving off some equipment, eg the generator, spinnaker pole, jockey pole and the boat heater. We ended up giving him a cheque for £6,750. I will take most of the gear from him, but I can do it over a few months to lessen the shock. We should launch the boat tomorrow, at last. We left Garrard's and went into Bedford to see Dad, who has not been too well lately. I rang the boat haulage firm and found that it was not arranged for Tuesday. I rang Garrard and had another battle with him on the phone. In the end I agreed to go another £500 and leave in the heater.*

After waiting for years it was almost an anti-climax. What new schemes or goals would I give my efforts to? The business was in good shape and we were making money, the kids were settled into their new routine, we were living in a nice house with a good address. I was 38 years old and it seemed everything in the garden was rosy. Looking back to where I'd started from with a lot of self-belief and determination to succeed, no money and no knowledge of running a business, I had come a long way, but I realised that I still had a long way to go.

I planned to expand the factory buildings at the Telford Way site. I would need more land and hoped to purchase some from British Steel, who owned all of the surrounding land.

There was bad news from the Falklands. Landing craft RFA. *Sir Galahad* and RFA. *Sir Tristram* with units of the

Welsh Guards on board, were bombed by Argentine aircraft off Fitzroy. More than 50 men were killed.

Tuesday 8th June: *We were all up early, excited by the thought of actually seeing the boat launched. I dashed over to Fairline with an early delivery and arrived home at about 0800 to have a hurried breakfast before leaving for Bedford. I loaded the truck and we left about 0845, which was later than I had planned. When we arrived at Great Barford the boat was already hanging from the crane and ready to be manoeuvred onto the low loader. David was bustling around and Ron was also busy. There were still a few odds and ends to do to complete the boat but nothing serious.*

As soon as it was on the trailer I climbed aboard and started to fit the lifelines, the boat had to move out of the yard immediately to let the crane out. The crane driver was already moaning that he was overrunning his time. I was crouched in the cockpit as the boat lurched out of the gates on the low loader. I continued to fit the lifelines and David and Ron were still doing odd jobs. The boat took longer than expected to load, so it was decided not to launch until the following day. It took Mr Debbage, the boat haulier, another hour to finish strapping the boat securely onto the trailer ready for the 100-mile trip to Ipswich. We decided not to go to Ipswich until tomorrow and we then left Great Barford and called in to see Dad. I left Ann and the kids at Dad's and went to fetch the lunch, Kentucky Fried Chicken, one of Dad's favourites. We stayed with Dad until mid-afternoon and then drove back to Kettering. We all felt elated that the boat was at last on its way to Ipswich and we looked forward to seeing it actually launched. I had the standing rigging in the truck and didn't want to be late tomorrow.

After dropping off Ann and the kids at home I went into work to sort things out. Later on in the evening we watched a video of the day's events. It wasn't very clear and appeared slightly out of focus. This video, a Hitachi, doesn't seem as clear as our last one, perhaps because it is a portable unit.

Wednesday 9ᵗʰ June: We were all up early and soon had the truck loaded with equipment for the journey to Ipswich. We left at 0830 after first checking the oil and water levels on the truck. It was a beautiful morning, slightly misty, but the sun already felt warm. We were soon past Cambridge and on the A45, David Garrard whizzed past in his Volvo.

As we approached Bury St. Edmunds the truck suddenly seemed to lose power. I stopped and checked that all the plug leads etc. were still on. We set off again and the truck started to sound very sick indeed, then the big ends started knocking in a most alarming manner. Luckily a few miles ahead was a petrol station and Little Chef restaurant, and we just made it, with little power left and the engine sounding completely knackered. I went into the restaurant to phone the AA only to find the phone vandalised. Luckily the chap in the petrol station allowed me to use his. I rang the AA and also Debbage's boat yard asking them to ask Garrard to come and rescue me, we then went into the café to have a coffee and wait.

The AA arrived first and Garrard shortly after. We told the AA to take the vehicle to Ron's (Ann's brother) and then David took us to Ipswich. Blue Target was waiting on the lorry ready to be put into the water. Ron and David still had a few last minute jobs to do. Ann took some video film and Theresa and I went to the chip shop and got lunch for everyone. About 1400hrs the gang arrived to launch the boat. As the slings took the strain every creak and groan seemed so ominous. Slowly it rose into the air and swung round over the loading dock. As they started to lower it into the water I thought that now even if the slings did break she would not suffer any damage!

As soon as she was afloat David and Ron went aboard to check the sea cocks, and everything appeared OK. It seemed ages before they put the mast up and fixed the standing rigging. The engine started and ran OK, so as soon as possible we took her out of the berth and motored slowly into the river. As we approached Fox's marina I noticed that the engine was overheating. I stopped it immediately and Ron took off the filler cap and poured in some more water. Luckily the tide was taking us in the right direction, but the wind kept blowing her head round. David and Ron were looking through the engine manuals hoping to find an answer. I had to keep starting the engine to keep the boat out of danger and it was then decided to stop the engine, pour in more water and put up the sails to sail her the last 4 miles to Woolverstone. I was at the wheel and Ron was in the cockpit with me. James was in the fore-cabin and Theresa was standing behind David, ready to hand him the kettle full of water.

David put a small cloth over the filler cap and undid it. As the cap came undone there was a sudden roar and a blast of boiling water and steam erupted from the engine. David reeled back as the searing blast of steam hit him. Theresa screamed as she was showered with hot water and Ron and I tried to dodge the boiling spray that enveloped the cockpit. It only lasted a few seconds. but as the steam cleared I could see David doubled up in pain and Theresa crying in the cabin. Luckily she had been holding a kettle of cold water and had poured it over herself instinctively to cool down the hot water in her clothes. I was terrified that she would be scarred.

We then doused David with cold water. David seemed to recover slightly, and as we were drifting into shallow water we commenced putting up the sails. On the jib nothing worked and all of the snap shackles were too small. They had more luck with the main, but the operation seemed endless. The engine was refilled to be used just for taking us into our berth at Woolverstone. We were still in fairly deep water so I decided not to anchor.

As soon as the mainsail was up we tacked gently down the river to Woolverstone Marina. As we approached I could see Ann on the pontoon waving, oblivious to our problems. David and Ron took down the sail and I started the motor to take us into the berth. As soon as we docked Ann took one look at David's burns and took him to hospital. His arm was one enormous blister and his left side was also badly blistered.

David and Ron left at about 1900 hours and we started to tidy up the boat. We thought we would take a walk up to the But and Oyster Pub for a meal, but when we arrived they were not cooking so we had a drink and walked back to eat on board. What a day!

The problem with the engine was a worry. David did not know what to do and he was suffering with the scalds he had received on launching day. There were several lessons to be learned, the obvious one being never take the radiator cap off an overheated engine.

I had big problems docking the boat. The tide was flowing out quite fast and consequently I was bringing the boat into the berth down tide. The boat ended up across the end of the pontoon, pinned there by the tide. and it was a struggle to turn her and get her moored up. My excuse for the cockup was the malfunctioning engine! I decided that in future I would plan to always berth the boat when the tide was flooding or go alongside the end pontoon and wait till the tide turned. Another lesson was always to ensure that the sails could be hoisted without problems, with correct-sized snap shackles. We should have tried running up the sails before leaving the boatyard. It would also have been a good idea to hoist the mainsail as soon as we left the dock.

I couldn't understand why the engine was overheating. I thought perhaps that it was the thermostat, so I bought a new one and then decided to strip down the cooling system and investigate. I took off the heat exchanger and there found the cause of the overheating – one of the protective plastic plugs fitted to the heat exchanger had not been removed when the heat exchanger had been fitted to the engine. I reassembled the engine and it ran perfectly. I ran it for a few hours to ensure that I had solved the problem.

Woolverstone Marina on the Orwell was a good place to be berthed, as it had a boatyard and chandlery and was an ideal place to sort out teething troubles. We had a few trips down the river and into the estuary. We planned a trip across the North Sea to Ostend for our summer holiday, a trip of approximately 15 hours. We went to the boat most weekends, but the business was very busy and I was working all hours to keep customers happy. However as soon as I stepped onto the boat on a Friday night I forgot most of my problems until Monday morning.

I was still flying about once a month to keep my hand in. I would take the flying school's B121 and go off to do some aerobatics, or perhaps just a few circuits.

The Falklands War was going well for the British forces. The Argentine Air Force was being shot out of the sky; their pilots were no match for the British pilots and some days as many as ten Argentine aircraft were shot down. The British lost several ships, some to Exocet missiles and some to bombing by Argentine aircraft, but on 14th June white flags were seen flying over Port Stanley and General Menendez surrendered to Major General Jeremy Moore. The Falklands campaign was a great success for the British armed forces and also for Mrs Thatcher.

Over the next few weeks we had some beautiful sailing. The boat was as expected; she sailed well and was a comfortable "live aboard" boat. In August everything was working and at last it was time for our summer trip to Ostend. I had decided to do an overnight passage, hoping that Theresa and James would sleep for most of the trip. Ann and I had decided on a watch system so that we could each get some sleep. There was very little wind, so the engine was on for a lot of the time.

The fuel contents gauge appeared to be malfunctioning and was showing 'full' all the time. I was worried that we would run out of fuel before arriving. The fuel filler was in the cockpit floor and in the middle of the tank, so I decided to "dip" the tank to ascertain fuel level. All I could find to use as a dipstick was the broom handle of the deck scrubber. which showed that the tank still contained plenty of fuel, so I upped the RPM as we motored towards Ostend. The trip took 20 hours from leaving Woolverstone to mooring up in the Mercator Marina, and there was quite a sense of achievement. It was our longest trip as a family so far.

We stayed in Ostend for five days. The weather was beautiful, and several days were spent on the beach. We all liked Ostend very much, especially Theresa and James. The restaurants and bars didn't seem too expensive, but the facilities at the marina were not very good – the toilets were very scarce and there was only one shower for both men and women.

We left Ostend and sailed along the coast to Dunkirk. It was quite windy (force 5-6) at the outset, but then the wind died down to nothing. Dunkirk Marina had much nicer facilities than Ostend but was very expensive. Prices were much higher in France, especially in the restaurants.

The three days spent in Dunkirk were also sunny and hot, but it was soon time to head for home and Ramsgate. We were up early for the BBC shipping forecast but for some reason our area wasn't mentioned. It was Friday 13th, but I always considered this to be my lucky day as it was the date of my first solo flight back in 1978.

Two hours out of Dunkirk it was blowing a 6-7 and we were undecided whether to continue or head back for Calais. We decided to carry on and by the time the boat was half way across the wind speed indicator was reading 40 knots (full gale) and we were sailing with a deep reefed main and the jib rolled up very small.

Friday 13th August: We went onto a run to make the East Goodwin Lightship and with all sails down we were running at about 9 knots under bare poles with an apparent wind speed of 45 knots. When we reached the lightship we then had to turn into the wind to head for Ramsgate. We had the engine on and made remarkably good headway into the teeth of the gale. The spray was blinding. I promised everyone that when we got in I would take them ashore for a slap up meal and they could have anything they wished. We eventually made Ramsgate outer harbour and went alongside a UFO 31 with a bent mast, to await the opening of the sluice gate to the inner harbour. Several boats came in with damage, there were at least 2 broken masts and one boat had lost its rudder. According to the BBC, the weather was recorded as storm force ten. The trip from Dunkirk took about 8 hours. The boat really proved herself and never at any time was I doubtful of her ability to handle the conditions. Obviously I would not normally put to sea in those conditions. The only thing that stopped working was the water pressure pump!

I took the family ashore and we found a nice restaurant overlooking the harbour. I asked the children what they wanted and they said "rump steak and champagne" so that's what they had.

Blue Target was a beautiful sailing boat, but she had taken four years to build and I fancied something bigger. The boat was fitted out to a high standard, possibly as good as any UFO built. The cockpit was very exposed and I decided to fit a spray dodger, which provided a lot of protection for the cockpit.

Having sailed with Pat Patterson and Martin Smith I fancied a catamaran. The stability and extra room seemed to outweigh the disadvantages of extra berthing charges and poorer upwind sailing performance. The draught on the UFO was 6ft, whereas most of the cruising catamarans of around 35ft had a draught of under 4ft. which was more suited to east coast sailing. The cost of building the UFO was about £39,000, but second hand models were being advertised around the mid-20s.

In the middle of November Ann fell down the stairs and broke her left leg. She was plastered up to the knee and although she was able to get about it was most inconvenient.

End December 1982: The Christmas festivities are now over and we are looking forward to starting back to work on January 3rd. During November I managed to get a 12-month order agreement from Fairline and if they honour it, it should keep us busy for most of 1983. December was a very busy month with only 3 weeks to do 4 weeks' work. Most of the jobs were completed and delivered by 24th December. This year I did not hand out any booze to customers at all. Most years I hand out quite a few bottles, but in November I had a notice from Fairline stating that on no account was I to give out any presents of any description to their employees.

I've not been shooting very well this year. I replaced the gun I had stolen in June with a similar boxlock, but I can't seem to get used to it. I think that for next season I shall shorten the stock by about half an inch.

Work finished on 24th December and at 12 o'clock I gave the lads their wages and Christmas box and a bottle of booze each. I also gave them a day's pay, which I think was generous enough. I was most surprised when they gave me a bottle of vodka and a Christmas card signed by them all. This is the first time I have ever had a gift from the men and I was quite moved by the gesture.

I drove over to pick up Dad and we arrived home at about 1730. The Dewhursts (Ann's parents) came at about 1900. I spent most of the evening preparing the turkey, which was put in the oven at about 2130 with the timer set for 0730 am. The children were awake when we took in their presents at 1230.

Christmas was similar to other years and on the Monday after, I went to Kirby Hall for a morning shoot. We were finished by 1330 and when I arrived home for lunch as a special treat we had turkey and chips. Friday was the 31st December and we had booked into the Haycock for the New Year's Eve Ball.

31st December: We collected Val and Bryan and drove to the Haycock. It was a carvery with a choice of turkey, ham, suckling pig and rib of beef. It was quite nice but I thought very expensive, also the wine was extra. The dancing was in a marquee, there was inadequate seating, the band was far too loud and there was some jostling on the dance floor. Auld Lang Syne came and went and by 2 am we had decided to leave. We went back to Val's for coffee and Ann drove home. We had a drink before turning in. Another year over, it has been reasonable, we changed houses and cars and launched our yacht. The business consolidated for another year but no great progress was made. The turnover for 1982 was only about 6.5% up on 1981, we have yet to see what the profit will be.

At the Earls Court Boat Show the general feeling among the boat builders and the trade generally was one of optimism. Each day one or other of the main players would announce good sales figures. Shetland had restarted production at their Redgrave site and Bernie Reinman, the MD, was keen for us to supply them. They were hoping to produce fifty boats per month, and although they were small boats (up to about 23ft), the volume of small parts was a welcome addition to our production. Fairline Boats were selling very well. The Fairline

40 was up to full production capacity and the Sun Fury 26 was selling steadily at six boats per month.

I wasn't having much luck selling *Blue Target*. I had advertised the boat, offering to do a swap for a catamaran with cash adjustment, but only had one person to view. I looked at their Comanche catamaran and it was very nice, the accommodation palatial compared to my monohull. I think that after the cat, the accommodation on *Blue Target* must have seemed tiny.

I was still flying when weather permitted. I would take the flying club B121 and go off and do some aerobatics, barrel rolls and loops, or perhaps just a few circuits to keep my hand in. Ann was checked out on the Cessna 152 and would fly that also. As the business was so busy I was working in the factory alongside the men, doing most of the odd jobs that no one else wanted to do and also polishing, so most nights I was going home looking like a coal-miner.

19th March: Last month we had a record turnover, the largest since we sacked all of the men in 1980, about £17,000. We appear to have far more work than at this time last year and for the first time for two years I can see a steady increase in new business. We have a large amount of spar orders that are required for the end of the month. April 1st is Good Friday and everyone wants their fittings by then. Singh is unable to work so many hours as his wife is visiting her mother in India and Steve is off sick, so things are a bit tight. Cash flow is reasonable with the overdraft well within limits and the loan account is coming down well. The 1982 profit figure was slightly higher than last year, but the overall position is stronger and the bank is pleased.

Over the last few weeks we have been tidying up the boat. The exterior varnishing is now almost complete and she is beginning to look lovely. We had a chap look at her last weekend, who is interested in swapping a Quest 31 (catamaran), but I am undecided, she is such a beautiful boat and I wonder if it is worth changing while the market is so depressed. We are managing to stay on top, but I think in October we will have to make some spars for stock.

The swimming pool man, came round last night to mark out the position of the pool, work should commence in April. We are trying to keep the pool secret but the children seem to have guessed what's going on.

The Warkton Lane house had a large garden and I had always planned to have a swimming pool. Bryan had a very nice pool and I decided to construct one of a similar size. As soon as the enormous digger arrived it was obvious that the pool was to happen. Luckily there was enough room down the side of the house for the digger to get through to the garden and for the large lorries to take the spoil away. The hole looked enormous, but luckily the digger didn't encounter any drains, water pipes or electrical cables. It took just over three weeks to build the actual pool and another couple of weeks to finish off. It took a few days to fill, the water pressure being low. I bought a second-hand heat pump and together with an electric heater started to warm up the water.

May 6th: The pool is now almost complete. The pool itself is finished but the other groundwork, paving plumbing etc, will not be finished for another few days. We started filling it yesterday but the water pressure in the main is low so it will take a few days to fill up completely. Everything is going fine, cash flow is good, order books are full and although we are a bit behind with the work everything looks good, I think we are on the way up again.

Last weekend I sailed with Martin in his Catalac to Cherbourg, we picked up some duty free and sailed down to

Barfleur. The weather was quite rough and I am quite impressed with the sea-keeping qualities of the Catalac.

The trip to Cherbourg was mainly a booze run and we called in at Cherbourg to pick up duty-free alcohol. French wine in those days was very cheap and we loaded up the Catalac with large amounts of wine and spirits. On return to Christchurch we would have two customs declarations filled out, one listing the duty free and the other showing nothing to declare. The system for small boats was for only the skipper to go ashore and ring customs. If they decided to visit the yacht, then no one was allowed ashore until after the boat had been cleared. The customs form was placed in the customs postbox somewhere on the dock. On arrival we would take the contraband ashore and put it in our cars and then ring customs. Quite often they would say that if we had nothing to declare, we should put the completed form in the customs box on the dock and that they would not come out to visit the boat!

I had a phone call from Pat Patterson asking me if I would like to crew with him on a 50 ft. catamaran from Plymouth to Guernsey. The boat, *Typhoon,* was an aluminium catamaran that was to be sailed to St. Samson in Guernsey for a refit. The boat was a ketch and the largest yacht I had ever been on. The trip took about 14 hours sailing and motor sailing, the engines were overheating and the oil level was low, there was a problem with the cooling system but we made it!

10th June: Margaret Thatcher has won a landslide election victory over all other parties. I wonder what this will mean to the economy of the country. I think perhaps the recession may deepen for a couple of years and then there will be an increase in demand as we come up to the next election. I don't think we are heading for any big boom at the moment.

This weekend we are going to the boat for a sail. We have only sailed her once this year so far, although I did have a trip with Pat Patterson in the 50ft ketch Typhoon, delivering her to Guernsey. It was quite a good trip with a few minor problems. We left Plymouth 0510 Friday 20th. May and arrived St. Peter Port 1930 that same day. We went ashore and Patterson treated us all to dinner. On Saturday we moved the ship round to St. Sampson, where she is to be laid up ashore. We took a cab into St. Peter Port that evening and had a night out on the town. I flew back to Plymouth on the Sunday morning with Bill the other crew member. Pat couldn't get a flight until the next day.

For the last couple of weeks we have been swimming every evening. Last Saturday I bought a new barbecue, which fits a gas bottle. On Sunday we went for a swim at about 0900, and I then cooked breakfast on the barbecue. Sunday evening we invited Angela , Paul and the kids for a swim and barbecue, we had great fun with all the kids in the pool and afterwards we bored everyone with our video film of the pool being built.

I decided to have a log cabin in the garden to act as a changing room and shower. It would also double up as extra accommodation when we had lots of visitors.

11th June: *Over the last two or three weeks we have been under a lot of pressure to keep up with demand. The buyer at Fairline has as usual treated me like dirt with his poor buying practices, inefficiency and ignorant manner. It's a pity that we are so dependent upon this one company for the volume of business they provide.*

We have done very well over the last few years and in about two and a half years the factory will be paid for. I will then be much better off and less dependent on one customer. Even if the stainless business collapsed I would still come out of it quite a rich man. In fact if I were to sell the boat and pay the money into the loan account it could be paid off by next April. I will be 40 then. I always imagined that at 40 one was quite old, but now I am nearly there myself the age seems quite young. I do not look old and I am fairly fit, although I am sorry I gave up karate.

14th June: *At work we seem to have caught up a bit, I don't know whether this is good or bad. I went over to Fairline yesterday and Carter was almost pleasant. I am sure he is planning to stab me in the back in the near future but I don't really care, I shall have last laugh. The concrete base is almost complete for the log cabin. I'm really looking forward to having it there. I am hoping that we can then afford to have the paving done, which should give us a really nice feature in the garden. Ann and I are both booked to go flying tomorrow and I am quite looking forward to it. If the weather is fine I may go over Pitsford to do some aerobatics. Ann is booked in the Cessna 150, which she likes to fly.*

Ann and I were both very keen flyers and tried to fly as often as possible. I liked the Beagle Pup, which was cleared for aerobatics, although I also flew the Cessna 150, 152 and the Robin. Although Ann was checked out on the Beagle Pup she usually preferred to fly the Cessna. As we were flying the club planes we never went anywhere, as the aircraft were in demand most of the time.

In June Ann and I went sailing with Pat Patterson. I was interested to see the new Ocean Winds, which was fitted with both a Cooney jib reefing system and a mainsail reefing system. This worked on a similar idea to the jib reefer and was a luff spar behind the mast. It worked exceptionally well and made reefing the main much easier than with the old systems that rolled the sail round the boom.

We sailed to the Helford River, planning to spend a night at Gweek. On the Sunday morning we left Gweek and slowly motored down the river. We went into Frenchman's Creek to look at this beautiful place and then left the Helford, heading for St Mawes. The next morning we had a beat against an easterly 5-6 to Fowey. We had a good sail and the main and jib reefing worked well. I went ashore in the dinghy and set up the camera whilst Pat and Ann sailed the boat past the castle and I took some photos. We stayed the night in Fowey and the next morning motored back to Plymouth in a flat calm.

For our summer trip in *Blue Target* we planned to go to Holland. We set out for Ostend planning to sail on up to Breskens and Flushing, through the Walcheren Canal and into the Verse Meer. Although Theresa and James liked the "messing about on boats", long passages for them were boring and Theresa suffered with seasickness. When going over to Belgium, France or Holland we would do a night passage if possible so that they were tucked up safe in bed for the trip. Once there they liked going ashore, especially Ostend with the marina opposite the Winkelcentrum, the main shopping area.

From Ostend to Breskens is about 25 miles and the wind when we started was blowing from the NE at about 25 knots. It steadily decreased and by the time we arrived in Breskens it had moderated to NE I-2.

Breskens had an excellent yacht club, the food was first class and inexpensive and we stayed for a couple of days. Entering the locks at Flushing I dropped a fender overboard, and it quickly floated into shallow water so I couldn't retrieve it. I saw a man with a bicycle who saw what had happened; he quickly ran down to the water's edge and picked up the fender. I thought he would walk over to the lock and hand it back, but alas, I last saw my fender on his bike disappearing in the direction of Amsterdam!

The Versemeer is accessed, by the Walcheren Canal. There are various bridges and locks to navigate, but once in the Verse Meer there are small Islands to moor up to with barbecue areas. Some of the islands have resident deer populations. At the end of the Versemeer is a lifting bridge called Zeelandsbrug which only opens once a day, so it's important to arrive at the right time. We arrived at 1300, just in time for the opening. After the bridge we moored up in Colingsplaat; opposite Colingsplaat is Zeirikzee, which is where the majority of the mussels come from.

We left Colingsplaat on 20th August. We were clear of the Roompot Channel by 1335 and heading back to the Orwell river. There was another boat on our berth at Woolverstone Marina, so we tied up on the end pontoon at about 0600 on the 21st.

Thursday 25th August: This is the first day back after the summer holiday. I left Bill in charge and as usual everything ran fairly smoothly, with most of the work being done. We had a super cruise through Holland, the first time we have had three weeks off at one time. The boat was admired everywhere we went. She did look beautiful. This year we have fitted an Autohelm and a spray hood, also a blue sail cover. Under power she will do a good 7 knots and we had a very quick uneventful passage both ways across the North Sea.

Tuesday 13th September: Blue Target was sold today. I actually closed the deal and was paid. It was a funny day. I did a delivery to Fairline at about 0800, then went back to work and left at about 1030. I parked in Kettering and got Dad's watch from the jewellers and bought him a hat. I then drove to Bedford to his house, picking up lunch on the way. I needed to take Dad to the Hospital for some treatment on a skin complaint on his head and we left the hospital at about 1530. Dad felt a bit self-conscious with a large dressing on top of his head but the hat, a cloth cap, hid it well enough.

After taking Dad home I drove down to Woolverstone to meet Geoff Aspinwall, who was buying Blue Target. The deal was finally done and I went with them to the yacht club for a few beers. I left the yacht club at about 2300 and got a bag of fish and chips in Ipswich on the way home. I arrived home at about 1245, Ann had waited up for me. We looked at the cheque and had a few drinks. It was funny really, it took about four years to get Blue Target, during the dark days of 1980 the thought of her kept me going. I never lost sight of the dream until after she was launched. Next month the final payment on the factory will go through. I may buy another boat but will not be too disappointed not to have one in 1984.

Tuesday 27th September: Last weekend we went to look at a boat. The only problem was that it was on the west coast of Scotland, approx 450 miles away. We left Kettering at about 1530 Friday and drove to Carlisle, a distance of about 250 miles, where we stayed in the Crest hotel. The hotel was quite pleasant, all rooms having colour TV and a kettle with coffee, tea bags and milk etc. We left the hotel and drove to Crinan, where "Woodstock" a Moody 33, was lying. The boat was in a bit of a state, there was damage to the topsides and the interior stank of mildew and damp. We decided that it was still a good price and were prepared to make an offer.

We drove back to Carlisle and arrived at about 1945. We found an Italian restaurant and had dinner, returning to the Crest at about 2200. Sunday we drove back to Kettering, arriving at about 1500. Ann put the dinner in the oven and we went for a swim, the temperature was about 78F. At about 1830 I rang the owner of Woodstock and made him a low offer which he turned down flat! I talked it over with Ann and we decided to offer the asking price. I rang him 0900 Monday, but he had already agreed to sell it to someone else. What a bloody waste of time!

Today Ann and I were invited for a week on a Moody 41 in the south of France. The plan is to depart on Saturday 10th October and the trip will be from Montpellier via St. Tropez to Monte Carlo. I am quite looking forward to it.

The boat we would be sailing was called *Bagadag*, owned

by Geoff Millman, a former England cricketer. We had done various Jobs for him and he wanted to change his stanchion sockets, as the aluminium sockets were badly corroded and splitting. This tended to happen on Moodys as the aluminium stanchions reacted with the extruded toe rail. I made a set of stanchion sockets in stainless steel and planned to use zinc chromate between the different metals in order to combat electrolysis.

Saturday 8th October: We were up at about 0315 and out of the house at about 0415 arriving at Gatwick at 0615. We met Geoff Millman and his friends a little later. The other couple in the party were Susan Rothschild and her boyfriend Tim Jackson. There was another group that we met consisting of 5 chaps, they were to go on Ray Baron's boat. One of the group was David Morris, the son of John Morris, who was our first bank manager. On arrival at Montpellier we took a taxi to Port Camargue where Bagadag and Seatack were lying. It took most of the afternoon to unpack and sort out the boat as we gradually got to know our new friends.

The whole party (10) were meeting that evening for a meal. Some shopping was acquired and we were dressed and ready, gin in hand by about 1800. We had a smashing evening and planned to leave fairly early for a cruise down to Carro the next morning.

Sunday 9th October: We left the berth at 0715 and headed down the coast until we caught Seatack. We stopped the engine and put up the cruising chute. The boat moved well through the water and the wind gradually increased. Most of us felt queasy, but we took a commanding lead over Seatack and were about a mile in front when the chute blew out. We stayed in front and on arrival at Carro we were able to pick up a mooring buoy. Seatack followed us in and also found a buoy. During the evening they accused us of using our engine during our race, but

we told them where to get off! Sue and Tim had not sailed before
and seemed to settle into shipboard life quite well.

We had a bit of a lay in Monday morning and then sailed
down to Bandol stopping at Cassis for lunch. This trip was one
of the best sailing holidays that I can remember. We ended up
in St. Tropez and during the night we had a storm of violent
proportions, one of the bow warps parted and eventually we had
to use the anchor chain to tie her to a bollard.

On the way back from St. Tropez we stopped off at Hyères
and had a smashing meal cooked by Sue and Ann. It was pork
with roast potatoes and onions. the starter was prawn cocktail
and there was tart to follow. We went from Hyères to Cassis,
arriving fairly early, and Tim, Sue, Ann and I went for a swim
at the beach. We had a good laugh and splash about and went
back to the boat in time for a shower before happy hour. I really
came to enjoy these evenings, a few gin and tonics, a laugh and
a joke, it's surprising how friendship can develop in such a
short space of time.

We went for a meal with the crowd from the other boat and
found a super restaurant. After our swim we had popped into
Cassis to do some shopping. While we were having a coffee
David came along. He was cook on *Seatack* and we had a
wander round the shops with him. During the meal later that
evening Sue let it out that they were having chicken for dinner
and David was not amused, as he liked to keep the menu a
surprise!

We went from Cassis to Marseille, which was quite a rough
trip, but we arrived without mishap and decided to spend the
night there and eat on board. While the meal was being
prepared we ran out of tonic. Sue speaks quite good French,
so I took her ashore to try and buy some. We found a bar and
had a drink and then we found an off licence. Unfortunately

they only had five tonics left, but we were able to obtain other provisions.

When we left Marseille the next morning the wind was very light, so we put the engine on to about 2200 rpm, which gave us 7 knots. I was a bit sad, as this was to be the last time (this trip anyway) I would be at sea with my new friends. I used to feel this way towards the end of a trip when I was at sea on big ships. Under the circumstances everyone had got on remarkably well.

When we entered Port Camargue I took the boat alongside the fuelling berth to fill up the fuel and water. Sue took the boat back to her berth and we made her fast (the boat not Sue) and I started to change the stanchion bases for the stainless ones I had brought out. This was a very tricky job. All the screws had corroded into the bases and I managed to remove only two before I had to get ready for the evening. The crew from *Seatack* had cycled into Egmont and we were to meet them for a last meal together.

We had a devil of a job getting a taxi, but eventually Sue and Tim managed to track one down and we met up with *Seatack*'s crew in Egmont at about 2015. A carnival was in progress and hundreds of people were thronging the square, so there was a jolly atmosphere with a very loud group playing and people singing, dancing and boozing. We drank Pernod and sat in the square chatting to the others and enjoying the carnival atmosphere.

We went into the restaurant and had what I consider to be the best meal of the trip. We got through 10 bottles of wine between us. After the meal we went out to sit in the square, where we had some brandies and coffee and Ann and I danced to the rhythm of the band. The rest of the group were amazed at our cha cha and samba. Once back on board we drank whisky and played dice until about 0330.

Sunday 16ᵗʰ October: I awoke at about 0830 feeling awful. No one else appeared to be up, but I had a job to do so I got out of bed and had a drink of orange juice. I took the tools on deck and decided to wake up the rest of the ship. The stanchion bases that needed removing were corroded onto the toe rail and needed loosening. I chose the one directly over Tim's cabin and started belting it with a large hammer. The din was unbearable, just the thing to wake someone up with a dreadful hangover. It wasn't long before everyone was up on deck looking a bit frightened, bemused and astonished that anyone could make such a dreadful row.

As the morning wore on Ann and Sue cleaned up the boat while Tim and Geoff busied themselves with various tasks around the ship. I worked on steadily and gradually got on top of the job. *We had French bread for lunch and by 1430 the stanchions were on. I was absolutely knackered, so I asked the girls to clean up excess compound etc. and went below for a wash. After about 15 minutes I felt a bit better and took a walk round to Ray Baron's boat to measure up for some fittings he required. On the boat he asked me whether I had any news of the taxis to take us to the airport. As I'd been working all day I was not aware that there was any problem.*

I returned to Bagadag and we started getting gear off the ship ready to leave at 1615. The taxi didn't turn up and the flight was to be at 1745. What a panic, the members of the party that spoke French were working overtime. Eventually the lady from the chandlery shop managed to obtain some radio taxis, although we thought it unlikely that the taxis could get to Port Camargue and on to Montpellier airport in time for the flight. Several of the party started arguing and having a post mortem as to who was responsible. I thought this a bit unnecessary and childish.

One taxi arrived, everyone then started arguing who was to get in it. David Morris said that he was the most important and promptly put his bags in the boot and sat in the taxi. I decided that if possible Ann or I, preferably Ann, should go as we would have problems with work and the children if neither of us made it. No. 2 taxi then appeared. The taxis would only take 4 people so that meant 2 had to stay behind. Unselfishly Sue and Tim volunteered and ushered everyone else into the waiting cars, saying they would hitch a ride to the airport. The taxis took off at great speed and we arrived at the airport in record time. Geoff and I were very concerned and guilty about leaving the others behind, they had no baggage and very little money.

We tried to delay the airplane and had all sorts of delaying tactics planned, eg falling down the ladder or lying in front of the airplane etc. We had all checked in, Geoff had prepared an envelope with a letter, some money and the boat keys for the others should they not arrive in time The Dan Air desk told us to go through to the departure lounge, but we were still hanging around waiting for the others.

A car came speeding into the airport with Sue and Tim aboard, apparently the French Lady from the chandlery had taken pity on them and brought them in her own car, but even then their problems were not over as the car ran out of petrol when they were half way to the airport." All's well that ends well". We had two drinks each on the plane and quite a nice meal. The plane stopped at Toulouse to pick up some more passengers and we landed at Gatwick at about 2100 hrs.

Geoff travelled down with Tim and Sue and we decided to follow them to the M1, stopping for a bite on the way. We stopped at a chip shop in London and had chicken and chips and then came the goodbyes. I felt very sad to be parting company with Geoff, Tim and Sue, especially Sue, as I had become quite fond of her and I think I probably won't see her *again. We arrived home sometime after midnight, it was nice to be home. We looked in on the kids, had a few drinks and turned in.*

I was very impressed with Geoff's Moody, both the accommodation and the performance. Since selling the UFO I had been looking for another boat, although it was nice to have a substantial balance in the bank. After such a memorable trip I was keen to buy another boat and was scanning the pages of yachting magazines looking at brokerage advertisements. There was a Halberg Rassy 352 for sale and Ann and I decided to view it. The boat was ex-charter and although a bit knocked about appeared in reasonable condition. The accommodation would be ideal with an aft cabin, fore cabin and berths in the saloon. The asking price was £31,000, which was more than I wanted to pay. We looked at several other boats, but the Rassy was the one we really fancied, so I rang the broker, who said they would only consider an offer at the asking price.

Ann and I discussed it and decided that although we would be stretching ourselves financially we would make an offer. I rang the broker and was told that an offer had already been made, but they would accept £34,000. This was far more than we were prepared to pay.

Many of the boats we viewed were overpriced and in poor condition. The Moody in Scotland needed a refit and the Rassy seemed overpriced and was also a bit knocked about.

Sunday 23rd October: On Friday I rang Marine Secol to see if they had any second-hand Moodys on their books. They had a few but they seemed awfully expensive compared to new ones. I decided to consider buying a new Moody "34", they had one at their Brighton depot. Saturday evening we had Val and Bryan to dinner. They left about 0030. We got up at about 0730 Sun morning and had bacon sandwiches for breakfast. We left at about 0815 heading for Brighton Marina and a test sail in the

Moody 34. The traffic in London was awful and we arrived at the marina at about 1210. Our appointment was for 1200, but no one seemed to mind. We went to the boat and looked her over, she wasn't badly finished off although there were one or two rough bits. We took her out for a sail, it was only blowing a force 2-3 but she seemed to handle quite nicely under sail and the performance under power was quite impressive. I know Ann liked the boat and when we returned to the Marina we decided to buy it. I managed to negotiate a discount, and we were told prices were going up in the New Year. The price was £24,500, and it seemed a lot of boat for the money, the UFO had much smaller accommodation and we sold that for £25,000.

We went into Brighton and had a snack and then left for home. The car broke down on the M25 but luckily the AA got us going again. By the time we arrived home the dinner that we had left on the timer was cold, we soon warmed it up and ate it anyway.

In order to purchase the new boat, I went to see the bank manager for some finance. He agreed to my proposals but in the end we managed to do the deal without needing finance. I applied to the British Ships Registry to name the new boat *Bluejacket* – as the last boat was *Blue Target* I wanted to adopt a blue theme with my boat names. The name was refused as someone already had it. The way it works is you submit a list of names and the registrar then decides which one you can have. We ended up with *Blue Melody*, which I was quite happy about.

Now the swimming pool was complete I went over to Sywell and took UN for a flight to enable Ann to take some aerial photographs of the house and garden.

Wednesday 4ᵗʰ November: Last weekend we went to Brighton to visit the new boat. We didn't go until Sunday as we visited Dad in hospital on Saturday. We checked everything on the boat and found a few faults, nothing serious. We left a list with the sellers and hope all the faults will be remedied before handing over.

This week has been a bit dull. I have visited Dad every day since Tuesday, he had his operation on Monday and wasn't allowed visitors. Belbro moved out last weekend. I went down to get the keys yesterday but they refused to give them to me as they'd had had some cut. I refused to buy them back on principle. They were always scrounging bits and pieces from us and I was disgusted at their penny-pinching attitude.

Tomorrow is Guy Fawkes. I have a few fireworks for the kids, they prefer letting them off themselves to going to a firework display. Last Saturday Ann was bitten by next door's dog. I complained to Elaine (the owner), but she didn't seem very concerned. If they don't keep it under control I shall report it to the police. I think I would be justified to shoot the horrible thing but I won't in case it's against the law!

After packing up Shotokan karate I needed a physical challenge. There were several clubs around doing various martial arts; judo was popular and ju jit su, there was an akido club and I looked at various karate clubs. There was a fairly new club doing Kempo karate and I decided to give it a try. The training was in the Northampton road Drill Hall. The main hall was used for five-a-side football and the karate club used the rear room, which was quite large. The club wore black karate suits as opposed to white as worn in Shotokan.

Teri James and I all turned up for a training session. The instructor was the club secretary, John Summers. James and I wore our white karate suits and Teri wore one of my old judo kits. We were quite well kitted out compared to some of the other beginners, who were wearing Jeans and T shirts. As the training got under way Tony Conway the chief instructor arrived and took over the training. I had thought the Shotokan training was hard, but Kempo was much harder. Tony came over to talk to us and asked what we had done before and where I had trained. I told him that I had trained at the Shotokan club and wanted to take up the sport. "This is not sport" Tony said, "This is combat."

Teri, James and I started training two or three times a week. Teri soon lost her "puppy fat" and surprised me with her dedication. We used to like the free fighting sessions where you would all be fighting each other, changing opponents every few minutes, giving the beginners the chance to spar with the more experienced fighters. When doing the various exercises Tony and John would be going round spurring us on shouting the numbers out in Japanese, Ish Nee San Shi Go. A few would drop out exhausted, and Tony would shout "Come on, you're like a load of poofters, this is a karate club not a gay club!"

The training was hard and demanding. There were several females and they were expected to train as hard as the men. The women wore a chest guard and the men a "box" to protect their manhood.

Wednesday 7th December: For the last week or two I have been taking the children to Kempo. The training is quite hard and I enjoy it very much. Both kids enjoy it and I think Theresa, if she sticks at it, will become quite useful. We have not been down to the boat lately, I suppose now it will be January before we get down to Brighton again. Work has held up all year and cash flow is better than usual at this time of the year. I was shooting last Saturday, I didn't hit much but I hope to do better next time, the next shoot is Christmas Eve. Fairline have two new models and there is a load of stainless on them, I hope they leave it with us. If we keep the majority of the stainless work, next year should be better than this year. I can't decide what to do with the reefing spars. There are now so many on the market I think sales could drop off.

Sales on the jib roller reefing were holding up quite well, the main problem being that there were new products coming onto the market that used our spar design and I needed to re design some of the parts. The mainsail version that fitted behind the mast worked very well – Pat Patterson had one on test and liked it. Several large sailmakers had brought out versions that worked quite well and they were prepared to invest a lot in design and development, whereas I had lost enthusiasm for the product.

Christmas 1983 went very much as usual. On Christmas Eve I was shooting for the day. We had quite a good day's shooting but unfortunately someone broke into my truck, which was parked on the road, and stole my shooting stick, a pheasant and a new coat. I picked up Dad later that evening and Ann's mum and dad came over for a drink. I stayed up quite late watching TV with Dad.

Christmas morning the children were not up too early and brought Ann and me a cup of tea in bed at 0830 to show us their presents. We had bought James a 48k computer and he was over the moon with it, while Theresa had a Walkman type radio cassette player, so they were both very happy. Ann had bought me some navigation equipment for the new boat and some new cufflinks, while I had bought her a gold necklace and other oddments.

We had the traditional family Christmas, going over to Ann and Tony's on Boxing Day. On the Wednesday we picked up the in-laws and visited Ann's brother Ron and family. Thursday we went to Brighton to spend a few days on the boat – it was quite mild but cold at night. The boat had beautiful accommodation and we now had most of the snags ironed out. It was blowing about a force 9 most of the time, so we did not go out for a sail. I fitted a new transom ladder which was designed for boats with high freeboard. We were selling a number of a similar design to boat builders making sailing boats.

We left Brighton on Saturday 31st December and were going to Angela and Pauls (our old neighbours from Woodford), taking the kids with us, for a New Year's Eve Party.

Friday 1st Jan 1984: We all had some drinks and saw the New Year in, then after 12 we all went round to "first foot" Malcolm and Jean who live two doors down from Angela. Paul had a tray with a lump of coal and a glass of sherry and led the way. Unfortunately he fell arse over head and broke the glass but, undaunted, he carried on with just the lump of coal on the tray. We had a drink and then all returned to Angie's house. Glad and Mike came round and the party broke up at about 0430.

Friday 6th January: This morning I had some people round who want to take approx 2000 sq. ft. of next door. They are to erect a partition themselves and it would be a good compromise for me. I will occupy the remaining 1000 sq. ft. and it should provide a good income for 12 months or so. 1983 has proved to be a very good year for business and we achieved quite a lot. We increased turnover by about 32% and kept on top of all orders, and I don't think we upset anybody at all. We built the pool at home and are well set up for the coming summer. We sold the UFO, and although we intended to pay off the loan and have a year without a boat we ended up buying the Moody 34. I still think this was a good move because the Moody will hold its price whereas the UFO, although a beautiful yacht, was no good as an investment.

I still consider that we are far too dependent upon Fairline and it would be nice to find another big turnover customer in 1984. It's funny really, when things are going reasonably well I rarely think of sailing into the sunset but when things are tough it's that dream which helps me through. With James now growing up, in five or six years he may be interested in coming into the business, it must be his decision however. Although James is not academically brilliant he is quite good at making things, rather like me perhaps.

I was employing some men part time, which worked out very profitable as they were working on piecework, that is, only being paid for what they produced. In a weekend an impressive amount of work would be produced. Bill Cullum was now working regularly and was probably the most highly skilled of them all. I would get Bill to develop any new jobs and set the time accordingly. All new jobs were costed at "double time", which meant they could be produced in half the time on the job card. some of the men would do the jobs even quicker, and earn perhaps two and a half times the time on the job. This must be the fairest way of working, as the employee is rewarded relative to the amount of effort they put in, while there was no place for the idle. The problem with this system is maintaining quality, hence the ruling that any rejects had to be rectified in their own time. The system worked very well.

Saturday 14ᵗʰ January: On Wednesday we went to the Boat Show with Brian and Chris Summerland. We met them on the train at Kettering station. I managed to see all of our customers except Fletcher's. Fairline apparently have already taken orders of £75m. We all went onto the Moody stand and met Brian Sharp (the broker from Brighton). We took Brian and Chris onto the 34 and they liked it, the one at the show is fitted out in the same colours as ours and it was like being on our own boat. We had a look in the 47. She looked enormous and although very nicely done, she didn't appeal to me. I quite like the 41, she would be quite big enough for a small crew to handle although in two years' time requirements may be different.

Today I am at work, I have a customer collecting a boat that we have been working on and there are four men working. I shall probably finish before 1400hrs and go home. I feel very tired due to a very full week and tomorrow I am going to the Boat Show again, this time to take the lads. I had intended to send them on their own but they're a bit worried about travelling alone on the Underground etc.

Although I am not drinking, I still get very tired during the day, maybe it is boredom, I seem to be doing less and less work. I am also eating less in a bid to lose weight.

The company accounts for 1983 were finalised at the end of January. It had been a good year with a turnover of £189,233, an increase of £64,500 on the previous year. A 34% increase in turnover was a good result and the net profit at £61,573, an increase of £11,962, was 13.6% of turnover. In 1982 the net profit was 13.4% of turnover, which was almost the same as the previous year. It seemed that this was the level of profit we could expect whilst working on this system.

I wanted to increase profitability, and although we were successful, we were still a partnership with the vulnerability that entails. If anything went wrong Ann and I were responsible for all the business debts. On the positive side, all of the money was ours, and we could do whatever we wanted. It was far more convenient being a partnership and more tax efficient. We were also in a freehold property. I think the worst piece of advice I have ever been given was by that estate agent in the 1970s who told me, "Why do you want freehold? You would be better off renting and investing all of your money in the business." This might have been a way of building the business, but if problems arise it is nice to have some assets to fall back on and I consider freehold property the best asset you can have.

We did have a limited company I had formed to handle the sale of fibreglass mouldings and kits of boat parts, but we never sold any and the company lay dormant.

3rd February: *Had a good year in '83, the accounts were in late January and it seems that we may have to start paying tax. Last weekend Tim (Sue's boyfriend) came over and asked my advice on buying a boat. I agreed to go and look at one with him on Sunday. We went down to Burnham on Crouch and looked at a Colvic 31 Motor Sailer. I quite like the class but unfortunately a lot of them were home completed and are pretty awful. The one we went to see was supposed to have been boatyard completed, but I thought it was very poorly fitted out and I pointed out a few things for Tim to look out for in future.*

We left Burnham and then went to Essex Yacht Marina. The only reasonable motor sailer there however was a Finsailer 35, which does not have much accommodation for its size. we returned to Bedford and had a cup of tea and I then left for home.

We now have some new tenants for next door, they are only using about 2000 sq. ft. and have partitioned off the rest, which I am using as a finished parts store. The jib roller reefing is in a state of limbo. I can't decide whether to redesign or drop it. The last time I dropped it I had to bring it back due to popular demand, but unfortunately in the meantime there were many more on the market. I also fancy putting up another factory unit on the car park, I think I could probably get a about 3000 sq. ft. for about £20,000, the only problem being that I don't have 20 grand to spare and I have nothing big to sell to raise anything like that amount. The Bank would probably help but I already owe them quite a considerable amount.

I could also do with a car. I am driving around in the filthy works pickup and Ann uses the Sierra. It is quite embarrassing for me, although Ann seems to think that a filthy truck suits my image. I don't like looking like the richest tramp in Warkton Lane!

Now we have the pool we are reluctant to consider moving house, but really that would be a good way to generate a bit of cash. Although I would like a Jaguar or a Mercedes I think perhaps if we bought a smaller car for now just so that we didn't have to run the truck so much I would be more content.

Next Thursday is the grading at Kempo. Over the last few weeks I have been training very hard and I am looking forward to next week. I don't know how high a grade I shall achieve but I hope to do well. I feel quite confident and tough at the moment.

10th February: *Last night was the Kempo grading, Theresa went in for it against my better judgement and we were both graded 7th Kyu (yellow). I was pleased for Theresa, she worked very hard and put a lot into it. I was very disappointed. Several of the beginners were graded up to 6th and really I can't understand why I didn't make it. I train very hard and during normal training sessions Sensei always puts me with the top grades. Still "You can't win em' all". I wonder what will happen next time, there will be another grading in about six months. If I train hard for six months I will be as fit as anyone there, especially now I am not drinking. I have been doing Kempo now for about three months and I am thinking of having another go at Shotokan in the near future, I think one style would complement the other, my biggest problem being coordination.*

18th February: *Last weekend we went down to Brighton to spend a few days on the boat. We left Friday night at about 1730 and planned to have a meal on the way, calling in at a Little Chef and then went on to the Marina. When we arrived on the boat the agents hadn't left us the shoreline electrical lead and so we couldn't put the TV on. The children were a bit disappointed, but it was fairly late and they were tired so they turned in early. After they had turned in I decided to try the TV on the 12-volt system. There was a plug provided to fit a car cigar lighter so I removed the plug and fitted a spare 12-volt plug. I switched on and was amazed and shocked to see smoke billowing out of the back of the TV accompanied by crackling noises. The poor TV was dead and I was to blame!*

Saturday morning I was in a foul mood and the kids were not speaking to me, what an awful day. Ann and the children went shopping whilst I fitted the VHF radio. Sunday morning I prepared the boat for sea whilst Ann prepared breakfast, and we left the berth intending to catch the lock at 1230. The children were very good handling the boat through the lock and after taking on diesel we gently motored out of the marina with Ann putting up the sails. Everything is new and takes a bit longer to sort out.

The wind was blowing a force 4-5 and we tried the boat on various points of sailing. On the port tack she seemed to handle beautifully but on starboard she seemed a bit hard mouthed. Suddenly the steering went 'ping' and we had about three turns of backlash in the wheel. We headed back to the Marina, Ann taking the sails down, and went alongside the visitors' berth to have a look. I found that the wire had come off the quadrant, so I replaced it and tightened the wires. it seemed to work perfectly so we went back through the lock and returned to the berth. I reversed her in and while I was putting sails away etc. Ann cooked the dinner. We left Brighton at about 1830, arriving home 2125, quite a good run.

Towards the end of February Ann and I went to Geoff Millman's for a dinner party. There was Ray and Valerie who own *Seatack*, the Moody 36 we sailed with in the South of France, Danny and Pam who sail with Geoff, and Tim and Sue. Tim told me he had been offered the Sea Wych moulds and all the parts necessary to build the boats including the plans. I was quite interested, having worked with John Sadler in the 70s. in fact it was Sadler who got me into the boat industry. His advice and encouragement were invaluable to me in the early days and I spent many hours at "Summer Place" talking to him and learning about boat building and the industry.

I rang Sadler and he was in good spirits, it was nice to speak to him again. He had no regrets about selling his business as he had got out at the top, when he was winning. It was a pity that the people that took over *Sea Wych* failed, it wasn't a bad boat. I was quite interested in the cost of the project, which at £3000 was fairly cheap, and I did have the space to set up a moulding shop.

29th February: *Over the last few days I have been looking at the Sea Wych project. Tim came over on Monday and we have agreed to build it in the end unit. We have just enough space and I think it could do well. The biggest problem I can see is that the design is quite old, but with the tooling available at only £3000 it can't be bad. To tool up for a new 18ft. boat would cost at least £25,000 and there would be considerable time to develop the project, whereas the Sea Wych is a known quantity. If all goes according to plan the moulds are being delivered on 9th March and we hope to complete a boat in time for the Brighton Boat show in May.*

Tim and I formed a partnership to build the boats, and we both paid half of the initial £3000. We agreed to split all other costs 50/50. Fibreglass moulding is a specialised job and although I had done some fibreglass work on my own boats I was not up to moulding a complete hull and deck, so I decided to hire a professional moulder to do the first boat.

The moulds when they arrived took a lot of cleaning up. There were two sets. The set we decided to use for the first boat needed the hull flange repairing and there was a lot of work to prepare the moulds for boat no. 1.

My 40th birthday came and went. I was expecting a surprise party but nothing happened, I wanted a party and we told a lot of people that I would be having one and that they would be invited, but it didn't happen.

The first boat was being moulded. I had employed John Martin, a moulder, to do the work during the weekend. this wasn't a very satisfactory arrangement but then John suggested that I employ his brother Phil, who was unemployed, on a full-time basis.

Friday 6th April: The hull of Sea Wych 801 is now complete and the deck is well on the way. Phil the laminator seems to be making a good job. There are quite a lot of reinforcing pads to go into the deck and these seem to be taking forever. This weekend we are going down to the boat, I had hoped to go this evening but we have a dinner dance to go to, what a bore. Now I am not drinking I find I have a very low boredom threshold and doing gropey dances with fat old women I find embarrassing and degrading. I went to Kempo last night and had a good session. My weight is quite low again and I feel very fit.

The work on the first boat was progressing well and it looked as though it would be ready for the Brighton Boat Show. The rest of the business was booming and we were having difficulty keeping up with demand.

I had heard from Dad that mother was ill. He and my sister often spoke about her and I knew she was ill, but I had not seen her since Granddad's funeral and then we didn't speak. I used to see Dad at least once a week and quite often on a Sunday we would all go over to see him. I would often visit him on a Wednesday and take some lunch, either fish and chips or his favourite, Kentucky Fried Chicken. On this particular occasion I asked "Have you heard how mother is?" He hesitated, looked up at me and said "She died last Monday". It came as a shock. I didn't realise she was that ill. She had died on my 40th birthday and no one had told me. Apparently she was asking for me just before she died. If I'd known I don't know what I would have done, but luckily I didn't know so I have no feelings of guilt. I didn't grieve; I grieved in 1961 when she left, although I knew she was OK as Anne kept in touch with her. Dad never got over her leaving, I think he always hoped that one day she'd come back.

Pat Patterson

Cornish Crabber

Blue Target in Ostend

Sailing in France with Geoff Millman

Moody 34 in Woolverstone

Moody 37 showing company name

Sailing with Martin Smith

Martin's Catalac in Cherbourg

Ann and I in Holland

Enjoying the sun

Kevin and Ann sailing Finesse in the Caribbean in 2015

CHAPTER TWENTY THREE

A following wind

The fear of another miners' strike like the one that had in effect brought down Heath's Conservative government in 1974 had resulted in power stations around the country building up massive stocks of coal. British coal was now so expensive to produce, due to excessive wages and restrictive practices in the coal industry, that it was cheaper to import the coal needed for the power stations. The National Union of Mineworkers was demanding more and more, and seemed determined to disrupt the Government, but Margaret Thatcher held her nerve. Arthur Scargill, president of the NUM called on the miners to strike on 12th March.

Despite violent picketing and intimidation by the strikers, life carried on. Running a business is challenging at the best of times and there always seemed to be something lurking around the corner ready to throw a spanner in the works.

The first Sea Wych came out of the mould on 16th April, and it looked really good, almost like a sea creature wanting to get back to the sea. I was optimistic, I'd always wanted to be more involved with boats. Making the deck hardware was what we were good at and we were fast becoming recognised as a market leader in this field, but I imagined that building the boats would be a natural progression.

I was looking forward to taking the new Moody round to our berth at Woolverstone Marina, and planned to do the trip over Easter, weather permitting. I had fitted a few new stainless parts to the boat but planned to do more when we were at Woolverstone.

24th April: Last Friday was Good Friday and we eventually left Brighton Marina at about 1800hrs bound for Woolverstone. Tim took us down to Brighton and we arrived about 1300hrs. We left the berth at about 1715 and had cleared the harbour by about 1800. it was a beautiful evening with not a breath of wind. The engine was doing about 2300 RPM and just over 7 knots through the water. I had pre-programmed the Decca Navigator and the waypoints slipped away effortlessly. I had hoped to reach the Goodwins in daylight, but we made such good time that we arrived at the South Goodwin lightship at about 0430 Sat. morning. Ann took over at about 0445 and I went down for a sleep.

I got up, at about 0830, it was a beautiful day I was dressed only in my thermal underwear and the sun felt surprisingly hot, although there was a slight sea mist. We berthed at Woolverstone at about 1300, and the trip down the Orwell was a delight. Yesterday just as we were leaving Ken and Jenny drove up. We'd noticed that their boat wasn't on its mooring and thought they had perhaps left, however they have now changed it for a large Westerley. We went on board for a look, it seemed quite a nice boat and quite different from their little Snapdragon.

15th May: Last weekend I went down to Pattersons. We fitted up the halyard swivel on his jib reefer and it worked beautifully. We had a good weekend sailing and on Sunday night we returned to Millbrook and met up with Tom Reese, who is going to Japan in convoy with Pat. We had a pleasant evening singing Sea Shanties. Pat has a small electric organ on board and Lillian Woods played the recorder.

This weekend I fitted a Mk. 3 jib reefer to our Moody. Everything went according to plan. I hate going up masts and luckily Ken Campling pulled me up. Ann is not too keen on pulling me up the mast although she does it when necessary. I also changed all the guard wires for plastic-covered wire and the ship looks really nice.

29th May: This weekend we took a trip over to Nieuwpoort. Our original intention was to sail Friday night, but by the time we arrived at Woolverstone and sorted the boat out it was 1945 hrs. and it was decided to postpone the trip until Saturday. We left the berth at 0600 Saturday morning. The wind was southerly and for the first hour we didn't sail at all, but then as we turned for waypoint no. 2 we started to get some drive from the sails and after an hour or two the wind was force 4 on the beam and with all sail set we were creaming along in fine style.

We arrived in Nieuwpoort at about 1900 hours. The Decca Navigator worked faultlessly, but the berth we chose was a bit difficult to get into. After sorting the boat out we all went for a meal. The first yacht club we went into had finished serving, so we rushed over to the larger club and had a superb steak au poivre. We also picked up a duty free list.

On Sunday we went for a walk round Nieuwpoort. James hired a BMX and entertained the holidaymakers with his many stunts. We went to the yacht again for the evening, this time I had a T-bone steak, Ann had pepper steak and the children had fillet. Theresa and James said they were the best steaks they had ever tasted. We planned to sail on Monday night at about 1700hrs, hoping to be off Harwich at dawn Tuesday morning. Monday morning we were up at about 0800 and had a large breakfast, then walked down to the beach. It was very cold and drizzly with the wind in the north. We hired an eight-person bicycle and went for a ride up and down the sea front. The forecast was northerly 4-5 with fog patches, not the ideal conditions, but we decided to go anyway, thinking we could motor back into it without too much discomfort.

We left the berth at 1800. There was a Heavenly Twins catamaran coming in and as we passed they shouted across that there was thick fog out at sea. When we cleared the harbour the visibility was about two miles and as we approached the first way point the wind had increased to about a five and the sea was quite rough. By 2000hrs. it was blowing force 6-7 and the going was getting quite bad. I decided to head back to Nieuwpoort and turned the ship around. As soon as we turned downwind the motion became easier, but as we headed for Nieuwpoort the wind steadily increased and the boat was yawing and rolling quite a bit. James had turned in earlier and Theresa was sitting with us in the cockpit. Neither of the children was sick and they made no fuss about the discomfort.

We found the entrance at about 2130 and motored back into the yacht harbour. There were storm signals showing from the control tower and it was quite a struggle getting moored up. I actually fell into the harbour, but luckily grabbed the pontoon as I did so and managed to pull myself out before my trousers got wet, and the self-inflating life jacket didn't go off!

When we were moored up Ann prepared some food. We decided to get the morning forecast and if necessary catch the

*ferry home. The morning forecast gave out northerly gales so we
packed up the boat and got ready to leave. I went over to the
Harbourmasters' office to pay a week's dues, intending to return
next week to bring the boat home. The weather was awful,
howling wind, pissing rain and we had no proper waterproofs
with us. I was wearing Theresa's, Ann was wearing James's and
they were wearing their anoraks.*

*We caught the train to Ostend and enquired about the
sailings of ferries etc. We decided to catch the Jetfoil and luckily
one was just leaving. I have never travelled on a hydrofoil before
and was amazed at the smoothness of the ride. However it was
a bit too much for some of the passengers and there were quite
a few ashen faces and people being sick. The weather must have
been just within limits, apparently they do not operate in wind
strengths over force 7.*

*On arrival at Dover we took the train to London Victoria
station. James was quite enjoying himself with all the excitement
of travelling. We took the underground to St. Pancras and then
the train to Kettering. From leaving Nieuwpoort it only took us
6½ hours to get home and I was able to ring into the factory to
discuss production with Singh. The polisher hadn't turned up,
which meant the month's turnover would be a bit low.*

The year was nearly half over. The Pool was a great
success. Ann and I swam most evenings, Theresa and James
were popular with their friends and the pool seemed to almost
be in constant use. I bought Ann a new Ford Escort and I was
using the Sierra, which was better for my image than driving
around in the works truck, although I was still doing all the
deliveries to Fairline. This was useful, as I could keep an eye
on what the individual boat lines needed. Their buying was a
bit haphazard – often they would ring up desperate for an item
and then it would not be fitted for weeks. I had a phone call
from one of the line managers accusing me of invoicing parts

and not delivering the items. I drove over and had to show the man where the items were in the factory. I think the problem was that Fairline had expanded so quickly the middle management were incompetent and hid their inadequacies by blaming their suppliers.

On the house we had all the windows changed. I used Stephensons Joinery, the company we had shared premises with in the early 70s. I planned to extend the house by building another room over the garage. I had the boat fully equipped so now I could start on the house.

I was negotiating with British Steel to buy some more land to further extend the factory, the thought being that if the Sea Wych, was successful I would require more space anyway. Ann designed a very good advertisement for the boat and I was optimistic that it would sell. Tim appeared to have lost interest in the project, and I thought that I would probably need to take it over completely.

Saturday 9th June: Last weekend Ann and I went back to Nieuwpoort to pick up Blue Melody, and we had an uneventful trip going via train, Jetfoil and tram, arriving back on the boat about 1600 hrs. Luckily the boat hadn't been vandalized and we were soon settled. The 1830 forecast seemed quite hopeful and that evening we went to the yacht club. We turned in at 2330 and intended to get the early morning forecast. The forecast gave NE 5-6 locally 7 with gale 8 later. I was so disappointed, I thought we might have to return on the Jetfoil again. We resolved to get the 1350 forecast and hoped the weather would moderate. As the morning wore on the wind backed and died down to about a force 3 and the sun came out. By 1030 it was such a nice day I decided to go anyway. The wind direction indicated to me that the low had already passed us by.

We left the berth at about 1115 and were soon out to sea in a flat calm doing about 7 knots under engine. The wind gradually picked up to about a 3 from the west, I put up the sails and we motor sailed at about 7 knots, and were off Harwich at about 1030. It was very dark and the shore lights made pilotage quite confusing, however we slid up the river and crept into our berth at Woolverstone at about 2315, in fact we were tied up by 2315 which made the trip from Nieuwpoort just 12 hours, at no time was the wind force more than force 4 and the direction was almost exactly opposite that given by the good old BBC.

The next morning we were feeling quite pleased with ourselves, we had made it and were ready to drive straight into work and have a slightly late start. The only problem was that I had left the car keys at home. I called out the AA and did everything we could to enter the car without damaging it, but eventually I had to give up and decided to hire a car to get us back to Kettering. We arrived back around 1645. What a cock up, a whole day wasted and we thought we were doing so well to have arrived back into Woolverstone during the weekend!

The year's production was on target and there was no indication that it would slow down as it had in previous years. I was under a lot of pressure as the industry ramped up production. I planned to sail down to Alderney in the Channel Islands for the summer holiday trip, which was quite a challenge. Most of the boats on the marina went to local ports with a few going as far as Holland.

The boat was now shipshape and fitted out as I wanted. We had a sailboard, water skis and a powerful engine for the dinghy. The first Sea Wych was nearing completion, and I had bought the hardwood from David Garrard as he had it in stock. Tim seemed to have lost enthusiasm for the project and I decided that I would probably need to take it over. The boat was turning out a lot better than expected; Phil the laminator was an accomplished carpenter and he was enthusiastic and concerned for the project.

Thursday 5ᵗʰ July: Any moment Fairline are going to ring chasing their fittings. I promised them for today but it will be tomorrow before I can deliver. We are under a lot of pressure and I am looking forward to the summer holiday. Last weekend we went down to the boat and took her round to Woodbridge, I'd bought an 18hp outboard and the children were anxious to try it out. We anchored off Ramsholt and put the engine on the dinghy. It took a bit of starting but once it got going it ran nicely. I set off with James and it went like a bat out of hell. I let James have a go and found it exhilarating.

During the weekend we had a good time and I found that I unwound very quickly. At the moment I am dreaming of that 45ft Brigantine that I will cruise to far places, I don't know how much longer I shall keep this lot going.

Saturday 21ˢᵗ July: Saturday morning, and I am in the office looking forward to the summer break. After the holiday I'm going to clean up the office and redecorate the entrance. We may also employ an office junior to try to work in a tidier way. The office is efficient, it just doesn't have time for unimportant things like cleaning up and tidying things away. The entrance porch needs cleaning up, repainting and organising as a reception area, we could then use the front door for visitors.

British Steel have now agreed to swap some land for part of our car park and I will probably go ahead with it and put up a 4000 sq. ft unit across the end of the existing site. This would fully develop the land available and create a good-sized unit for investment. I will probably build in similar materials to the existing units. If we get a slack period this autumn I shall try to expand by getting more customers for the stainless and I may start travelling again.

Inshore Marine is a bit dead, Tim has done absolutely nothing to help since April. We have sold one or two items for spares on Sea Wych but I don't think much will move until about October.

The plan for the three-week summer holiday was to sail down to Alderney and the Channel Islands. Martin was there with his catamaran, Berry Head, and Val and Bryan were staying in the Sea View hotel. If we could get there it would be a great achievement especially for an east coast boat. On 5th August the boat was loaded up with the sailboard, water skis and the toys necessary to keep teenage kids occupied. Ken and Jenny wished us good luck and hoped we would make the Channel Isles. We left Woolverstone at about 1030 and had hoped to make Brighton our first port of call. The wind was a NW4, which was ideal and we made good speed, however as the day wore on the wind steadily increased and veered westerly. As evening approached it increased to westerly force 7 and as the seas increased and with the boat surfing down the waves I decided to put into Ramsgate rather than spend an uncomfortable night at sea. By 1930 the boat was safely tied up in the outer harbour.

By morning the wind had moderated and I decided to set off for Brighton, leaving at 0630. The wind was light and variable and by 0900 it had died completely. As we approached Brighton the wind steadily increased and as we entered the marina at 2030 it was a steady southerly force 6. I decided to sail overnight to Alderney, planning to arrive mid-morning, and calculated that the trip should take about 15hrs if we averaged 6 knots. The weather forecast was favourable, promising clear skies and moderate north-westerly winds, and we cast off the ropes and after refuelling cleared the harbour at about 1730. James cast a mackerel line and soon had three fat fish wriggling in his bucket. It was a beautiful clear moonlit night with only the odd ship.

The watch system that Ann and I use for night passages is

three hours on and three hours off, and it was a pleasure to sail under the canopy of stars with the gibbous moon lighting our way. The Decca Navigator was a superb navigation aid when it worked, but occasionally it would lose itself and we had to tell it where it was. I always kept a chart with position lines and fixes, just in case.

13th August: We have now been in Braye for about a week and plan to sail to St. Peter Port tomorrow. We had quite a good trip round, we had hoped to make Brighton our first port of call but the weather turned foul so we went into Ramsgate for the night. We were tied alongside a Prior Coaster and the skipper told us he would be away about 0630 Monday morning. We left at the same time but unfortunately the tide was against us for most of the way to Brighton. We left Brighton about 1700 Tuesday and James put out a mackerel line. I reduced speed to about 5 knots to allow the trolling board to work. We managed to catch about 5 mackerel before dusk.

The wind was flukey and on the quarter, so we motor sailed most of the way. On approaching Braye I called up Martin Smith on the VHF, he answered immediately and as we were entering harbour Martin, Bryan (who was holidaying at the Sea View) and Richard came out to meet us in a borrowed Micro Plus. We moored up to a buoy and after sorting out the ship we went ashore. I liked the place immediately and we spent a few days with Martin and Bryan until they left on Sunday. James has been water skiing, we all had a go but James was the only one successful and he will be quite a good skier. Ann and I have been sailboarding, and both kids have nearly mastered it.

I think the magic of Alderney is getting through to me. The people are so beautiful and helpful and every time I think of the island I get emotional.

We said a sad goodbye to Alderney on the 15th at 1500 to catch the tide down to St Peter Port. The tide around the island runs at a fearsome rate, with the Alderney race on one side which runs between the main island and the French coast. There was a slight mist as we cleared the breakwater, which then turned to thick fog. I thought "We'll be OK in the fog with the Decca Navigator" but then the Decca beeped and a red light came on telling us it had lost signal. The visibility was down to about 10ft, so I hurriedly started plotting our course on the chart down to Guernsey and the Little Russel. Ann was steering and Theresa and James were on the bow keeping a lookout.

The fog was with us for most of the trip until it lifted at 1800. I had estimated our position to be between the Tautenay rock and the Platte Fougère lighthouse. and we were exactly where my estimated position said we should be. The Decca beeped and came back on line and we were tied up in St Peter Port by 1900. The marina in St. Peter Port is only accessible when the tide is high enough. The tidal range in the Channel Islands is at times 12 metres and sometimes a yacht gets stranded on the sill at the entrance to the Marina. A Prout catamaran trying to beat the tide sat on the sill for several hours, much to the embarrassment of the owner!

Our next port of call was St. Helier. We went into La Collette Yacht Harbour to await the tide prior to entering the Marina. Mick Webb was on holiday in Jersey and Mick, Monica and their friends came on board and accompanied us on the short trip into the main St Helier marina. We stayed in Jersey for a few days before heading home, calling in at Alderney. It seemed a bit quiet without our friends there.

The wind was in the NE, the worst direction for Braye harbour. After an extremely rolly night we upped anchor and headed for Brighton.

26th August: We had an uneventful trip back to

Woolverstone. We did Alderney to Brighton in 16hrs and Brighton to Woolverstone in 19hrs. We motored most of the way, hardly putting the sails up at all. The boat performed really well and I think Moody's have a winner in the 34.

28ᵗʰ August: Back at work today, Bill had coped very well as usual most of the jobs had been done. it usually takes me quite a time to acclimatise after a long holiday. I always plan to sell the business and do something different during the holiday but then, when I get into the day to day routine, I start to enjoy the feeling of security. The problem is nothing ever changes no matter what you do.

In September it was boat show time again. The company wasn't exhibiting but Ann and I went with Martin, Richard Smith and Bryan Essam. We all went in Martin's new Peugeot, which was ideal as it had three rows of seats instead of the usual two. I was impressed with the new Moody 419 and would have bought one if I had the money, the finish was very good and the accommodation similar to Geoff Millman's "40. "

We had another visit to the show, taking Theresa and James. Whilst Ann and I were interested in the yachts, James and Theresa were more interested in the speedboats and inflatables!

30ᵗʰ September: This weekend we all went down to the boat, the object being to strip out the units in the aft cabin to enable me to fit strengthening pads to the inside of the transom to take the davits. I have decided to design a range of davits and use my own vessel for development and testing. I managed to get most of the units out and now all that is necessary is for me to get some plates made up for fitting various davits. The Sea Wych is now almost complete, but until I have had a concrete road put down I probably won't be able to get the boat out. I have had Tim's resignation letter but wonder if I am taking on a bit of a white elephant. There has not been the degree of interest I had hoped for. I bought a life raft last week which I will fix on to the deck of the Moody during the winter. We should be well set up for the sailing season next year. We plan on keeping her in commission this winter in the hope of some winter sailing.

Last Wednesday was the Kempo grading. I was looking forward to it but was a little nervous, although I do quite well in the free fighting (I win most contests) I always feel a bit frightened at the thought of it. This is quite normal apparently. I suppose it's like anything else, I always feel the same way about flying a plane but as soon as I sit in the cockpit I enjoy every minute. On Wed. I had three contests, the first was against a purple and white belt. He was fast but a bit lighter than me and I beat him fairly easily. The next contest was with an orange belt (I am a yellow belt). He was similar weight and the fight developed into a bit of a slugging match. After a short time he became very tired and I managed to score several times with punches to the face and body. I stayed on and my opponent sat down and my next opponent was another orange belt. He was fast and agile, but I managed to floor him with a leg sweep and finish him off with a double punch to the head, twice! and so won the contest.

I don't know why I am so good at free fighting, I think probably it's because I don't get excited or afraid of my opponent. I just spar a bit to get their measure and then I go in and demolish them like a ton of bricks! I was graded up to green and white and I was delighted, mind you I had to work damned hard for it. Theresa got her orange belt, she is getting quite good now, James did not grade but will have a go at the next one.

6th October: Saturday morning again, the summer is now long gone and the weather is quite cool. Singh is the only one working today. Bill and Steve promised to come in but have let me down. I am especially annoyed at Bill because there were some jobs he promised to do this weekend that are required for Tuesday and he has been paid for them as well. I wonder if it is in my interest to pay people up front!

On Wednesday Ann and I went flying. As it was the first flight for about 12months we both needed a check flight. I went with Paul Smith and did two circuits. During these we managed to fit in an engine failure and some stalling. It was nice to fly again and I then went off to do some solo. I only did three circuits but all of my landings were very good.

The chap who was supposed to be planning the factory extension informed me that we didn't have enough land for the required number of car and lorry parking spaces, and if I bought more land I would be liable for road maintenance charges. Building land on the estate was at a premium and I needed more manufacturing area and a larger office, so the best option was to extend the existing units. Uncertainty in Industry generally and the continuing miners' strike was causing a lot of companies to put their expansion plans on hold, but I was determined to keep pushing forward.

On 12 October Irish terrorists tried to murder the Prime Minister and her cabinet by exploding a bomb in the Brighton Grand Hotel, where members of the cabinet were staying for the Conservative Party conference. Although five people were killed and 34 injured, luckily the Prime Minister and her husband escaped serious injury. At Mrs. Thatcher's insistence the conference opened on schedule at 0930. In her redrafted speech to the party she declared "This attack has failed. All attempts to destroy democracy by terrorism will fail".

The Prime Minister was an inspiration to the country as a whole. The economy was recovering despite militant unions and the Irish terrorists.

The Sea Wych project had not been the success I had hoped

and I had the laminator, Phil, doing other jobs and decorating the house. After that the strengthening on the transom to fit the davits on *Blue Melody*. The productivity for the year was very good, we had met most of our targets and cash flow was excellent.

11th November: Yesterday I was shooting, I had quite a good day out but had a terrible headache. I did not get to bed until about 4 am the night before as we'd been to the Kettering Golf club dinner. It was quite a good evening but didn't break up until about 2am and then Bryan and Val came back for coffee. Last night I went to a party with Paul and Angela Brinkman, we left about 11 pm and it was a pleasant evening. Bill has Just finished the radar mast for Mr Sharman's Nelson 44. It's quite impressive looking and I shall probably photograph it to go in the brochure.

Last week the cat was run over and had to go to the vet's for a couple of days. She looks very sorry for herself with her middle all bandaged up, but she should recover OK and will be having the dressing off tomorrow.

As the year drew to a close there was a lot of pressure from customers for items on their London Boat Show exhibits. Fairline had a new 33ft boat that they had high hopes for, the first of their "Targa" range, aimed mainly at the Mediterranean market. Pat Patterson, who was in the Caribbean, wrote to me inviting Ann and me out for a couple of weeks in February. We were far too busy for both of us to go, but I thought I would like to go on my own if I could persuade Ann. Pat had fitted a prototype Cooney mainsail reefing system that used an aluminium spar behind the mast. He also had a Cooney jib reefing system fitted. Pat had already tested the Cooney reefing on his first circumnavigation, "In the wake of Drake", and was now using the newly-designed mainsail system.

24th December: Christmas Eve again, it is pissing with rain and I will soon be driving over to Bedford to pick up Dad. I gave the lads their Christmas bottles and they have all gone down the pub. I don't feel in the Christmas spirit but I'm looking forward to seeing everyone tomorrow.

I had planned to fly out to visit Pat at the end of January or early February, it depended where he was going to be. He was calling the trip the 'Ocean Environment Expedition' and he was sailing in company with his mate Tom in another catamaran called *Morvran*. He had one crew, Brenda, who had sailed with him on one of the passages during his previous circumnavigation. Although I had always sailed in monohulls, with Pat's influence I thought I would like to swap to a cat. Martin had a Catalac and was always singing the praises of cats, especially their stability. Ann wasn't too keen and liked monos, but Pat and I'd spent hours discussing the different designs and characteristics of the two types.

1st January 1985: Last night we went to Chris Stokes' house for dinner, it was a super evening. We arrived about 2015 and soon got to chatting with the other guests. Chris lives in Roade Manor, which is a very nice manor house near Northampton. The first course was soup followed by salmon mousse, the main course was a massive lump of gammon which had been roasted. Chris carved this at the table and there were roast potatoes and roast parsnips, carrots and French beans. It was a magnificent feast washed down with copious amounts of wine. There were three sweets and cheese and biscuits to follow. To finish the meal there was vintage port and coffee. We saw the new year in and the merrymaking went on until about 0500 hrs. Ann and I slept on a double air bed in the lounge. We got up at 0900 and started to help the other guests to clear up. We left at about 1000 as I was invited to Smithy's for a clay shoot which started at 1100.

I arrived at Smithy's at about 1115 and everyone looked like death warmed up, apparently their party finished about the same time as ours. There was a gale blowing and the clays tended to rise fairly vertically and then curve round and dive back at the trap. Nobody shot very well apart from people who had never held a gun before. On my stands I got to hitting about one in three clays and Bryan came and stood behind me shooting at the same clays. Apart from being very dangerous I found this very distracting and I eventually walked away and left him to it. On my last stand the trap was set to give a fast-crossing bird and I was hitting most of them. After the shoot we all went down the pub. I only drank non-alcoholic beer, I will not drink or smoke again until next Christmas.

I had invested in a new truck, which I collected on January 2nd. It was much more comfortable than the old Sherpa, with a larger back. The delivery loads were getting larger as we expanded the business and the Sherpa was very tatty. Pat's wife Ethel has flown out to the Caribbean with a load of spare parts for his rigging, his mast had come down but luckily he was able to lash it alongside and not lose it. I was due to fly out there in February and needed to ascertain where the boat was and what spares I needed to take.

14th January: I've now received a letter from Pat Patterson asking me to join him in the Caribbean for a couple of weeks and take some parts for his reefing systems. I have been down and booked my flight, I'm hoping to go on 5th Feb. for about 2 weeks. I shall fly to Antigua and then we will sail from island to island, day sailing up to Puerto Rico. We've had some snow and the weather is getting colder, the compressor is freezing up every night and it takes a couple of hours to thaw out each morning. I have ordered a large container of anti-freeze and hope this will sort out the problem.

Today we had a summons from the VAT office for not

putting in a return on time. We were amazed, the return may have been a bit late but the tax was paid weeks ago. To me their actions seem vindictive. Everyone I know puts their returns in late and some people only pay on assessments, which we normally receive about one month after the VAT return is due. I think the action they are taking could be in response to our appeal to have the VAT back on our firm's yacht. Ann was furious but luckily didn't get too aggressive toward the patronizing worm that served the writ. I have not decided what to do about it but will be seeking advice from my solicitor and accountants on Monday.

The Ocean Winds and Pat's earlier design, the Heavenly Twins, were being marketed by Heavenly Cruising Yachts, a company owned by Brian North in Petersfield, Hants. Brian had asked me to obtain some photos that he could use for marketing purposes. I had decided to take the train to Heathrow, which would save Ann the trouble of driving me there. The spare parts for Ocean Winds were ready with some subtle design changes.

Tuesday 5th February: Left Kettering at 0715 and arrived at Heathrow 0930, the plane took off at about 1145. During the flight I watched "For Your Eyes Only" and slept for an hour or so. The flight was uneventful and it seemed that we were descending and preparing to land at Antigua's VC Bird airport in no time. As I left the aircraft and walked towards the arrivals hall I saw Pat standing on the observation balcony. I waved, slightly relieved that he was there to meet me. I cleared customs and was surprised that I got through without questions regarding the amount of spare parts I was carrying for Ocean Winds!

I looked for Pat but couldn't see him anywhere. I knew he was there because I had seen him on the balcony. I walked up and down at a loss to know what to do. He wouldn't have left me there and gone back to the boat, would he? I walked out to the taxi stand and turned round and there he was, leaning against one of the support pillars reading a book, what a relief!

We took a taxi to St. John's, where Ocean Winds was lying on a mooring alongside Tom's boat Morvren. Brenda rowed over and took us back to Ocean Winds. After chatting for an hour or so we went over to Morvren for a drink. Tom had only one guest and we had a good yarn.

6th February: Last night I woke up in the early hours with a headache. There was a sound of hundreds of cocks crowing, so it must have been nearly dawn. I went for a walk on deck and then went back to bed. We all got up at about 0815 and pottered about until 1030, when we went ashore for shopping. The prices seemed quite high, but the local people were very nice. We returned to the ship about 1330 and had lunch, we then went for a swim and about 1500 we rowed ashore and visited a Canadian warship. We returned to Ocean Winds at about 1630 and upped anchor and left about 1800. It is now 1940 and we are at sea heading for St. Barts. It is a beautiful starlit night and we have been identifying the different constellations. My watch starts at 2100 until 2400. There is a slight swell but it is generally calm, Pat is making some sandwiches and Brenda is steering.

St Barts is a beautiful spot, we went ashore this afternoon and wandered around. The place was spotlessly clean and the people were very friendly. Most of them spoke English and there seemed to be very few black people. We ended up in a café and I bought dinner. It was coq au vin and was OK but not brilliant for the money. We returned to the ship at about 2000, had a few drinks and Brenda turned in at 2130. I sat up yarning with Pat and then Tom came aboard. Pat turned in at about 2200 and Tom eventually left about 0030.

8th February: I woke up in the early hours, then slept fitfully until about 0730, when I got up and made some tea. Brenda,

Tom, Brian and I went ashore. I wanted to post a couple of letters and we needed some bread and a few provisions. The shopping was done and as we returned to the dinghy I noticed that there was a sign advertising cold beer. We went and had one and then noticed it was very cheap, so we bought a couple of cases. We returned to our ships and were making ready for sea when the customs came alongside and insisted that the two captains went ashore to complete formalities. While Pat was ashore Brenda and I prepared lunch.

We sailed at about 1345 heading for L Forchue Bay, where we intended doing some snorkelling. We anchored at about 1500 and I put on my newly-bought fins, mask and snorkel and leaped over the side. Just off the beach there was a reef, and Brenda and I swam around looking at the myriads of coloured fish and the fingers of coral swinging back and forth like beckoning fingers. We saw a moray eel and some small barracuda glided past. Brian and Pat were also on the reef and on one occasion I had a head-on collision with Brenda. I swam back first as I felt a bit tired, I've caught the sun quite a lot but it is not too painful. Pat and Brenda came back and I took a couple of photos around the bay. Pat showed us how to work out a sight with his sextant and I was only 1¼ miles out. We will probably stay overnight here and sail down to St. Martin tomorrow.

9th February: I awoke from deep slumber at 0515 and then dozed until 0730 when I decided to get up. I went on to the foredeck and did 25 knuckle press-ups whilst the kettle was boiling. I made some tea and had half a grapefruit for breakfast. We had decided to go ashore and take some shots of the boat. We all went ashore at about 10 am and photographed some of the cacti and a variety of small lizards. We climbed right to the top of quite a high rocky outcrop –the view was stunning. There were some people on the island hunting and we heard a few rifle shots, however they left in fast power boats before we returned to the beach. I found quite a nice brain coral, which I shall take back home.

We had an early lunch and then we all went over to another coral reef for some snorkelling. We went in Tom's inflatable and tied the anchor rope to a large rock about 15 ft. down. The snorkelling on this reef was far better than the one we swam over yesterday. We returned to Ocean Winds about 1500. we had decided to go ashore this evening for a barbecue and Brenda baked some large rolls (they were about the size of a small Hovis) and we went ashore at about 1730 - it gets dark at about 1830.

While Brenda, Tom and Brian made camp Pat and I walked to the weather side of the island to collect driftwood. When we returned there was already a cheerful fire going and it was just getting dark. While the food was cooking we had a singsong. Tom has a beautiful voice and the scene was pure magic with the sunset over the bay and the waves gently lapping against the shore.

The meal was very good. Tom had brought a large sausage about 18 inches long and we had brought a couple of tins of Frankfurters. We put them all in a saucepan on the fire. We then realised that Tom's sausage should have had the plastic skin removed! We did this and the whole saucepan cooked away merrily.

After we had eaten we had some more songs and Brian gave us the benefit of some dancing, I wasn't quite sure what the type of dancing was, but it was amusing and very lively. The embers of the fire were getting low and Brenda wanted to get some photographs, so I put some of the empty beer cases on the fire to flare up to give enough light for a time exposure. The fire then died down and the songs became quieter as the effect of an active day, alcohol and food gradually made us mellow. We gathered up our gear and tramped back to the dinghys. Although I rolled up my trousers (I was the only one wearing trousers, because of sunburn) I still got wet trouser bottoms, but not a wet arse. We returned to Ocean Winds and yarned for half an hour, then Brenda turned in and half an hour later Pat turned in. I am still awake writing this log and drinking Pat's whisky.

Filipsburg, St. Martin: After the Spanish left in the 1600s the island was jointly claimed by the Dutch and the French and there were several battles between the two powers, but a treaty was signed in 1648 which divided the Island between them. Local legend claims that a Dutchman and a Frenchman stood back to back and walked in opposite directions round the shoreline, drawing the boundary from the spot where they met. This may be true, but the French have more land.

Six months ago I could never have believed that in such a short time I could be in such a situation. It is 0850 and the sun is already becoming hot. Brenda is doing some embroidery and the Captain is thinking about making ready for sea. I can't decide whether to go for a swim just yet, I suppose sometime I shall return to reality.

We sailed about 1000 hrs for St. Martin and had a leisurely sail at about 2 knots, arriving at about 1400. This is a delightful place and we went ashore to weigh it up. We returned to the ship at about 1600 and went for a swim. The water was not as clear as the last anchorage but it was nice and warm. It was my turn to cook tonight and I cooked up some beef and dumplings in a stew. It is now 2115 and I can't decide whether or not to go ashore. Tom is fah-la-la-ing away on the next boat but I think I had enough of that last night.

It is quite a long row ashore in the dark and Brenda and Pat are not keen on coming with me. I think I am getting over my initial sun overdose and starting to feel like adventure, sex or "a good run ashore". When I return to England I shall try and obtain some songbooks.

11th February: We went ashore this morning to look at the duty free goodies on sale in this freeport. Tom bought a pair of binoculars and Brenda a waterproof camera case for underwater work. We left at about 1400 hrs. and hoped to stop on the way to Marigot to look for a bay for some snorkelling and reef diving so that Brenda could try out her new toy. Unfortunately, when we arrived at a suitable bay, there was a heavy swell running into it so we decided to carry on. The visibility decreased and soon it was raining incessantly, but we arrived in Marigot just before dusk.

The Captain has a game leg at the moment, so after dinner he decided not to go ashore. Brenda and I picked up Tom and Brian and we rowed the 200 yards to the shore. It was a quiet, clean town and everywhere there were restaurants full of quite well dressed people stuffing their faces. We found a bar and the barmaid informed us that this was the dearest bar on the island. We only stayed for one drink and then decided to row back. We were just casting off when a big drunken bearded man asked for a lift back to his ship. We started out and I thought this might be a mistake. The drunk did not seem to know where his ship was lying, but after rowing around for about half an hour we came to a big black ketch and the man climbed aboard. I hope we dropped him off on the right ship!

We returned to Morvren, declined Tom's invitation for a drink and then returned to Ocean Winds. Brenda turned in straight away and I read for an hour before turning in. Not the most exciting of days!

12th February: The weather is not so hot today. My trip is almost half over and I have not finished the work on the jib reefer. We decided not to go to Anguilla today, Pat decided to fill up with water and diesel and whilst he went ashore to make arrangements Brenda cleaned the ship and I had a go at the jib roller reefing.

I had a nice chat with Brenda about the problems of a platonic relationship when one is constantly in someone else's company. There must be friction, but I think Pat and Brenda get on very well. He has the greatest regard for her easy-going manner and the seamanship she has acquired over the months. Brenda is probably more competent than most weekend yachties you will meet. I personally have the greatest regard for her abilities.

We had to go alongside a small ship to get water and at first the chap in charge seemed a bit aggressive. I went and chatted to him and by the time we had tanked up we were buddies. We returned to the anchorage and then Pat and I went ashore for diesel. We took Tom and Brian ashore, borrowed a couple of supermarket trolleys and Pat went for the diesel while Brian and I went to buy booze. We returned to our ships about 1730 and it was my turn to cook. After going ashore this afternoon my opinion of the place has mellowed, it is a duty free island and wholesale beer and wine are fairly cheap.

Tomorrow we sail for Anguilla and from there to the Virgins. I start to wonder about connections and whether I can get back to the UK as planned. I am hoping to fly from Puerto Rico direct to England.

13th February: We upped anchor at about 0800. Brenda is sailing on Tom's boat as he wants advice on camera equipment and intends to take the bus into Filipsburg, where things seemed cheaper. We had a cracking sail, first on a run and then on a broad reach straight up to Road Bay. As soon as we were safely anchored Pat and I started work on the jib reefer. We had a couple of bottles of Guinness as we slaved away under the merciless Caribbean sun. We finally finished at about 1815 just as the sun disappeared in a glorious sunset. Tonight after dinner I shall row ashore and see if Anguilla is as quiet as the guidebooks claim it to be.

It's Pat's turn to cook and it looks as though we are in for a gastronomic delight. I have spent very little money, as Pat wouldn't allow me to contribute to the cost of my stay but suggested that the jib reefer spares should more than cover it.

14th February: We all except Brenda went ashore this morning, she stayed on board to develop her films. As we walked ashore, we were greeted by a big black chap who welcomed us to the island. We decided to walk the four miles into town. Anguilla seems very nice, all of the people were friendly and helpful and we did shopping in order to use up our Eastern Caribbean dollars. The prices in the shops seemed reasonable compared to other EC islands.

Whilst waiting for the bus to take us back to Road Bay we stopped for a few beers. We returned to our ships at about 1500 hrs. and after having a swim, set sail for Tortola. I took the first watch until 1900 hrs. and Pat cooked a chicken for dinner. The chicken was very nice but a bit tough. I stood out with Brenda looking at the twinkling stars and went down for a sleep at 2000 hrs.

We were running with twin headsails and the trade wind was giving us a good six knots. The Autohelm could only just cope with things and the wind vane required fiddling with to make it work satisfactorily.

15th February: Pat called me at 0100 hrs. It was a beautiful starlit night with only the odd ship in the distance. Pat then turned in and I was alone with the swishing of the water under the Keels and a canopy of a million stars shining down onto the blue Caribbean. A couple of satellites came through, enabling me to fix our position fairly accurately. When Brenda took over at 0400 the lights of Tortola were just visible in the distance. I turned in at 0430. We were approaching Round Rock Passage at about 0745 and Brenda turned in a short time after. Pat casually asked "You do have an American visa Kevin, I hope?"

I replied "No". He then informed me that I required one to enter the American Virgins.

After anchoring in Road Town we rowed ashore and I went to immigration to ask whether it was possible to obtain an American visa. I was told the only way was to fly to Antigua and process an application at the American Consulate. This of course is out of the question because of the cost involved, also the time. I dare not risk entering the American Virgins and Puerto Rico with no visa, so unfortunately I will have to fly home from Tortola.

I went to the British Airways office and arranged to fly to Antigua and then to Heathrow on Tuesday. Pat was very good and agreed to take us off to Virgin Gorda for a couple of days snorkelling and then bring me back to Road Town to catch the plane. I was so disappointed I felt like crying. I was having to cut my holiday short by a week, missing some of the best boating I have ever experienced, all because of my inadequate preparation.

The Cruising Association port officer came aboard this evening and we had an interesting chat while Brenda cooked dinner. Tom and Brian came aboard and a good yarn was had all round. After they'd left we had dinner. Brenda had cooked up the rest of the tough chicken from last night, making it into a broth with onions, carrots and potatoes. She also did some cornbread to go with it – it was superb! – after she had made a beautiful bread pudding. The Captain and I could hardly manage our portions of pudding, but it was so delicious we couldn't resist it.

We finished our wine and the Captain decided to go ashore to place an ad in the local pub for crew to replace me for the next leg of the voyage. As the Captain seemed very tired and pissed, I agreed to accompany him. We walked to "The Pub" and I was immediately impressed with the place. There was a calypso band thrashing away, loads of unattached females with lascivious eyes darting around and an atmosphere of happiness and wellbeing. I had only been there a moment when a nubile black wench grabbed my hand and led me into a bold samba. I think she was surprised that I could do the dance, however although I enjoyed the dance and the company of the maid I remembered that both the Captain and I are married and we made our apologies and left.

16th February: We left Road Town at 0730. Morvran decided not to join us as Tom was expecting to pick up another charter in Puerto Rico. We had a cracking sail up to Virgin Gorda. It was blowing about a four and we were close hauled most of the way. We took the passage between Virgin Gorda and Mosquito Island, anchoring in Gorda Sound. We took the dinghy and with snorkelling gear rowed over to where we thought there would be some coral. Unfortunately there wasn't any, so we rowed back to OW and moved to a different place. We all went swimming. There were some isolated patches of Coral but nothing as pretty as L Forchue.

The Captain is typing an article and Brenda is sunbathing in the cockpit. I started to cook dinner at about 1700 hrs. I did spare ribs of pork and chips and even though I say it myself it was delicious, everyone remarked how good it was and meant it!

I went out after dinner and had a breath of the warm Caribbean air. A few stars twinkled in the cloudy sky and it was warm in the gentle force three breeze. A few minutes ago as I stood outside I felt that pang of regret as I remembered that in a couple of days I would be leaving OW and her unusual crew and going back to the pressure of everyday life. I know the grass is always greener on the other side, but I cannot understand why I don't do something as exciting as Pat. If I re arranged my finances I could do exactly the same. The only difference is that

Ann would take an active part. This is a good point in many ways, but I think my life lacks a certain amount of freedom.

Tonight we looked at Brenda's slides, she develops them herself and they were good. When I saw the pictures of OW dismasted I was sorry that I had not been along to help out. After the slide show we discussed a slide copying attachment to go onto her camera so that she can send some slides out with me to go with Pat's articles. I suppose the easier way round it would be for me to take some slides back with me, have them copied and then mail the originals back to Brenda. However tomorrow I shall make up a device which I hope will do the trick!

17th February: This morning I was awakened by a loud crashing noise on the foredeck. I went on deck to investigate and found that one of the hatches had blown open. I sorted it out and Pat appeared on the scene. It was blowing like hell, so we let out another 50ft. of cable. I returned to my cabin and turned in, rising at about 0745. We had a fairly lazy morning, I made Brenda a slide copying attachment for her camera with an old beer can holder, and discussed with Pat his new catamaran design. We were hoping to be able to do some sailing while Brenda photographed us from the shore or another boat, but the weather wasn't suitable.

We decided to move Ocean Winds round to the coral reef lying to the north of Virgin Gorda. We moved the ship round and anchored just off the reef. The snorkelling was superb. The coral was better than the reef at L Forchue and the fish were more abundant. Brenda tried out her new waterproof camera case and took some pictures of fish. Pat decided to stay the night where we were. It was Brenda's turn to cook and she did a beef stew, it was superb. Pat got a little merry and after we played dice he turned in. Brenda and I had a couple of games (of dice) and then she turned in. I am not very tired. Tomorrow is my last day. I've grown to love the easy way of life on OW. Both Pat *and Brenda are the sort of people we meet very rarely. Brenda and I are now firm friends and I hope to keep in touch.*

18th February: We got up at about 0745 and decided to drop Brenda off on the jetty near Mosquito Island to photograph the boat under sail for advertising and publicity purposes. We dropped her off at 10 am and there followed a hectic time as Pat and I tacked the boat through the coral reefs on all points of sailing. Brenda took about three films and then as she was packing up she dropped her tripod into the water, so we anchored off and Pat rowed over with her snorkelling gear and retrieved it. We then sailed to another coral reef and did more snorkelling. I think this was the best reef so far, the fish were startling in their colours and types.

We only stayed for about an hour and then sailed down past Virgin Gorda to anchor off a beautiful tropical beach covered in beautiful rocks and palm trees. Brenda is going to develop the films she took today and tonight it is my turn to cook. After dinner we looked at Brenda's newly developed slides. There were some very good ones. I am leaving tomorrow. I have packed my case and am ready.

Over the last two weeks I have had long discussions with Pat on the advantages of catamarans over monohulls. I think I would like to buy one of Pat's new designs and do some extended cruising.

19th February: We were away from the anchorage by eight and had a nice run down to Tortola, anchoring in Road Harbour. On arrival Pat rowed ashore to get a loaf and on his return cooked breakfast. After breakfast we rowed ashore to clear customs and immigration. I bought us all an ice cream, they were two dollars each and melted faster than you could eat them. Pat and I looked like two little boys with faces and hands plastered in ice cream.

We returned to OW and had a Guinness. We like our daily Guinness, do Pat and I. I will be going ashore in about an hour to get a taxi to the airport. Pat rowed ashore and Brenda came too. Pat helped me to carry my bag to the taxi rank in the Moorings hotel. I agreed the price with the driver and put my bags in. I shook hands with Pat and gave Brenda a goodbye kiss. As the taxi drove out of the car park I waved and smiled. They waved back and just as I was going out of earshot Brenda called out" Come and see us again sometime". I shouted "Yes OK" and then I was gone.

On the taxi radio they were playing "I Just Called To Say I Love You" (Stevie Wonder). The taxi driver seemed a jolly chap but didn't say much to me apart from the odd question about plane times etc.

While I was waiting for the plane an American chap started to chat. He was an interesting guy and our conversation on such subjects as politics (we both admire Reagan and Thatcher) whiled away a pleasant hour. The plane was a Jetprop 748 and looked quite new. Just after we took off the stewardess brought around cheese and biscuits and I ordered a gin and tonic. I paid in EC dollars, giving her a five-dollar bill. I didn't get any change, no wonder she smiled. I think we are about to land at St. Kitts, either that or the pilot is about to ditch.

We landed at St Kitts at about 1930 and took off for Antigua 1945. It should take about 20 minutes to get there and there is a two-hour wait until the next plane. I had a hamburger and a couple of beers at Antigua and boarded the plane at 1015. I was lucky to have three seats all to myself. I wonder what the film will be and if there will be any food?

The film wasn't a lot of good and I read a little and had a nod. We were served with a light meal and I read until 1230, then tried to sleep. I slept until about 0245 and then read some more. Breakfast was served at about 0430, which is 0830 UK time. We should be arriving at about 1015. The temp. in London is 2 degrees C, 36F, quite a difference from Antigua at 78 degrees when I left.

My trip should have lasted another week and I hadn't told anyone I would be home earlier. I was met with astonishment when I walked into the house. Ann's mum and dad were there and Ann was at the office. When Ann walked in and saw me her face lit up with a mixture of surprise and relief that I was back. I think she had come to realise what a responsibility running the business was with the day-to-day problems.

I was in fantastic shape both physically and mentally and had dreams of sailing off on a long trip, possibly fitting out one of Pat's new designs. I had spent hours with Pat discussing different rig designs for extended sailing. The Sea Wych project was coming to nothing, there was very little interest and I was considering selling off the finished boat and the moulds. The boat that we had completed was beautifully finished to a very high standard, which probably made it too expensive, but I thought it would make the sets of mouldings seem a good buy.

I received details of a set of OW mouldings from Brian North. My enthusiasm for the boat after my trip with Pat was as strong as ever. I thought perhaps sell off the Sea Wych and obtain a set of OW mouldings to build over the next three years, if possible keeping the Moody, so I would still have a boat to sail in the meantime.

At the end of February, I had a phone call from Pat Patterson to say that he had agreed to sell the Ocean Winds moulds to a guy in Puerto Rico and he was now back in the UK to arrange transport. He'd left Brenda in charge of OW and planned to be back in UK for about three weeks. When he returned to the boat he would sail it to Panama, finish it off and put it up for sale with an American broker.

11ᵗʰ March: I have decided to exhibit the Sea Wych at the

Brighton Boat show in May. This may result in a few sales, and as she is being exhibited afloat will show her off in her best light. She really looks nice and I will be glad of the opportunity to show her off.

Ann is off with the flu and just lately it seems someone is off every day. I have practically decided that I shall go for an Ocean Winds as soon as finances allow. I hope I could get some mouldings without having to sell the Moody so that I don't lose too much sailing. Also if I could do this and build Ocean Winds out of Cooney Marine, when she is complete I could sell the Moody and pay off my loan account. I don't know what sort of a deal I could do with Brian North but I think I could possibly screw him to the floor on price as I think he is keen to get some boats turning over.

The business was getting busier by the day and I was working a lot of hours. Fairline were updating their current range and introducing new models every year. In March we did the Beaulieu Boat Jumble, an excuse to sell off any rejects or old design parts. We stayed on Martin's boat at Christchurch. Martin had a Citroen with three rows of seats and seven of us were crammed in with a trailer behind full of our bits and pieces We managed to sell quite a lot of junk. Martin is a good salesman and one guy came up and wanted to buy a small bow rail. He asked the price and Martin said 20 quid. The guy said "Cor that's cheap, if I went to Cooney Marine it would be twice that price". Martin took his money and then introduced me to him.

The Brighton Boat Show was on May 8th, and was opened by the actor and comedian Frankie Howerd. The opening party entered the marina on the steam yacht *Amazon,* owned by Kevin Lowe, the son of the late Arthur Lowe, star of "Dad's Army". A jazz band was playing traditional jazz on the stern deck as the clipper-bowed yacht slowly motored round the marina to the landing stage, where Frankie Howerd alighted and after a brief speech declared the show open.

The Sea Wych looked well presented and the fit out was of a high standard, but although there was a lot of interest we didn't sell any, so the decision was made to sell off the finished boat and the moulds and use the workshop for other production.

Every year Theresa and I organised a pool party for the karate club. They were a good crowd from all walks of life, karate being the thing we all had in common. The two main instructors, Tony and John, were dedicated to the principles of Mushashi, Japan's greatest warrior, and the training was extremely hard.

29th June: The karate party is tonight. I worked until about 1300 and then collected a fresh bottle of gas for the barbecue. When I arrived home Theresa and her friend Jody were quite excited, most of the preparations had been done. Ann had made 30 beefburgers, and there were chicken drumsticks, rice, loads of salad and odds and ends. She had made some strawberry tarts with fresh strawberries and also some apple and blackberry. Mick and Graham were first to arrive and then Kipper and Old Mick, and by 1800 everyone was in the pool.

Theresa, Jody and I had planned a bit of fun, the three of us being thrown in fully clothed. Everyone seemed to be having a whale of a time, and I was surprised that they all mixed so well. Luckily the weather stayed fine and the rain stayed away. The food was much appreciated and the wine and beer was flowing freely.

At about 1030 everyone went for another swim. The water in the pool was very warm and with the light on everyone loved it. When they came out of the pool I put on a Bruce Lee film. I drank rather a lot and fell over towards the end. Everyone left about 0200.

The business was doing exceptionally well and I was working a lot of hours, the only cloud on the horizon being Inshore Marine. That company was not doing very well. We were not selling any Sea Wyches, although there were some orders for spares. Phil the laminator was doing other work. I thought he could be trained as a welder, as he was intelligent and had a natural ability for making things.

Inshore Marine made a £3,580 loss in 1984 and the decision was made to wind it up so as not to incur further losses. The same year Cooney Marine turned over £195,161 and made a net profit of £33,763, which worked out at 17.6% of turnover. This was an excellent result; not many companies performed so well and it was mainly due to the piecework system. The men were earning far more under this system than they would on the clock. The 1984 production was only about 3% higher than 1983, but the profit was considerably higher. Recruitment was a problem, there were welders and fabricators out there but most of them needed extra training to work stainless steel to the Cooney standards. I was doing a lot of the lathe work and machining and sending a lot of repetitive machining work out to subcontractors.

I was looking forward to extending the house. I had accepted the price from Clipstone Builders and they were due to start in August. The work would extend the house to four bedrooms with extra bathrooms.

The summer cruise was planned for August and we hoped to sail the Channel Islands again.

11th September: The summer is now fading fast, it must have been one of the coldest, wettest and windiest summers for many a year. We had to abort the plans to sail to Alderney. We set off and ended up in a full gale, so we went into Ramsgate. After leaving in a 4-5 the wind steadily increased and when we were abeam of Dover it was blowing a 7, but we kept beating into it. The wind kept increasing and the swell was building up, so I decided to turn back and run for Dover. We had to stand by off Dover to wait for the traffic to clear and when we eventually had clearance the wind was gusting to 45 knots and with the strong tide across the westerly entrance it was touch and go.

The weather was bad for a few days and when we left I decided to head for Ostend. The wind was astern and blowing about a six, it only took about 8½ hours to get to Ostend from Dover and at times we were surfing down the waves at 10 knots. We left Ostend in a force 3 on a run, eventually the wind died and a few thunderstorms were around.

We were just about to cross the Westerschelde when we were struck by a 65-knot storm, which reduced visibility to about 20ft. It was dreadful, all we could do was run before it. We knew exactly where we were but I was concerned about the many huge ships anchored in the Flushing roads. After about 20 min. it moderated enough to allow me to get the mainsail off and then I decided to head for Breskens.

We motored up to Veere the next day and went into the Verse Meer. We met some nice people and cruised in company with them for a day or two, ending up in Courtgene. Theresa became pals with their daughter Ingrid and we managed to get her water skiing. We left the Verse Meer on the Thursday and thought we might head straight back, but the wind was on the nose and the children were unhappy so we went into Zeebrugge. I thought it was an awful dump but I am pleased I went there. I now only have to visit Blankenberg to have done all of the Belgian ports.

We waited in Zeebrugge, as the BBC were giving out gales in all areas and I had almost decided to leave the boat there and return on the ferry. I asked the Harbourmaster for a berth in the marina but he refused, so I thought that if the weather looked at all reasonable I would take the boat down to Blankenberge and leave it there.

We left Zeebrugge at 0800 Sunday morning. It was blowing a SW6 and I found I could sail about 285 degrees with a reefed main and a tiny jib, so I decided to head for England. I knew it would be a rough ride, but the opportunity was too good to miss. Ann and Theresa were ill so I had to steer for most of the way. It was still daylight when we passed the Roughs Tower and the Sunk light vessel, but by the time we were off Harwich it was dark. We crept up to Woolverstone at about 1030 Sunday night. I decided against my better judgement to take her into the berth downwind and downtide, we had to go in fast but made it OK. We'd been in about half an hour feeling elated but very tired when Ann reminded me that we were still flying the Belgian courtesy flag, which I quickly changed for a Q flag.

We were back to work on 27th August, and production for the month was surprisingly good. I think August will probably be the highest turnover month since 1979. Usually, due to holidays, August is a low production month. At the Southampton Boat Show I viewed the Hallberg Rassy 352 and 38, they are both beautifully finished off and after the Moody the 352 seemed small. The 38 would be a nice step up but the price was high at £65,000.

I looked at the new Moody 37 at the show. This was available with a fixed windscreen and the boat was better finished off than the 34 but not as good as the Rassy.

15th September: Today we went to the Southampton Boat Show. We took Jody with us, she is a nice girl and good company for Theresa. We were most impressed with the HR 352 again. She is a beautiful ship and I would really like one, the only problem is the price. The accommodation, although nice, is smaller than the Moody 34 we now have. Ideally the HR38 would be a logical progression, but then the price would come out somewhere over £65,000, which is too high.

We were impressed with the Moody 37. It seemed extremely good value for money and had a good write up in the current Yachting World. A Perspex windscreen is also available, I have yet to see this but if it is nicely done it would be a great improvement. The write-up on the boat claims that it will motor at 8.3 knots and also sail at the same speed, so good passage times are possible. I wonder what sort of a deal I could screw out of Brian Sharp?

On September 19ᵗʰ at the show we had a meeting with Brian Sharp and John Rubython, the Managing Director of Marine Secol, the Moody selling agent. We hammered out quite a good deal, trading in the 34 and placing an order for a new 37. I decided to take the option of a larger engine and the fixed windscreen. I decided to go for the roller headsail in lieu of the working jib and supply a Cooney Mk. 3 to be fitted when the mast is erected in Brighton. After sea trials, as soon as the weather allows the boat can then be sailed back to our berth in Woolverstone. Blue Melody would need to be moved to Brighton as soon as possible. After placing the order for the 37 we spent the rest of the day looking at equipment. I was very impressed with the new Vigil Radar and we were interested in various autopilots, navigators etc.

28ᵗʰ September: Marine Secol rang yesterday to say they had a chap interested in buying Blue Melody. We went down early this morning as we had some clearing up to do and at about 1400 Mr Taylor arrived to view the boat. At the moment he has a Fairline powerboat and although he seemed very keen his wife seemed a little unsure. He was very impressed with the boat and said he would like it if Marine Secol could take his boat in part exchange. He left about 1530 and I wondered whether he really would go ahead. If he does it will save me the trip round to Brighton next weekend.

Mr Taylor went ahead with the purchase of Blue Melody and took her away on October 5th. He seemed delighted with her. The new boat was due to be delivered in January and I planned to keep her longer this time. It seems that I only keep boats for two or three seasons and I planned to fit radar and a lot of expensive equipment on the new vessel.

October 11th: Today is the Flying Club Dinner. we are taking Chris and Ruth and Bryan and Val. Bryan is interested in an old wooden Heavenly Twins that is down on Pat Patterson's patch at Plymouth. We plan to go down there tomorrow to have a look. Bryan is turning into a catamaran bigot and keeps going on about how much better they are than monohulls. Although I like cats and have sailed on them on occasion I personally prefer monohulls.

The boat Pat was selling was the original plug that the Heavenly Twins moulds were made from. Quite often when a Fibreglass production boat was conceived it was customary to build the first boat in wood and use this prototype to make the moulds for the production run. The boat looked the same as the production twins and was only a fraction of the price, but Bryan didn't seem impressed, and decided against it.

2nd November: Today we went to Turkey. We had a taxi at about 0815 and caught a train to St. Pancras at about 0910. The train was full, so we travelled first class, paying an extra £200 each. On arrival at St. Pancras we then struggled to the Underground in the middle of the rush hour and crammed ourselves and our bags on the train to Heathrow. We met up with Geoff Millman and his party in plenty of time. There was Geoff, Danny, Colin and Dougie, and all except Colin had some experience of sailing. We bought some brandy, gin, tobacco and cigars from the duty free shop. Everyone seemed to hit it off at once and by the time we boarded the A310 Airbus we all felt at ease.

The flight to Istanbul took about 4½ hours. We then had to catch another flight to Izmir, unfortunately there was a two-hour wait for the connection, however we had a drink and the time seemed to go very quickly. Istanbul to Izmir only takes 1½ hours but by the time we arrived in Izmir it was about 11pm local time. We cleared the airport and boarded our minibus for the final 4½ hours to Bodrum. Geoff incidentally put all of our bags in the hold of the wrong bus, but luckily we realised in time and swapped them over.

The trip to Bodrum took over 4 hours. After about an hour someone suggested that we had a drink, so Dougie opened his bottle of Armagnac. Luckily we had kept some plastic glasses from the aeroplane. I opened my box of cigars and very soon we were having a super time laughing and telling jokes, the Journey seemed to take no time at all. It was 0330 when we finally boarded Bagadag. It was a relief that the journey was over although I quite enjoyed the day. Bagadag was all ready for us with the gangway down, groceries in the fridge and everything clean and ship shape. As soon as the gear was stowed we all turned in.

Geoff had placed the boat with a charter company and when we joined it was set up as if going out on charter. The gangway was a bit wobbly, so caution was needed when going aboard, but the boat generally was in good shape.

The booze stocks needed building up, so we went ashore to stock up. The load of beer on the dock looked as though we were going for a month, not just a week! Carrying the beer onto the boat up the wobbly gangway was a challenge, as I found out. I was halfway up the gangway when it wobbled and overboard I went. My leg became tangled in the guardrail, leaving me suspended over the water. Ann screamed 'My camera, my camera!' while I hung there clinging onto one case of beer as the other disappeared into the turgid depths of the harbour.

Ann's camera, a new Olympus that I had bought her for her birthday, was dangling off my shoulder and was rescued. Next came the remaining case of beer, while I was left dangling! I was eventually pulled on board. My right leg had nasty grazes and a rope burn from the guardrail that had twisted around it. Ann's camera seemed OK, but within 24 hours it had seized up solid and was useless.

At the airport in Istanbul I'd changed some pounds sterling into Turkish currency. Our first port of call after leaving Bodrum was the Greek island of Kos. At that time the Greeks and Turks were at loggerheads and Turkish money was not acceptable anywhere, but I eventually found a bank which agreed to change the Turkish currency into Greek (drachma). We sailed around some of the islands, calling in at Kos, Simi and Rhodes. Doug had an old Leica camera and was constantly taking photographs. He had a wicked sense of humour and liked to take charge when we were sailing.

Danny went to the same school in Bedford as me and although a couple of years older I vaguely remembered him. He had left school and gone into the police force, first as a cadet and then as a police officer. He'd frequently sailed with Geoff on *Bagadag* and was a very competent seaman, Colin had little sailing experience but was keen to learn and would have a go at any tasks requested of him. Ann and I had sailed with Geoff on *Bagadag* in the South of France and had a high regard for Geoff and his abilities as skipper.

The week flew past and all too soon it was time to return to Bodrum. When we docked we found that there was no alcohol on sale anywhere as it was the anniversary of the death of Mustafa Kemal Ataturk, the first President of the Republic of Turkey and the founder of modern Turkey, and as a mark of respect alcohol sales are banned on the anniversary of his death. We'd run out of booze on board, but then Geoff remembered the case I had dropped overboard at the beginning of the trip. Doug said he was a diver and offered to dive in and retrieve the lost case. The depth of the water was 5-6 metres and I thought it a bit dangerous, but Doug insisted on trying to recover the beer. The cardboard case would be sodden and would fall to pieces, so we tied a rope to a bag. If Doug could dive down with the bag and put the beer in it we could then haul the bag up to the surface.

Doug dived down and surfaced with a big smile on his face. The beer was in the bag, and it was soon on board being drunk. Doug was the hero of the hour and said that now he wanted to visit the fleshpots!

11th November: Today we go home or at least some of the way home. I didn't get up that early, I suppose it was around at about 0800 and Ann a little later. When I went into the main cabin I saw that Geoff had the drill and the new stanchion sockets out, so I knew what my job for the morning was to be. I started drilling out screw heads and trying to remove the badly corroded sockets from the Pushpit and toe rail. It was a laborious job, but gradually I succeeded in removing the stbd. Pushpit half. Danny helped from time to time but I thought we probably wouldn't succeed in replacing all of the sockets on the Pushpit. One of the sockets on the port side wasn't too badly corroded, so I decided to leave it on. I managed to fit all of the others in the nick of time although some of them still need a couple of screws to fix them to the toe rail. Geoff was delighted and I felt I had achieved something, if I get another trip out there I shall do the work on day 1, not the last morning. There is only the pulpit to do now and that shouldn't take long at all.

We left Bodrum Marina at about 1430 and the minibus was a lot quieter than when we had arrived. It seemed only a few minutes since we had arrived and everyone seemed a little sad to be leaving. The driver of the bus was quite talkative and offered to sleep in his bus and run us to the airport at 0530. He also said he would take us to a typical Turkish restaurant and afterwards a nightclub. I was a bit suspicious, having had experience of pimps in South America, but my suspicions were unfounded. The restaurant he took us to provided remarkable value for money, and the meal was only about half the cost of a similar meal in England.

After the meal we had a tour of Izmir and then went on to the nightclub. Our guide negotiated cheap drinks with the management and the floor show was first class. The belly dancers were superb and the locals kept stuffing banknotes down their brassieres and knickers. We left the nightclub at about 0300.

It seemed that we had only just closed our eyes when awakened by the early morning call on the bedside phone at 0500. We struggled awake, I had a blinding headache. We stuffed our belongings into our bags. Even an early morning shower did nothing to improve the hung-over feeling. I nodded off on the plane from Izmir and also on the plane from Bodrum to Heathrow, which arrived there at 1200. I had started to feel a bit better by then.

We said our farewells to our friends and made our way to the Underground. When we arrived at St Pancras we had just missed the Kettering train and had an hour to wait until the next one!

23rd November: Last night I missed karate and drank far too much. I woke up at about 0700 feeling awful. I went downstairs and had a handful of Paracetamol and then started preparing my shooting gear. Ann got up and made me some breakfast and a packed lunch. I had to go into work to pick up the truck and by the time I arrived at Kirby Hall it was about 0920. As I drove down the road I felt awful and hoped that perhaps I had got the wrong day so that I could go home and *get back in the warm. It was a bleak morning, cold and grey with a promise of rain to come.*

As I drove up to the meeting place I saw the other shooters, beaters and dogs ready and waiting. They all looked happy, even the bloody dogs looked cheerful, and I switched on my smile and tried to be pleasant. During the morning the mists of alcoholic depression began to clear, but it was the third drive before I had a shot. A woodcock, very low, darted straight for me, seemingly intent on knocking my hat off. As I swung my gun I burned my hand on my cigar and even as I fired I knew I had missed. On the next stand I was lucky, I had three lovely shots and downed three nice cock birds. I didn't have a shot at the triangular spinney, but on the next stand I had two very high birds, the last one probably my best ever shot. It was an extremely high bird going like a jet plane and it came down and never moved.

This evening, we had the Summerlands to dinner, it was very pleasant. We had carbonnade of beef, which was very good. They left at about 0230.

5th December: This morning the invoice arrived for the new boat. Our accountants inform us that if we pay for the boat during December we should be able to claim capital allowances, which should help no end with next year's tax position. It is now only about five weeks to delivery and I am getting excited. We plan on having a lot of useful equipment fitted to this boat and there should be a lot of planning and dreaming time from now till the spring. I would like to fit radar, but I think the cost this first year may be too high.

I have the flu and feel awful. Last night at Kempo I had to pack up halfway through the session and go home. Tomorrow Ann and I are going to a dinner dance at the Ritz, I hope I feel a bit better than I do today.

We have the decorators in and the house is a bit of a tip. Brian Summerland is doing the actual decorating and Phil from work is fitting an archway where the old front door used to be.

The development work on the new Fairline 36 Sedan is now almost complete. There are a few alterations to do but most of it is good. The year so far promises to be one of the best ever and I am looking forward to the results of the accounts in January. I think next year we may see quite a lot more business from Shetland Boats, as they now have a good range and there is a strengthening of the market generally.

I visited Father yesterday, he is very frail and seems to be deteriorating quite quickly. It's a shame to see him so weak and Ann and I are keeping an eye on him.

14th December: Christmas is nearly upon us and the year seems to have flown past. I trained twice this week and I am training again on Monday and Friday next week. I am quite fit and the karate training I am doing is very good for me, without it I would be in poor shape. I am drinking more than is good for me but will go on the wagon in the New Year.

The decorators are almost finished at home and next week we have the tilers and carpet fitters in. The house will be very nice when finished, Brian and Carl have done a good job. The carpentry work wasn't brilliant and there were quite a few gaps here and there, but the overall job on the extension is good.

The house extension was a successful project. Warkton Lane was at that time a prestigious address and a nice place to live.

Production at Cooney Marine was very efficient and we could barely keep up with demand. I was looking forward to the January boat show, as it was possible to get an idea of how the industry was performing from the sales claims of the boatbuilders, although they were often exaggerated.

We were looking forward to Ann's parents 50th wedding anniversary and had organised a surprise celebration party. Ron, Peter and their families were coming. I had organised a 'Naughty Vicar' and Ann's Mum and some of the other guests thought it was a real vicar to bless their anniversary. When his cassock fell off and he stood there in a pair of boxers they couldn't believe it!

I'd booked the works Christmas dinner at a restaurant called Barnaby's. Over the years I had tried various venues, but the sort of night out I liked wasn't suitable for everyone. Most of the youngsters only wanted to get plastered, whereas the older people with wives or partners preferred a more sedate evening.

24th December: Last night I took the lads to Barnaby's for the works Christmas dinner. I was surprised that most of the lads took a girl. Some of the girls were very attractive and I chatted to some of them for some time. Bill came with his new lady friend. She was very nice and apparently they plan to marry in the near future.

Tony rang this afternoon, he was at Dad's house. Dad had been sick over himself and couldn't walk. I drove straight over, arriving at about 1515 hrs. Just after I arrived the doctor came and said Father should go to hospital for a few days. They took him in an ambulance and I felt so guilty, I felt as though I should have taken him home with me.

I went home and started preparing the turkey. I made some chestnut stuffing and also some sage and onion. I had just finished and was having a drink, feeling slightly depressed, when there was a knock at the door. It was Father Christmas (Phil dressed up). He came in for a drink and we had a good laugh. It cheered us up no end although I still felt sorry for poor old Dad stuck in hospital at this time of the year.

25th December: This morning after breakfast the children and I went to the hospital to see Dad. We met Ann Tony and Ian there, Michael is in America. We spent an hour or so with Dad, then everyone came back to our house for the traditional Christmas. We had a very nice lunch, somewhat subdued due to Michael and Dad being away, then during the afternoon we had a phone call from Michael in New York. We all spoke to him and cheered him up a bit. As usual I ate too much and felt rather uncomfortable most of the afternoon. At about 2000 the phone rang and once again it was America. It was Theresa's friend Doug who had stayed with us in the spring. Theresa was so surprised and it really made her day.

The past year was fading into memory. The turnover for 1985 was £317,778 compared to £195,161 in 1984, an increase of 63%. Considering the problems that we encountered this result was remarkable. Net profit was up from £33,763 to £61,913, an increase of £28,150 or 83%.

CHAPTER TWENTY FOUR

Plain sailing at last

In 1986 I had plans to extend the factory by building another 3000 sq. ft. unit on the car park which would be used for the larger pulpits (bow rails). The boats seemed to be getting bigger, with Fairline planning a 50ft. boat. I was looking forward to the delivery of my new boat. It didn't arrive on 22nd January as promised, but the weather was so awful I didn't mind. As the men were working so efficiently they seemed to be flying through the work. We were on time with deliveries and I was having to go out chasing more business. As the industry was expanding I was having some success, but having to quote for less glamorous work. I also needed to watch quality standards, but overall the system was working well, with the men rectifying any substandard items in their own time.

Dad was not doing very well and was still in hospital. The nurses were very good. He was up and down – one moment he seemed anxious to come home and the next he was at death's door. I called in to see him most days and one day he told me that one of the patients just admitted was Granddad's sister Cis. She was in a poor way and didn't know much about what was going on around her.

Saturday 15th February 1986: On Thursday I called to see father again and he seemed slightly better. I met Cousin Sylvia at the hospital, who had called to visit her mum, who is also a patient. I hadn't seen Sylvia for about 20 years and wouldn't have recognized her, although she is still an attractive woman. She came over for a chat and said I still looked the same. People always tell me that, I must have one of those faces. She seemed to know a lot about me considering our families haven't really kept in touch.

The weather is still bitter cold and apparently there is a bit more snow to come this weekend. Tonight I shall take Ann out for the evening for a bar snack at the Star. We will visit Dad this afternoon and look around Bedford for some furniture. I am still quite slim and the lightest and fittest I have been for years.

8th March: This morning I returned the hired truck to Corby Motors and then went to look at some new cars. I fancy a Capri, but Ann likes the Granada. I probably won't do anything for a month or two and may wait until August and the new registration. Our pickup truck is still in the garage, it's now four weeks since it broke down and I am disgusted with it, the service from the Renault dealers is shocking.

Father came out of hospital yesterday and we will go over and see him this afternoon. I am so pleased that he recovered and I hope he will continue in good health. The hospital was such a depressing place.

2nd April: I am 42 today, I don't feel any older. Apart from the fact that I drank too much last night I feel very fit. Today is the first day back after Easter. We went down to Brighton for the Easter break, leaving here on Good Friday. It was blowing about a force 9 all the time we were there but we did most of the jobs and sorted out most of the problems.

I went down to the Florists today to order the flowers for Aunt Cis's funeral on Friday, I don't think I shall go although Anne (sister) will go.

25th April: I left work at about 1630 today, I am off to Brighton to pick up the boat and hopefully sail her round to Woolverstone. We left home, James Ann and me at about 1810. Theresa is staying at her friends for one of the days of the weekend. At the Little Chef we had a meal and arrived at the boat at about 2130. We unloaded all of the light gear and had a few drinks and I had a cigar, then we turned in at about midnight. The alarm went off and I climbed wearily out of bed and switched on the radio for the weather forecast at 0625. At 0626 I thought something a bit peculiar was happening as the BBC are usually very punctual with things like weather forecasts. I checked the almanac and found that the time had been changed to 0550 for the morning forecast. I decided to go back to bed for another 10 minutes' kip and awoke at about 0905!

I started rushing about trying to get everyone motivated but was wasting my time, so I put the kettle on and made some tea. It was a beautiful day, the sun was shining, birds singing and just enough wind to turn the Windex. We plodded through the day getting the ship ready for sea, and were almost ready by 1530, eventually clearing the harbour at about 1630. It was good to be at sea again, I was a bit worried about "sea sickness" but the weather was calm and everything was working OK. The log seemed to be under reading, but everything else worked all right.

It was a beautiful spring evening which started to cloud over at about 8pm. At 2200 I decided to turn in for a couple of hours. At about midnight Ann called me, we seemed to have total electrical failure. The radar had gone haywire, as had the navigator. I changed over to no. 1 battery and everything came back on. I was concerned that even with 2 alternators working we had managed to flatten one battery. I turned in again for an hour and then relieved Ann. The wind was on the nose most of the time but I had the sails up and I think they helped a bit. The visibility was poor and it was raining a lot of the time, I had to alter course off Dover for a ferry but the night went fairly smoothly. I called Ann at 0430 and she did until 0800, it was cold and wet and visibility was half a mile or less. I never saw the Sunk lightship except on radar and the Roughs Tower was only just visible as we passed.

We arrived at Woolverstone Marina at 1045 and as the tide was in the wrong direction we stayed on the end until it turned. It was great to be back and we went for a walk to see if anyone we knew was around. Ken was there and we had a quick chat. We then went back on board and had a meal, a couple of beers and turned in for a couple of hours.

Manoeuvring into our new berth went without incident, and I tried to obtain a hire car but the garages were closed so we accepted that we would have to stay until Monday. The Godfrey Davis hire car arrived at 1045 Monday morning and by the time the boat was packed up with all gear stowed it was 1200 before we left. On the way home we had lunch at the Happy Eater, arriving home at 1430, I got into work at about 1500. There was no training tonight, so we spent a quiet evening at home.

There were a few problems to sort out with the boat. The log, which measured speed and distance, was not working, there was a leak from the anchor locker into the bilge and the electrical problem. The boat had two batteries, no. 1 for the engine and no. 2 for the domestic, lights, radios etc. it was important to keep the engine battery charged, as the alternators for charging both batteries needed the engine running.

We spent a few weekends sailing around the local area sorting out the problems. With the electrics it was a case of managing the two batteries to ensure that the engine could always be started. I was looking forward to taking the boat to Ostend, which was only about a 12-hour trip across the North Sea and the navigation was easy. In clear weather from just over half way across there is a tall building, and if you head for it it guides you all the way to Ostend's Mercator Marina.

Saturday 3rd May: Today I am in the office. Only two men turned up, Singh and his son Bindy. About three others said they were coming in, but I suppose the weather is so nice they decided to have a day off. I am really looking forward to the new boat, she is so beautiful. Last weekend when we left we switched on the dehumidifier, so the boat should be keeping nice and dry inside and free from condensation. I like everything about this boat so far, the only grey area is the electrics. When we do our summer cruise this year I shall take a generator with me for emergencies.

I don't know whether Theresa will be able to come to Ostend with us at Whitsun as she has to work on the Saturday. It would be a pity to leave her at home alone, so we may have to abort the trip. My car is still at Brighton and Tim has offered to collect it for me on Monday.

19th May: Went to the boat again last weekend. The plan now is for James and me to sail over to Ostend on Friday and Ann and Theresa are coming over on the Jetfoil on Sunday. We took the boat over to the fuelling pontoon to fill up on Sunday and spilt diesel all over the deck and coming back into the berth there was a cross wind that blew us into the pontoon. We bumped, but on examination there was no apparent damage. We let James do most of the work coming into the berth and Ann and Theresa kept out of the way, he coped very well and told me off for coming in too fast!

The boat is now ready, with everything working, and I am looking forward to another long trip.

Thursday 22nd May: I shall finish work soon and go home. Tonight James and I are going down to the boat, hoping to take her over to Ostend tomorrow. I am really looking forward to the trip and if we leave at about 0530 by this time tomorrow we should have the harbour in sight. James is quite excited and looking forward to the trip. We will stop on the way down for a meal in the Little Chef. Today at work has been busy and the weather is a bit warm and sticky.

I got home from work at about 1735. Ann had gone to get Theresa from work and her mum and dad were there. I went up for a quick wash and brush up and loaded the car. Ann arrived home just before we left and we made a few last-minute arrangements and said our goodbyes. We were in the Little Chef by 1930. James had his usual burger chips and beans and I had liver and bacon with a fried egg on the top.

We arrived at Woolverstone at about 2045. I then discovered that I had left the hatch key behind. We were both disappointed and I had visions of having to drive all the way home to fetch them. Luckily I had my sailing knife with me which has a screwdriver on the end, and I was able to remove the screws in the hatch-retaining strips and prize the hatch open. Once in the boat I was able to get at the tool kit. The hacksaw made short work of the cockpit locker hatch and I was able to fiddle with the engine ignition to make it start. As the engine burst into life James smiled from ear to ear and grabbed my hand, giving it a vigorous handshake.

I found a note from Ken and Jenny to say they were lying at

Pin Mill, approx. one mile down river, and they would be sailing for Ostend at about 0500 hrs. We plan on leaving at about 0530-0600 so with luck we should arrive at about the same time. I will call up Ken on the VHF in the morning and have a chat.

As it took about an hour to break into the boat and sort out the engine it was about 2230 before were sorted out and James turned in. It is now 2345 and I am ready to turn in myself, I hope the alarm goes off!

23ʳᵈ May: As I sit here at 1035 supping gin & tonic I can't help thinking what a day it has been. We got up at about 0500 and it was pissing down. We did what we could down below but soon had to venture out and sort out things like ropes and sail covers. We eventually cast off at 0615. The weather forecast hadn't been too bad, but I was resigned to a cold, wet and depressing trip. By 0700 we were off the Shipwash and to my surprise Holly Mills called us on VHF, it must have been such a shock when we answered. They were about an hour ahead of us and the weather was just as miserable there as where we were.

Around noon we saw a sail ahead which turned out to be Ken. They called us on radio and we decided to photograph each other's ship. We hauled away from them and made good progress. The weather was improving and the sun burst through the clouds. With 10 miles to go the sun was shining and James was sunbathing on deck. We entered Ostend harbour at 1830, I called the Mercator Marina and they opened the lock at 1845. Going through the locks was the part of the trip I had viewed with apprehension, but we got through with no damage. We tied up in berth 52 at about 1930, Ken came in about 1 hour later. We had a wash and brush up and I took James ashore for a meal which was expensive and poor quality.

Ann and Theresa arrived on the Sunday by Jetfoil. James and I had cleaned the boat from stem to stern and put fresh flowers on the main cabin table and in the aft cabin. Ken and

Jenny came aboard and remarked that the boat looked as though it was at a boat show!

Theresa and James knew their way around Ostend and liked to wander down the Kepplesraat to buy waffles or bags of frites. The weather was hot and we spent time on the beach. We'd planned to leave on the Tuesday but the wind started increasing on Monday night and by 0550 Tuesday morning gales were forecast for all areas and the decision was made to return to UK on the Jetfoil. The Jetfoil docked at Dover, and as our car was at Woolverstone we decided to return to Ostend the next weekend, sail the boat back and then pick up the car. In Dover I hired a Godfrey Davis Ford Escort, they did a one way hire and the drop off was in Corby.

While I had been away over the weekend we were having a new pool dome fitted and I was keen to see it. It had a rigid steel frame and a vinyl cover and could be left up all of the time, unlike the inflatable, which collapsed when the fan was turned off.

11th June: Ann is having a day off today, the weather was no good for flying. Unfortunately Wednesdays always seem miserable. I missed karate on Monday, I find it difficult to get enthusiastic about it any more. I won't pack it in, as I still want to get a Dan grade but I have lost a lot of interest. Theresa also seems less keen, in fact the whole club seems a bit lethargic, perhaps it's the weather. Clubs never do well in the summer as people have other things to do during the light evenings.

14th June: Today is Tim's wedding, it is a beautiful day, not a cloud in the sky, it would be nice down at the coast this weekend but today is the wedding and tomorrow there is a family get together over at Anne's. The weather has finally broken, yesterday was beautiful and after work we spent the evening round the pool. James and David swam with us and Theresa was round Jo's house. Theresa returned about 0930 and James went to David's to spend the night there. Ann, Theresa and I then went for another swim at about 1030. It was a lovely warm balmy evening, Ann and Theresa went topless but then Theresa went all bashful and put her top back on.

Tomorrow on the way to sister's we will pick up Dad, who is now at Clapham Hospital. He seems to be quite healthy, probably the best I have seen him this year. I have applied for a council flat or bungalow for Father and I hope he will move into a flat rather than go back to Kilpin Close. He doesn't like the Idea of a residential home due I think to the cost. He's been thrifty and saved all his life but now he is reluctant to spend his money on himself. I don't think he realises that the rainy day he has been saving for has finally arrived.

I am seriously considering taking Blue Amazon to Portugal to get some sunshine sailing. Ann isn't too keen as she likes weekending on the boat. If I do take the boat to Portugal I may build a smaller boat to keep locally for weekending, fishing etc.

The business seems to be building up nicely and we are at the stage where we may consider employing a manager again. Our tenants are moving out next week and we will expand into their unit ourselves. I will need some extra plant but will try to keep it to a minimum.

Tuesday 7th July: Last Friday evening we went down to the boat. Sheila came with us and on the way down we stopped at the Happy Eater and it was dark before we eventually arrived on board. On Saturday James and I inflated the Zodiac and fitted the engine to the transom, always a back breaking job. We left the berth at about 1330, it was very hot but there was plenty of wind and we put up full sail. We sailed down the river leaving a Contessa 32 behind and then had a beat down the coast to the Deben entrance. We motored down past Ramsholt and picked up a buoy. I put the fuel tank into the dinghy plus oars, anchor, flares and children to give them a whiz. The engine was a pig to start and as soon as I cast off and put it into gear it stopped. It was difficult to row back to Blue Amazon against the tide with a boat full of people but I managed it. I cleaned the plugs and restarted the engine, under load it was only firing on one cylinder.

I took the kids ashore to find a camp site, as they wanted to camp ashore. I found a nice spot and we returned to BA for dinner. I barbecued some steaks and it was a pleasant meal. After dinner I took them ashore again complete with camping gear, dropped them off and then collected Ann for a trip to the Ramsholt Arms. In the pub Ann remembered that the kids had left their matches on board. We left the pub and motored down to the camp site to take them a lighter. As we approached I could see Theresa and Sheila waving frantically from the shore, apparently they had been trying to attract our attention, thinking we were aboard Blue Amazon. The tent was in a nice sheltered spot on top of a low cliff, they seemed quite organised so we left them trying to light a campfire.

Back on BA it was a super warm balmy evening. The wind had dropped, so we sat out sipping gin and tonic until 1145 and then turned in. I was up at 0730 Sunday morning and I went ashore to pick up the campers at about 1000. They looked a bit bedraggled, having fallen in the mud. Theresa had fallen down the bank and Sheila was wearing only a bikini and a shirt, James however looked quite at home. He'd rigged his hammock between two trees and was swinging from side to side beaming from ear to ear. They'd been for a swim at 0730.

We loaded the dinghy and set off back to BA, where they all had a cup of hot soup and a good wash down. we cast off the mooring at 1500 and ran back to Woolverstone with just the jib. as we came onto the berth it was blowing force 5 on the beam, which made coming into the berth a bit tricky, but we made it OK.

23ʳᵈ July: Today is Royal Wedding day. I went for a flight, the weather was foul with rain winds and clouds rolling in. I almost decided not to go but Paul Smith said it would be all right. I only did two circuits as the weather seemed to be deteriorating. Steve asked if he could bring a portable TV into work to watch the wedding ceremony. I agreed, rather surprised, I didn't think Steve was a royalist.

Today I am going to Bedford to visit Father, apparently he is a lot worse than when I saw him last week and Anne is quite worried about him. I shall call in and see Geoff Millman to pick up one of Anne's presents as it's her 40th. tomorrow. We are having a big pool party on Friday and we are expecting about 30 guests.

The summer cruise was a trip to the Channel Islands via Brighton. I always liked to do the first leg of the trip overnight and we were ready to go with all gear stowed and the boat fuelled and watered at 1830 on August 4th. The weather forecast was NE force 6, occasionally gale 8, backing westerly force 4, rain, some fog. As long as it was as forecast, the trip shouldn't be too bad. We made good progress to Dungeness despite being chased off by the Channel Guard ship at 0600. At 0930 Holly Mill called us on VHF, they were about five miles astern of us also headed for Brighton. The wind by now had moderated and we motored into Brighton Marina and tied up on the visitors' pontoon at 1510.

We stayed a few days in Brighton. There was so much to do and Theresa and James enjoyed their time there. I decided to leave for Alderney on 8th August, departing at 1300. The wind was SW force 4 for the first few hours, gradually decreasing until around midnight, by which time we were motoring in a flat calm. At 0615 we picked up a buoy in Braye Harbour. The few days spent in Braye was the usual round of partying, most nights ending with friends on board bellowing sea shanties into the early hours, but all good things come to an end and we set off for St Peter Port on the 14th, eventually rafting up outside the marina. We refuelled but then found the shops to be shut; however we managed to obtain a few necessities, tonic, cigars and cigarettes.

We then motored round to Havelet Bay and anchored. Theresa and James were keen to improve their water skiing. They could do it OK behind our Zodiac but wanted to have a go behind a proper ski boat. So Ann, James and Theresa donned their wetsuits and I took them ashore to the ski school and returned to *Blue Amazon* to video their exploits.

While we'd been away the works had performed as well as usual, and preparations were under way for the Southampton Boat Show. I planned to be at the show for the whole time and was looking forward to seeing Pat Patterson, who was exhibiting his new Summer Twins and the crowd from Palamos Boatbuilding who were exhibiting their Banshee catamaran. The Banshee was designed by Richard Woods and was very fast. His wife Lillian was an accomplished sailor and had also built some of the earlier designs.

I discussed with Richard whether it would be possible to tow a water-skier behind the Banshee. I thought this would be great for publicity and an interesting thing to do.

Saturday 11th October: Last weekend we all went down to Cornwall to sail on the New Summer Twins and the Banshee catamaran. We stayed on the Banshee and the accommodation in the hulls is quite spacious. We had hoped that we could get James water-skiing behind Banshee but unfortunately there wasn't quite enough wind, although on one occasion she surged up to about 16 knots for a short time. I sailed the Summer Twins and was surprised at her performance, and also the accommodation, which had been fitted out quite nicely. We didn't come home until Monday. We called in to Palamos to look over the factory and discuss their requirements for the two boats they are building. We decided not to go away this weekend, I feel a bit tired and could do with a weekend at home to recuperate. I am not sleeping too well and I am drinking too much.

I am training quite hard at karate and I think I am doing OK. The only problem seems to be the other people in the club of the same grade are much younger, lighter and faster than me, so although I can beat them in free fighting I don't look as good.

On Sunday we started taking a few items from the boat ready for the winter lay up, we'll take the remainder off next Sunday. There's not much work to do on the boat over the winter but I suppose it will be a rush at the last minute. The factory is very busy but somehow production seems slow and the men are a bit lethargic. I am losing a lot of time, I visit Father two afternoons a week and with visiting customers I am getting behind with drawings and machining that only I can do. In the New Year I shall consider employing a machinist.

This morning on the way to work I pranged the truck. I met an oncoming truck on the Warkton Bridge, I braked, the truck skidded and ended up broadside on across the bridge, blocking it completely. In the process I had demolished part of the railings. The vehicle was still drivable and I managed to manoeuvre it off the bridge. Some kind person had called the police but I don't think I shall be prosecuted.

With the volume of new business Ann and I were under a lot of pressure. I was reluctant to employ any more non-productive staff in an effort to keep profit percentages as high as possible. Ann did all of the buying, wages and accounts, keeping our customers on 30-day terms and paying our suppliers on the same basis. Fairline and Shetland Boats were no problem, but some of the smaller boat builders tried to drag the payment terms out. I would immediately put them on stop and refuse to supply anything further until the account was paid. This worked like magic, it was only fair that everyone was on the same terms. Cash flow was good as long as everyone paid on time. It promised to be another good year although we seemed to be working harder to achieve the monthly turnovers.

26th October: Production this month has been quite good so far and as long as nothing goes wrong it should be a good month. We are now into the party season and have quite a few dinner dances to go to. I get bored with the Wicksteed Park functions, the crowd always seem slightly geriatric. On Saturday we are going to the Ritz at Desborough, usually a good night. I've been on the wagon for about five weeks but may have a drink on Sat.

Ann took delivery of her new car on Monday, it's a Volvo 345 GLE and today she's had a day off to go Christmas shopping in Northampton. Only four weeks to Christmas Day, it seems to have arrived so quickly this year. It only seems five minutes ago that we were sailing every weekend.

15th. December: Dad has now moved to an old folks' home in Bedford, it's a beautiful place and although he seems a bit worried I think he will come to realise that he is better off in the home than in that depressing hospital. I wrote to Sylvia on Saturday sending her some old photos of her mother and wishing her a merry Christmas. I think she will be pleased to know that Dad is now out of hospital.

Last week was very busy, most evenings I worked until 0730 and one evening after driving to Barnsley I didn't get home until 0930. We had the decorators in all last week and this added to the confusion, although the office looks very nice and we plan to keep it clean and tidy.

The truck engine is knackered again and I may put a new engine in it as soon as possible rather than bodge up the old one. Tonight is the works Christmas party, we have booked in at the Ideal in Wellingborough. Apparently the cabaret is quite good and the food comes highly recommended.

24ᵗʰ December: Christmas Eve again, the work is all done, the lads have produced a lot this month and finished the year off quite nicely. All the shopping is done and we are all looking forward to a few days off. We are hoping that Dad will be able to come over tomorrow with Anne and Tony. Theresa has to work all day today but here we are finishing at about 12.

I was looking forward to 1987. Although the company had a reasonable '86 it was a struggle from month to month to keep to production targets. We were supplying a company that had started up in Corby called Cruisers International, an offshoot of Cruisers Inc. of America. They were producing two boats, a 19ft cruiser and a 26ft cruiser. Sam Newington was not very happy and tried to get me to stop supplying them. I was in a difficult position, if I didn't supply them someone would and then they would be knocking on Fairline's door after our business!

The boats Cruisers were producing had a lot of stainless steel on them and they appeared to have a lot of potential as a customer. I was supplying them, keeping them on 30-day terms. Their boats were not such good quality as Fairline and they had a lot of warranty issues, but I hoped the quality would improve as their production increased.

2ⁿᵈ January 1987: I wonder if the pleasure is worth the pain. New Year's Eve was a super night, we had a dinner party with Ann and Tim, Ron and Kate, Paul and Angela and the four of us. We cooked gammon and the meal didn't finish until 1130. After the food we all went into the front room to sing "Auld Lang Syne" (I think that's how you spell it). We then all did the conga out of the back door and in through the front, and had cheese, coffee and brandy. At 0130 I cleared the coffee table away and put on the dance music. We all had a good dance about and the party broke up at about 0530. Everyone stayed over.

I woke up at about 1200 and mooched about a bit like a

zombie for an hour or so and then had a beer that killed the pain. We had Ann's mum and dad over for lunch and everyone had left by 1700. We went down the pub at 2100 and I had about four pints and two cigars, Ann had two gin and tonics. We walked home and then had a few gin and tonics before turning in. I felt awful this morning and I am looking forward to a fag and booze free year. Today is Friday and by Monday I should be back to normal.

During January the amount of new business coming in was threatening to overwhelm us. Fairline were increasing production and giving us a hard time over the fact that we were supplying Cruisers International, who were rejecting items for no apparent reason. I think they were trying to justify the non-payment of their account. I had a meeting with Mike Phillips, the MD of Cruisers, and explained that this was unacceptable and if the account wasn't paid on time supplies would stop.

Our accountants were in during January to produce the figures for 1986. The turnover was about £8000 less than 1985, but the net profit was £2000 more. I was quite happy with these figures, a 20% net profit was an excellent result. I was keen to expand the business and increase turnover but didn't want to compromise profitability. Luckily being a partnership our customers couldn't look at our accounts. If they knew the sort of margins we were making they would be after price reductions!

Martin and Pat were now living in Alderney and he was a partner in Mainbrayce, the island chandlery. They also ran the water taxi that operated in the summer months. If he was back in the UK he would call in and pick up parts that we had made for the shop, and often he would stay with us.

Now Dad was in the care home I needed to clear his house. I used the works truck to take any unwanted items to the local auction house. The planning for the new 3000sq. ft unit was approved and I was looking forward to the project. It should help my expansion plans, we intended to do the large pulpits (bow rails) in the unit and as the unit was 60 ft long it would give us plenty of capacity. I planned to take the boat to the Mediterranean and spend some time sailing in the sun, possibly ending up in Majorca.

12ᵗʰ March: It is 1823 and I am at work, we are under quite a lot of pressure and I am going over to Fairline early tomorrow morning to check some fittings and do a stock take. Cruisers seem to be expanding at a dangerously fast rate and I hope they maintain control. At the moment they are as good as gold and pay up dead on time. Shetlands are doing very well and I am pleased to see their success. I think our biggest problem is keeping the lid on Fairline. They have such a large range and designs keep changing, making it difficult to keep track. Their ordering system is a bit haphazard and on all of the smaller boats (under 33ft) I have to tell them when to order so I need to keep an eye on stock levels. Their middle management are great buck-passers and everything has to be someone else's fault, and some of them are as ignorant as muck.

In April we did our usual trip to the Beaulieu boat jumble. I was undecided whether to carry on with these events, as we were now possibly the largest independent manufacturer of high quality stainless yacht fittings and a boat jumble didn't really suit our image.

Theresa had Just passed her driving test (4ᵗʰ attempt) and as she had to work on the Saturday she drove herself down to the hotel where we were staying. She did well to undertake such a long journey with so little experience and I was very proud of her.

Although work was started on the new factory unit, it was unlikely that it would be finished much before August. The boat was almost ready for the trip to the Med. I had fitted a new satnav but was taking my sextant, almanac and sight reduction tables just in case.

30th May: Blue Amazon is now in Plymouth ready for the trip across Biscay, which will probably be in July as we will be very busy in June. The autopilot packed up again on the way from Alderney to Plymouth. I am not sure of the reason this time, but I have now decided to dismantle the whole assembly and refit the sprocket with a keyway and new shaft.

We arrived in Alderney on Sunday having had a run all of the way there before a NE 3. The tides worked for us and we motor sailed at about 8 knots. The visibility was quite poor, down to about 2 miles or less for most of the way. When the island eventually appeared it was quite eerie as she lay slumbering in the early morning sun. I called James up and we both had tears in our eyes as we sailed past the mighty Breakwater and into Braye Bay. We had two goes at the mooring, losing a boathook first time around. When we were eventually moored up I fixed the anchor chain to the buoy as the wind was getting up.

As Martin came past in the water taxi he nearly fell off when he saw us waving to him. He came aboard for a beer, absolutely delighted to see us. After lunch we went ashore and saw Pat at Mainbrayce, who made us welcome and lent us her car for a drive around the island. It was Pat and Martins' 25th. Silver Wedding anniversary and as a present we gave them a silver-handled crystal Ice bucket. We went up to the house and Pat invited us to stay the night as the harbour was very rolly. We had a bit of a party that night, Pam and Roland came over and we drank quite a lot.

We had a leisurely day on Monday and that evening we took Martin and Pat for a meal at the Georgian. The trip from Alderney to Plymouth was uneventful, we arrived at the Mayflower Marina at about 2015. Customs came out to see us and we stayed the night on the visitors' berth, moving to a different berth the next morning.

While the boat was at Plymouth we had a visit from Pat Patterson and we took him sailing - it was a change for him to sail in a monohull. It was good to talk to Pat and discuss the trip to the Med. as he had done the trip so many times. We had some good sailing around the local area and on Sunday we anchored behind Rame Head for lunch and a snooze, returning to the Mayflower at about 1800. I worked on the autopilot for most of Saturday and was disappointed to find that when I had it all fitted together, although I had replaced all of the steel parts with non-magnetic stainless steel, it deviated the compass by about 15 degrees. This was annoying because with the ordinary steel parts it only deviated it by 6 degrees.

It was nearly the end of June before everything was ready and we could at last get away, the crew for the trip to Gib. were Ken, Carl, Danny and myself. Ann took me down to Plymouth and we said our goodbyes. It was a flat calm when we cast off at 0630 on 29th June and we were clear of the Eddystone lighthouse by 0830. I'd decided that during the day we would do four-hour watches and at night three-hour watches. The position was plotted on the hour, which was quite easy as the Decca navigator was behaving itself and we soon dropped into a sea going routine. The wind was fickle, so we motor-sailed when it became light. I'd decided to pass outside Ushant rather than through the Chanel du Four and the Raz de Seine.

Crossing Biscay we had a NE 4-5 and the ship was flying along until we were approaching northern Spain, when the wind became light and variable. I'd decided to call in at Vigo, as I had happy memories of the last time there when I was an engineer aboard RMS *Amazon* in 1966.

It was 0900 on 4th July when we tied up in Vigo. The trip had taken five days and one hour, there were no problems with the crew and we all felt a sense of achievement after five days at sea. The boat had performed well and I was looking forward to the next leg of the trip.

We were approached by some girls who offered their services and when we refused they said we must be gay! We all went ashore and ended up in a bar plastered and singing along to the disco.

The ship was low on diesel, so we had to go alongside the town quay to fill up. I was concerned at the lack of depth at the quay, which was only 1.5 metres, but we didn't touch bottom and we were able to pay in sterling. It was noon before we left and the visibility was only about half a mile. The Decca had stopped working and the satnav only gave us an accurate fix every few hours. The radar was invaluable down the Portuguese coast, both for radar fixes and avoiding the numerous fishing boats.

At 0230 I was off watch and sleeping in the main cabin. Carl was on watch. I heard a shout and Carl leaped down the hatch shouting "There's a f*****g great duck just landed on me!" I rushed out into the cockpit and sure enough there was an enormous goose waddling around. It must have flown into the sail and flopped into the cockpit, landing on Carl. It appeared uninjured and unafraid of us humans and just kept waddling around and defecating on the cockpit floor. We couldn't decide what to do with it we had several days at sea ahead of us and in the short time it had been aboard the cockpit floor was disgusting and slippery, which was dangerous. I decided it had to go, so I grabbed hold of it, holding the wings together, and threw it overboard. There was a sound of frantically flapping wings and off it flew!

The visibility down the Portuguese coast was poor for most of the trip and with the fishing boats heading in all directions it kept us on our toes. At one time we had eighteen boats surrounding us. After checking in with Gibraltar Customs we moved to a stern-to berth in Shepherds Marina on 9th July. Both legs of the trip had taken five days and one hour, which I considered to be a success.

23rd July: Quite a lot has happened this last month. The June turnover was the biggest ever and I spent the first two weeks of the month sailing Blue Amazon down to Gibraltar. This was the longest trip I have ever done in a yacht and I enjoyed it very much. There were four of us aboard and the biggest problem was that I ate and drank too much. I usually have only one meal a day, but we were having at least three even in poor conditions.

The weather in UK has been diabolical for the last week or two and I am looking forward to our holiday in the Med. The new factory now has the roof on and the builders should start the walls on Monday. These building jobs always take months longer than quoted and I don't expect to move in much before November.

The work going on at home is taking longer than expected, the builders seem to work one day and have two days away. It is frustrating as we are sleeping in the spare room and it is far too small, clothing seems to be everywhere.

I am going to visit Father this evening. He is back in Henrietta House now and seems to be keeping well. He will be 79 next month and the last two years he has become quite frail, although he remains cheerful most of the time.

On the 5th August we flew out to Gibraltar for our summer holiday in Blue Amazon. As we left Gibraltar astern heading for Estepona, the wind steadily increased, and by the time we entered the marina it was blowing a Force 7 and the sea was rough. We were glad to tie up. After a couple of days we headed for Benalmadena, calling in at Malaga for fuel and water, but there was no fuel available there so we continued on to

Benalamadena, where we were able to fill up. Over the next few days we called in at Almeria, Gerrucha, Alguilas, Mazzaron and Alicante, finally arriving in Calpe on the 19th. We were all surprised to see our old boat *Blue Target* on the opposite pontoon, but no one was on board.

We decided to moor the boat for the next few weeks in Alicante Marina, the main problem being the fact that I couldn't speak Spanish. One of the locals who had a reasonable command of English offered to translate and I eventually agreed to pay the office in pounds sterling, or 'livres' as they called them. I planned to fly out again in October and paid the £450 cash up front to the guy in the office. I was not given a receipt.

25th September: This month the turnover has been abysmally low and I think it will probably ruin most of my euphoric predictions for record profits this year. The main problem is the polisher and packer were both on holiday, together with one of the most productive fabricators, and two men were off sick. I had to sack one on Tuesday because of constant absenteeism and another has given in his notice. It's been one of those months when I think of selling up and becoming a tax exile, but I shall be very busy next week getting everything out for the end of the month.

Cruisers have been carping on about prices and have taken away the tank business. I am a bit surprised really, when they started I designed just about everything on the boats and supplied them at the risk of upsetting Fairline, and at the first opportunity they stick the knife in. Sometimes I am tempted to pull the rug out from under them and watch them struggle, but I always decide to keep smiling and take their money.

Over the next couple of months I was under a lot of pressure. Some of the plant was breaking down, and there were issues with employees not pulling their weight.

7th October: Everything has gone wrong today. The packer has been on a go-slow due to a hangover, the truck wouldn't start so we missed the Fairline delivery and Teri pranged the new pick up on the way back from Gt. Dunmow. The press broke down and I have the main Linisher and a cut off saw out of action. Nick, one of the most productive workers, is off with the flu and the job he is working on should have gone out today. I could go on and on but I won't, I just get fed up sometimes when people you rely on don't pull their weight.

I went to see Dad yesterday, he seems to be recovering a bit now and the hospital want him to move out and into a nursing home so I now have that to sort out.

Although everything seemed to be going wrong, production levels were very good and I kept pushing everyone to increase productivity. This was working and the men were earning a lot of money. I didn't mind how much they earned, the more they make the more I make, it was as simple as that. Some jobs paid better than others and the attitude was to get the poor paying jobs out of the way as soon as possible to then get into the better paying work. The beauty of the system was that the men were constantly looking for ways to improve efficiency. We had no official tea breaks, I told them they could stop for tea any time they pleased and I wasn't worried about supervision as they were only being paid for what they produced.

On 24th October we flew out to Spain for a few days on the boat and to move it to Calpe for the winter. As we left Alicante Marina the Engine would only rev at about 2000 rpm and was low on power. I anchored off Villayoyosa and went overboard to investigate. I found that the propeller was completely encased in barnacles and resembled a ball rather than a propeller. Using a snorkel I was able to scrape off the fouling, although I cut my hand painfully. We had a nice week sailing with the engine working as normal and then laid her up for the winter.

On the 18th November I had a phone call from the hospital; apparently Father was very ill indeed. I drove to Bedford immediately, arriving at about 1300. Father looked dreadful and although his eyes were open he appeared to be in a coma. During the afternoon Mrs. Connelly, an old friend of Father's, came in and sat with me for an hour. I tried to talk to him but he could not answer me. Ann and Tony arrived at about 1800 and he showed no sign of awareness. I tried to moisten his lips with a sponge, he responded to this but did not wake.

Around 2130 Ann and Tony popped out for something to eat, and while they were gone I noticed his breathing was becoming very shallow. I felt his pulse and it was so weak I could hardly feel it. Suddenly he stopped breathing. I thought he had gone, but after a few seconds he started breathing again. Then after a few more moments he stopped again, then the nurse came in and he started again.

The nurses decided to move him to make him more comfortable, and I stepped out of the screens while they turned him on to his other side. I went back in and his breathing was very shallow. Anne arrived back just as he took his last breath.

We went to the dayroom while the doctor came to confirm that he was dead and the nurse made us a pot of tea. I rang Ann and told her the news.

On the 19th I arranged Dad's funeral. I decided to go for a solid oak coffin, the undertaker has them specially made. Dad was going to be the first person to be buried in the new Norse Road cemetery.

26th November: I woke at 0600 and could not get back to sleep. I tossed and turned and eventually got up at 0745, and we were all ready to leave at about 0900. Although it was a sad day I was relieved in a way that it was here at last. Theresa looked absolutely stunning all in black with a black hat and veil. Ann also looked good, black must be their colour or something.

We picked up Ann's father and mother at about 0930 and set off for Bedford. The car seemed sluggish and heavy with four people in the back, but we made good time and were in Bedford a lot earlier than planned. Anne, Tony and the boys were already at the undertakers when we arrived. Anne looked awful and had aged 10 years in the last week. We went into the undertaker's office. Joan Simcoe, an old family friend, was there and in all there were about eleven people including us. The funeral director took me to one side, introduced himself and explained what to do regarding following the coffin and also in the church.

We went outside, where the coffin was already in the hearse, covered in flowers. I went in the first following car with Anne and held her hand. We arrived at the church and waited in the cars for a few moments while the undertaker went in to see the priest. We disembarked and followed the coffin to the church door, where the priest blessed it. As we entered the church the congregation were singing "The Lord is My Shepherd", it was quite moving and there must have been about 50 people in the congregation. It was a beautiful requiem mass with most of those present taking communion. I think there were only about four people there that had actually known father, but Catholics do like a requiem mass and I was glad of their support.

The journey from the church to the New Bedford Cemetery seemed quite long. As we drew up to the graveside in the cars I saw Sylvia and as we gathered round the grave I said hello and introduced her to Ann. The grave was nicely presented with the pile of earth covered in green matting which extended into the hole. The priest did the burial service and the coffin was lowered into the grave. We all walked over to look at the flowers, which were nearly all from the family with just two from friends. Before getting into the car I walked back to the graveside and had a last look at the coffin. At the head there was a beautiful brass crucifix and below this a brass plate with Father's details on. When I walked back to the car everyone else was already in it. It seemed a long drive back to the undertakers' car park.

4th December: *Last month the turnover was lower than I had hoped for, and at the end of the month there was a lot of work that didn't go out. However if we get our act together this month shouldn't be so bad. The year so far has been successful and I think that probably there will be a lot of tax to pay. It is 1725 and there are Christmas songs on the radio, although I don't feel very Christmassy.*

The work seems to be going through nicely and now that we have an additional polisher it has taken a lot of the pressure from that department. I have trained for the last three sessions and I can feel my returning skill and fitness. Last Wednesday I had two fights and did reasonably well, but I am feeling very tired and I am looking forward to the holiday.

Theresa has now taken all of her exams. She has so far only had one result, 97%. Considering the pass mark was 60% I think she has done exceptionally well. James is trying to teach himself to play the guitar. He practices every night and I think he is hoping for an electric guitar for Christmas.

In about another four weeks the Boat Show will be here again. I usually look forward to it, but this year I am not really excited at all at the prospect. Last Saturday I went shooting, I took Graham West as my guest. We had a good day, although after lunch I couldn't hit anything. The bag was sixteen brace of pheasants, one rabbit and a pigeon. That evening we went out with Bryan and Val to Nicky's 40th. birthday party.

22nd December: *Most of the month's work is now done and we have two deliveries to do before closing. With it being such a short month it has been quite hectic, but I've been able to clear a lot of stock items that were lying around outside. We moved into the new unit today, most of the machines have been delivered and are being wired up. I think in the New Year we are going to be very busy and I can foresee a lot of pressure to maintain the sort of turnovers I shall be expecting to maintain. The biggest problem seems to be getting the products wrapped and delivered, although we now have another good polisher.*

4th January 1988: This is the first day back after Christmas and New Year. Christmas went off very well, we kept the kids' two main presents, a massage couch for Teri and an electric guitar fir James, in our room, so when they came in at 0830 to give us our presents we presented them to them. They were absolutely delighted and it was a pleasure to see their excitement even at their age. I gave Ann her presents and she seemed very pleased.

We had decided to eat later than the usual Christmas time so I still had the turkey to stuff. Ann's Mum and Dad came for the day and Anne, Tony and the boys. Boxing Day we went to Anne's as usual and had a happy day with lots of jokes and fun.

We went to Warners' holiday camp for New Year, it was an intensive few days but most enjoyable. The Earls Court Boat Show opens on the 7th and I shall take a busload of the lads on Sunday.

The Boat Show was one of the most successful for a long time with all of our customers claiming record sales. Our order book was stretching out till June and I was anticipating another record year.

Towards the end of January Ann and I went to Alderney; we stayed with Martin and Pat Smith and were looking at property to buy. I was going off the idea of keeping the boat in the Mediterranean and planned to perhaps base it in the Channel Islands. The accounts for 1987 showed an excellent result. The turnover for the year was £480,473, an increase of £180,000 on the previous year, or 55%. I had tried to maintain profitability during the year and the net profit was £108,605, an increase of 69%. On the £480,473 turnover the net profit was 22.6%, which was up on the previous year. With the level of forward orders, providing I kept control, I'd hoped that 88 should be as successful as 87, and I was already discussing the purchase of another half-acre of land adjoining our existing site. I was also keen to purchase a house in Alderney. Ann was quite insistent that we couldn't afford it.

The business couldn't run without us, and this became very clear when Chris, the office lady, decided to leave. Ann and I had considered her to be part of the team, but I suppose to her it was just a job. Luckily Teri decided to come into the business and joined the team on 11th February. With her experience working at Yorks Travel she was good with people and with her experiences of boating from an early age she had a knowledge of boats and sailing.

18th March: A lot has happened in the last month. February was the highest turnover month ever, I was delighted with the result and I am looking forward to another good year. On 1st March Ann and I went over to Alderney to look at property, once again we stayed with Martin and Pat. I was determined to do a deal on a property. but the one I really wanted was taken off the market due to the vendor's ill health. We looked at four houses and ended up deciding on the smallest of all. We also confirmed to BSC that we wished to go ahead and purchase the land behind the factory.

On 7th March I had a meeting with Fairline's buyer and agreed a price increase. I didn't get 10% but we settled for 7½% after a long discussion and a bit of haggling. We flew to Spain on the 8th. I didn't really feel like going, I felt a bit over pressed with everything that was going on, but as soon as I stepped on board the boat I immediately unwound. I found that there was no fresh water available, only salt, but Jack on the next boat kindly gave us a 5 litre container of fresh for immediate needs.

We took the boat to Campomanes for fuel and water and had a nice sail down to Benidorm. We met Geoff Aspinwall and his friend Doris, who were on Blue Target. We went on board for a drink. She looked really small (Blue Target not Doris) and then I remembered I used to think of her as enormous. The next evening we went out with them for a meal and they flew back the following day. When we arrived home Dennis the carpenter was busy fitting the new Kitchen, Teri came home from work and was so relieved to see us back. Everything at work had gone OK. although Teri was mentally exhausted!

24th March: Teri's birthday today, she is nineteen and it seems only yesterday she was a baby. we are all going out tonight to the Bell for a bar snack. Last weekend we were buying for the new house in Alderney. We have just about finished now, although probably there will be all sorts of things we have forgotten. For the main room we have bought a magnificent Indian rug to cover a large part of the main floor. We decided against settee beds as the ones we looked at were neither a comfortable bed or settee, instead we bought a normal three-piece suite and a couple of fold up beds for emergency. We are taking the furniture down to the docks on Sunday and it should arrive in Alderney on Wednesday. Martin will take it up to the house and we are hoping to fly out on Friday morning to spend Easter fixing the place up.

We flew out to Alderney on 1st April. We arrived at Southampton at 1530 and as we walked onto the airport we met the pilot of the charter plane, an Islander that was to take us to Alderney. The pilot said one of us could sit up front with him so I quickly volunteered. I did not tell the pilot that I also could fly and he seemed quite chatty, telling me what was going on regarding carb heat etc.

We had a wonderful flight and Pat and Martin were there to meet us at the airport. When we went up to the house, it was nice to see all the furniture in place, although it was not unpacked. We all had a drink to celebrate and then the Smiths left us to it. It didn't take long to unpack, although the fastenings for fixing the bunk beds were missing. We also had a water leak that flooded the bathroom floor and caused a fuse to trip out.

Saturday was my birthday and Martin, Pat and Mickey (their German friend) came round for dinner. As we were a bit unprepared, having just moved in, we had a simple meal of soup followed by Kettering sausage and baked spud, then freezer shop cheese cake and gateaux. On the Sunday Teri and Dave went for a cycle ride round the island whilst Ann and I went for a walk down to the harbour. It was a beautiful day, sunny with just a slight chill in the air.

We walked back up through the town and went into the museum. I am very interested in the history of Alderney, particularly the German occupation, so I bought three books on the subject. It's a pity that all of the big guns have been scrapped. If just one had been preserved it would have been a fascinating historical feature.

I had also decided to base *Blue Amazon* in Alderney and had arranged for Jersey Yacht Management, a company that specialised in boat deliveries, to collect the boat and sail it from Calpe to Alderney. She arrived in Alderney on 5th May. She survived the trip without major problems, apart from a bent stern ladder and some wear and tear. The autopilot also packed up and they had made some ingenious modifications to bodge it up.

9th June: May was another good month although it could have been even better had it not been for Whitsun at the end of the month. We have several people off. I had to sack the driver yesterday and two others are off with injuries incurred playing football. Last Friday we flew to Alderney for a long weekend.

We had supper in Braye chippy, which was not too good, the chips were very poor and the fish was tasteless. We went out to Blue Amazon, she looked very nice and did not appear to have sustained any serious damage.

During the weekend we found that the autopilot was wrecked and the satnav inoperative and one battery was dead. It should not take a lot of effort to sort it all out and everything should be OK for the summer holiday. I always hate to leave Alderney, although I like living and working where I am, I suppose it is nice to have something to dream about. I've started flying again and I am hoping to do my IMC rating. The last two flights have had to be cancelled due to the weather.

2nd July: I am on holiday tomorrow for two weeks, we fly tomorrow at 11 am. We have quite a busy schedule, which includes sailing to Guernsey and Jersey, so probably the time will fly past. Anne and Tony are joining us for the first week, they have not sailed before so it will be new to them.

At the weekend I bought a share in an aeroplane and I was checked out last night. We did some stalling and circuits and I did OK. The plane is a Robin Dr400/160 which is a full four seat with baggage aircraft. I am looking forward to doing some flying in Alderney, one of the syndicate members is going there in the next few days for his week's holiday.

26th August: This month has been very eventful. We flew to Alderney on the 3rd and Ann and Tony Joined us on the 4th. On the 5th we sailed down to St Peter Port, locking into the marina at about 2300. We stayed there for a couple of days and then left for Herm and anchored off Belvoir Bay, near Shell Beach. I took James water skiing, and Tony sat on the front of the dinghy for ballast, I think he had a shock when I opened up the power. The next day we had a good sail from Herm to Sark, although we did not go ashore due to the high wind. Instead we returned to Havalet Bay, Guernsey, and stayed a couple of days there.

Before sailing to Guernsey Ken sailed into Alderney in his new Moody 422. We went aboard for drinks and I was impressed with the overall finish and accommodation plan. On Sunday Ann and I are going to Brighton to have a look at one. The chap who bought our last boat rang and asked if Blue Amazon might be for sale, which got us thinking.

The holiday was a great success. Ann and Tony fitted in OK and I think they had a good time. While we were away Teri and Singh did exceptionally well, a lot of work was produced and the new quality control system worked OK with only a few arguments. This weekend is August Bank Holiday and we are closed until Tuesday. It's nice to have the time off but it plays hell with production for the month end.

September production was a struggle as we had problems with polishing. The best polisher was on holiday and in order to get production moving I went and did a few days' polishing myself. I also hired one of my former employees part time, which got things moving. At the end of the month some of the men had a protest and were rioting over the next year's holiday dates. I called them all together and told them that if they didn't like it they could leave! This seemed to work and they all went back to work.

Martin and Pat and their friend Mickey came to stay. Their son Richard was getting married and they stayed with us for a few days. In October we moved the boat round to Brighton, where there was a lot of police and security due to the Tory party conference. Offshore there were soldiers in RIBs patrolling the waterfront and in the marina there was a heavy police presence. We were questioned by them and asked not to leave until the next day.

On Tuesday morning I went to see Brian Sharp and ordered the new boat. I did not get a brilliant deal out of him, but at least I know he is straight and would stick to his word. The price was high, so I did not order many extras.

2nd November: October was another hard month, we just couldn't seem to get everything together. We still seem to have bottlenecks in certain sections. Our storeman-packer left on Friday, so I suppose I shall have to do quite a bit of driving this month until we get another driver.

Friday night was the Ladies' Night and we went and had a super time. After the function we were invited back to Peter Tye's house for coffee. Ann dropped me off but did not come in as she was tired. John Turner gave me a lift home. I went into work on Saturday until about 1230, now the pool is switched off there always seems to be a lot of spare time at the weekend. It was fairly quiet and perhaps a little boring.

Next Sunday we may go to Brighton to do trials on the new boat, that should be interesting although the driving is a bit traumatic. There is a lot of development work going through and it is a bit of a nuisance slowing down production, although when it is done the new jobs will be slightly more profitable than the existing. All of the Fairline boats from 31ft upwards will now have a full-length pulpit. Shetland have also changed a few of their range, the Sovereign being the most tricky. Corvette Cruisers are in trouble, their cheque bounced and I am a bit concerned as they owe us £8000.

The year, although at times a struggle, was turning out to be the most productive ever, and it seemed every year we did more and more. Productivity was the key, but the bigger the business grew, the harder it was to keep control of everything and everyone. Boats were getting bigger as people traded up for the next model.

We bought the Alderney house, intending to fly over in the Robin at weekends. The boat was changed from the Moody 37 to a Moody 425, which was a much larger.

20th December: Christmas will soon be here, I am quite looking forward to it for when we close the factory doors on

Friday that is in effect the end of our financial year and I shall feel that the pressure is off for a while. I have plans for next year to try and raise production but it will be tough going. I am looking forward to Alderney, we plan on going out on 28th December to return on 2nd January. This year I have been under considerable pressure and I can't think of any easy answers, the business seems to take up my whole life, we rarely go out with friends or meet new friends and life feels claustrophobic. I am drinking more than is good for me and I feel depressed and irritable most of the time. Perhaps I have the winter blues and as soon as spring approaches it will cheer me up.

I am looking forward to the Boat Show and to using the new boat. I have the stern rail in the workshop being modified to incorporate a life-raft holder, life-buoy holders and a pole for a Decca aerial.

James went to the Duke's Arms at Woodford for his works Christmas dinner. We arrived home at about 1215 and found James asleep in the log cabin in the garden, he had forgotten his house keys.

When we arrived on Alderney it was Martin's birthday, so we were straight into a party. I got absolutely legless and don't remember much about it. On the night of the 30th I was wandering around upstairs with the light out, didn't realise that I was on the landing and fell down the stairs from top to bottom. No one came to help me. I was sure that I had broken some ribs or something, I was in agony. I crawled into bed, but every time I moved it felt like someone sticking a knife into my back and waggling it around. I took some painkillers in the morning but no one had any sympathy. I found it difficult getting up out of the chair and getting in and out of the car was sheer purgatory.

We all went to the sailing club New Year party, but I left at about 1030 and went back to the house. What a start to the New

Year! Whenever I go to Alderney I feel as though I've come home. I am getting to know a few people now and I would dearly like to move over there for good. I am fascinated by the forts, more the Victorian and earlier, and I would like to learn more about the history of them.

The 1988 production figures once again showed an excellent result. The turnover at £575,066 was up by £95,000, 20%. The net profit for the year was £140,810, an increase of £32,000, which worked out to around 25% of turnover. These figures were exceptionally good and I didn't know of any other company in our area that was as profitable. At the time we were probably the largest independent supplier of stainless steel rails and fittings in the UK. Our main strength was the ability to supply rails for bigger boats of 50 ft. and over.

The work on the new boat, which we named *Blue Dancer*, was almost complete. I'd fitted an autopilot, a Decca navigator and refitted the stern rails complete with life-raft holder. The topsides on this boat are fairly high and coming into a marina berth with low pontoons is tricky in all but the calmest conditions, so I planned to fit side boarding ladders to make this easier. I had also ordered a radar, which was due to be fitted in February.

Ken Campling asked me to crew on his boat *Happy Hobo* down to Gibraltar and I was looking forward to another long trip. His boat was a Moody 422, which was almost identical to my 425. The plan was to sail from Falmouth to northern Spain and then on to Gib, similar to the trip we had done in *Blue Amazon*.

3rd March: I am off to Brighton tonight on my own, Ann is staying around as her dad is in hospital recovering from prostate surgery. I am fitting new stainless stanchions and gangway stanchions to accommodate side boarding ladders. The weather last weekend was awful. I managed to fit one side but then decided to move the gangway to a different position, so this week I have some repair work to do. I am looking forward to going sailing again, so far we seem to have done nothing but work on the boat every weekend.

The month grinds laboriously on. We can't quite keep up with demand and there is a lot of pressure. I've had a heavy head cold since Christmas and at the end of the month I'm going into hospital to have a job done on my sinuses. I hope this will improve things, although I can't really spend the time. The doctor said I need a couple of weeks to convalesce, but I won't be able to stay away for more than a couple of days.

The boat is almost ready for the season, there are just a few jobs to do when she comes out of the water next week. I am having a rope chopper fitted and also a three-bladed prop.

11ᵗʰ April: Friday 24th March was Good Friday and Ann and I went down to the boat for Easter. It was also Teri's birthday, so we couldn't get away very early. Teri, James and Dave went to Wales for the holiday. The forecast was not very encouraging, so we didn't go to France, although the weather would have been OK.

On Sunday we decided to go out sailing. There was a wind blowing us onto the pontoon and it was a bit of a fiddle getting out. The berth at Brighton is only an 8-metre berth and it is a tight squeeze for a boat of our size. We had a nice sail but I think she is not very fast, I have yet to give her a good thrashing in a bit of a blow so I shall reserve judgement. I would also have expected her to be a bit quicker under engine. Although the three-bladed prop is now fitted I couldn't get her over 7½ knots. The motion under way is quite pleasant and I think she performs quite well overall, and she is more comfortable than the 37.

On the 29ᵗʰ March I went into hospital to have my sinuses sorted out. I came out the next day and then had to have a week and a half off work. There were no problems and now I feel quite well. I don't know whether it was the time off or the operation that has made me feel better, I am not at all depressed. This weekend we are going down to the boat again, the family may be coming and I shall hope to go sailing.

Tomorrow I have a busy day ahead of me. I am going to the dentist at 0900, the bank manager is coming in at 1100, the hairdresser is coming at 1645 and it is lodge at 1830.

At the end of the month I am sailing down to Gib with Ken Campling. I am quite looking forward to it as I enjoy a "deep sea" trip once in a while. Ken wants me to be second in command, I don't know why. I'm sure his wife Jenny is quite competent enough but I am flattered that he rates me so highly.

I am thinking of changing cars, I fancy a Jaguar. Ann is not too keen on them but I have always wanted one, so we are going for a test drive next Tuesday.

25th April: The month is now drawing to a close and production is reasonable but not too clever. I am trying to get turnover up to £60,000 per month but we seem to be a bit below this figure most months. With the present work force and market conditions this is about the figure we should be turning out each month.

Next weekend I am joining Ken Campling on Happy Hobo and we are sailing it to Gibraltar. I am hoping to fly down to Truro and then get a taxi to Falmouth where the boat is now lying. I am working on my flight plan at the moment and only hope that the weather is OK.

Last Tuesday I ordered my first new Jaguar, it's for delivery in August to get the new registration, I'm really excited by the project and am looking forward to it very much.

On the trip to Gibraltar there were five of us, Ken, Jenny, and Ray, one of Ken's RAF colleagues, myself and two crew that were paying passengers. Ken used the boat for training and was an RYA instructor. We'd been friends since the days down in Wells-next-the-Sea. The Moody 422 had plenty of accommodation, but the leeward main cabin bunk was most comfortable at sea and the watch-keepers tried to ensure that the next person on duty had this bunk. As there were six of us it was fairly easy to sort out the watch system, there was always one of the experienced crew members on watch and it worked out that whoever was duty cook didn't do a watch. The boat had two heads (bathrooms). The aft cabin head was for the captain and his wife and the rest of us were to use the forward head.

2nd May: we sighted our first dolphins this morning. So far we've had a good trip, I felt queasy for the first couple of days but now I feel OK. Today I am duty cook so I will not stand a watch. I cleaned the heads this morning, they were disgusting. I suppose with four men using one bog at sea it's inevitable. The only problem was that one hour after I had done them they were as bad.

We may reach Vigo sometime on Wednesday. The last couple of days the weather has been cold but we've had light winds so although having to motor-sail we are making good progress. We are sailing at the moment on a port tack and it is nice and quiet, we are making about 5 knots.

Later: the wind is increasing to about a five and I had problems cooking this evening. With a beam sea and feeling queasy I had to cook a Chinese meal. It consisted of stir-fry chicken chow mein and prawns. I also did a tin of Spam cut into chunks in a sweet and sour sauce. It was too rough to use plates so I flopped it all together into dishes. They all said it was lovely, it didn't taste too bad, it just looked disgusting.

3rd May: The wind freshened during the night and Ken got up to put a couple of reefs in the mainsail and to roll up some jib. I gave him a hand, but he had it all under control. I was on watch from 0500 to 0800, it was a lovely morning and I watched the sun rise. The wind has remained in the east, giving us a good reach at 6 or 7 knots, there was not much shipping around. At 0700 I made breakfast for myself and Colin who shares my watch. Most of us have our sea legs and are enjoying the trip. With luck we should get into Bayona some time tomorrow morning. I have not been there before and I am looking forward to it.

1600: we have made good progress during the day. This afternoon Ken and Ray reefed the mainsail to the third reefing point. This made the motion a lot easier and we are still making over six knots. I am on watch again in an hour and I may sight land. we are only about 20 miles off Cabo Villano.

4th May: We arrived in Bayona at about 1100. The visibility was poor, we couldn't see a thing until about three miles off. It is very hot and everyone is a bit quiet, possibly an anti-climax after four days at sea. The trip took exactly 3 days 23½ hours. Ken and Jenny went ashore armed with a phrase book to report to the Harbourmaster and when they returned we went ashore for a walk. We had showers and went for a wander around. Once past the sea port there did not seem to be many shops, but it was enjoyable just being in a warm and friendly place.

5th May: After breakfast I went for a walk on the beach. It was absolutely idyllic and I felt perfectly content to just sit on a rock and admire the view. When I returned to the boat we moved to the fuelling pontoon and topped up the diesel and water. We then washed the boat down. When we'd finished she looked an absolute picture and I took a couple of photos.

6th May: This morning it was quite cool. I had the 1100 to 1400 watch and by 1400 it had really warmed up. We were all in shorts and funny hats and I got quite a bit of video. Although I have seen quite a few dolphins they have not come close enough to give me any good pictures.

As the afternoon wore on it got hotter and hotter until at 1630 the wind started to increase and we put up the sails. The wind was almost directly astern and we tried both gybes before getting it right. At the moment we are running at over seven knots! I have the 2000 hrs watch, which should prove interesting. Jenny is cook today and whatever she is cooking looks and smells quite interesting. We have just topped up the diesel tank from containers and it is now drinks time.

The trip so far has gone really well apart from the first 48 hours when everyone felt "sea sick". There have been no problems, everyone is getting on well together and we have had some good laughs. I don't know our ETA for Gibraltar, but it should be some time Monday or Tuesday, I shall get the earliest available flight back hopefully on Wednesday.

7*th* May: We are now off Cape St Vincent and we only have 175 miles to go. Today has been a lazy day with not much wind and very little shipping sighted. We saw dolphins today on a couple of occasions, but they did not come very close. We've changed the watch rota around so that I can be on watch during the night to cover the busy period as we approach the Straits. I have fixed our position quite accurately from a transit and a radar range.

As we rounded the Cape we only had one fishing boat that gave us trouble and we altered course for him. I also altered course for a small ship which approached head on. Roger is now on watch and will finish when Ray comes on at 0200. Ken is also around playing with the DF set.

8*th* May: This will probably be our last full day at sea. It dawned quite cloudy and the sea has the oily appearance of a flat calm. We are a long way offshore and there is some shipping about. We had home-made bread for breakfast, it made a change from the packet stuff which has lasted very well.

Now the trip is nearing the end it seems to have flown past.

The crew have all mixed in remarkably well and there are no tensions or problems that I know of. The boat has handled very well and I am pleased to own a similar craft. I am not sure whether our Moody with the in-mast furling will sail as well but there is probably not much in it. I am still not looking forward to work, having relaxed and unwound for a time it will not take long to screw me up again. I am duty cook today and consequently I don't do a watch.

9th May: We arrived in Marina Bay at 1130. We entered the harbour at about 1030 and then had to clear customs. After that we went to the fuelling berth and topped up with diesel. Ken took us into the berth stern first and it was nice to go for a wander ashore. It was very warm and we were all in shorts and little else. We all had showers and then went for a walk into town. We decided to take Ken and Jen out for dinner in the evening and we went to Chaplins restaurant. We were back on board about 2400.

10th May: We booked our tickets this morning to fly back to the UK and spent a leisurely time sightseeing. I went ashore and rang Ann to tell her I'd arrived safely. This afternoon I went shopping to buy presents for Ann and the children. I bought Teri a pair of earrings, Ann a brooch and James a watch. It was a beautiful warm afternoon and on the way back to the boat I stopped in the Marina Bay Café for a drink. I had a couple of pints and then returned to the boat. Colin was there, so we decided to have another drink. Jen did a spaghetti bolognaise in the evening and we had a couple of bottles of wine with it.

11th May: Today was my last day in Gibraltar and I felt a bit sad. I got up at 0815 and had some toast and coffee and then it was time to clean up the boat. I elected to clean the forward heads and removed the grating and hung it overboard on a piece of strong. I then cleaned the whole compartment and until it shone. On my own boat I always keep the heads spotless and I expect everyone to do the same.

Ray and I decided to donate a couple of scrubbing brushes with long handles, as Ken only had hand scrubbing brushes. When we'd finished the boat looked beautiful. I asked the man at the office if we could borrow a marina trolley to take the bags to the airport as it is only a five-minute walk. He refused and said the trollies could not be taken out of the marina complex, and there was also a £5 deposit to pay. We took the bags to the café and had a coffee, after which we borrowed a couple of Liptons supermarket trolleys and used these to take our bags to the airport.

The plane was delayed about 1½ hours and I didn't arrive at Gatwick until about 1630. I picked up a Godfrey Davis hire car and arrived home about 2000 hrs.

On 24th May James passed his driving test, and we were all surprised, but very pleased. He came into the office beaming from ear to ear waving his pass paper. On 27th we took the boat to Fécamp for the weekend. I originally intended to leave on the Saturday morning but the forecast wasn't very good so we didn't leave until Saturday night. We arrived at Fécamp in the early hours of Sunday morning, we turned in but we're up fairly early. The weather was gorgeous and there were dozens of boats visiting from Brighton and Shoreham. Unfortunately the craft we were lying alongside was leaving at 0500 Monday morning so I had to get up to move boats. I went back to bed and Ann did the forecast.

We left Fécamp at 0800. There was very little wind and we were motor-sailing most of the way. About halfway across we picked up a rope around the propeller. Luckily the stripper chopped it up and we were able to continue, but some of the rope remained on the prop and slowed us down, although we still had a fast passage.

In June I did quite a lot of flying. On the 8th I made an attempt to fly to Le Touquet, but the weather was awful so I turned back. On 17th I was more fortunate and Ann and I flew to Alderney. From leaving home we were in Alderney in about 4 hours, which is not bad considering that we wasted 1½ hours in Southampton on the way there. We flew back on the Sunday, so we didn't have much time to enjoy ourselves. The whole weekend seemed to be taken up with flight planning. It was super to be in the house again.

We didn't bother to get a taxi from the airport – it was such a glorious day we decided to walk. On the way to the house we stopped to buy Sunday morning breakfast.

20th October: The summer has flown past and I have done quite a lot. In August we went to the boat, which by then was moored in Alderney. We all went, including Dave, and I achieved most of the things I wanted. We ended up in St. Malo, having visited Jersey, Herm and Sark. Dave was excellent crew and a good person to have on board. Teri was seasick as usual and I don't think they will want to come with us in future.

On the delivery trip to Alderney we took Graham, Cesira, Ron and Don and went from Brighton to Cherbourg, staying in Cherbourg for a day, and then to Alderney. It was a very successful trip and everyone had a great time.

Back at work we have management consultants in as we are trying to double the size of the business. It will require a large investment in property and effort, but I think the next five years could prove very rewarding.

This year I have not done any karate and I am now training at judo again. Although I can hold my own with the others at Randori, my ground work is poor, I can't seem to beat anyone above green belt and some of the beginners tend to get the better of me.

18th November: Last night we took James to the annual prize giving at Tresham College. It was an interesting evening. We arrived at 1900hrs. and had a free drink. Ann had a sherry and I had orange juice. There were various speakers and then the actual prize giving. James's prize was for the best course work for the year and was donated by Alumasc, a local engineering company.

Last weekend Ann and I went to Alderney for a few days. We flew out on the Saturday afternoon, arriving at the house at about 1800. We booked into the Sea View at about 1830 for dinner and we got down there at 8 pm. In the bar there were only about three other people and the restaurant was also quite empty. It was however a super meal and we arrived back at the house at 2200. Ann then decided to ring Smithy and we had a good laugh over the phone.

On the Sunday we were up late and after an enormous breakfast of all the things Ann shouldn't be eating we went for a long walk down the Zigzag, arriving at the harbour late afternoon. We called into Mainbrayce and saw Pat, who invited us to dinner. We had an excellent meal and loads of booze.

On the Monday we pottered about and went for a long drive in the car. We had a quiet evening on our own and Ann did a Joint of beef. Tuesday we were due to fly back but the mainland was fogged in, so the flight was cancelled. That evening we decided to try the new chippy that Dick, Sue, Alan and Tess are now running. The food was very good. We watched TV for the rest of the evening and flew back Wednesday.

It seems every time I go away for a few days we have problems with Fairline regarding their orders. Teri was under a lot of pressure to deliver items that had not been ordered and their purchasing really cocked things up for a few days

7th December: We are now well into December. October and November were excellent months for production and at the moment I am not as depressed as last year. We had our report from the consultants doing the work for the DTI and it was interesting. The main theme seemed to be that we were too good *and they couldn't suggest much to improve things. It was an interesting exercise however, and I think we can expand the business considerably over the next few years.*

19th December: Singh is away on holiday until the 8th January, he's gone to India and I think he deserves a good rest. Bill Cullum starts back on the 2nd January in the position of General Manager. I hope it works out but I think there will have to be a lot of give and take on both sides. If it works things may be looking up for the future, I should be under less pressure and I hope to improve quality and individual performance. It should be possible to increase production by at least 25% and hopefully 33% with the existing labour force and facilities. Polishing and packing are completely up to date, previously this area has been a big problem. It will be interesting to see what the month's turnover will be compared to August when we were closed for two weeks.

We are going to Alderney for the New Year and I am looking forward to that, in fact I am looking forward to the whole year!

As the 80s came to a close and we looked forward to the 90s, I reflected on the last 20 years. Starting with nothing but a lot of enthusiasm, optimism and belief in myself, I had built up a business that was a serious player in the marine industry,

CHAPTER TWENTY FIVE

Atlantic adventure

As the 80s came to a close and I looked forward to the 90s, I reflected on the last 20 years. Starting with nothing but a lot of enthusiasm, optimism and belief in myself I had built up a business that was a serious player in the marine industry. 1990 was another record year for production, but as so often happens a recession was just around the corner. In '91 the industry was struggling again, I'd bought another half-acre of land and planned to erect another 10,000 sq. ft factory. I planned to build a house but was concerned that if work dried up these two projects would be a millstone around my neck!

I decided to go ahead with both projects and the factory was finished off in the middle of '91, the problem being that we now didn't have enough work to fill it, so it remained empty and I was trying to find someone to rent it. We started building the house early in '92 and it was finished in the November. James joined the firm that month and I kitted out a workshop for him. During his apprenticeship as a toolmaker he'd become a competent engineer was and an asset to the company. I now had both James and Theresa in the firm.

Business started to build up again and we moved into half of the new factory in March '93. We had some really nice products. I had designed a passerelle (gangway) that also doubled as a crane for lifting the dinghy and although superior to others on the market I found it difficult to persuade the boat builders to accept it.

In May '94 I took my Yacht-Master practical exam, as I'd decided that it was about time. Ann and I had both passed the theory and I had already done Coastal Skipper.

I bought the house next door, which was in a terrible state and was being sold as a building plot. The site measured about an acre and I was worried that a developer would get hold of it and build lots of houses there.

I eventually started selling our passerelles into Fairline, who were taking four per month, and production was about eight per month in total. Marine Projects in Plymouth were also interested.

I'd always had a dream of sailing the Atlantic, and another friend from the Shotley Yacht club, Dennis Knight, was also interested, so we decided to do it in Millennium year, 1999. We would then both be 55, so we decided to call it the 55 club.

I sold *Blue Dancer* and bought a Hallberg Rassy 42 ft. ketch, which we decided to call *Blue Jeans*. The Ships Registry wouldn't let us have *Blue Jeans*, so we eventually settled on *Forever in Blue Jeans*. Dennis sold his Moody and bought an Oyster 435 and called it Shilling of Hamble. Martin had also decided to sail the Atlantic in his CSY 43, *Ragtime*.

We had decided to join the Atlantic Rally for Cruisers, the ARC, which sailed from Las Palmas to St. Lucia, departing in November '99. I sold my share in Mike Uniform for the asking price. I was sorry to say goodbye to the aircraft, as I had enjoyed being in the group and the other members had become good friends. In January '96 we flew out to Tortola for two weeks' bareboat charter.

Production was at a very high level and we were producing about 18 passerelles a month. I had a trip to Singapore and Malaysia with Mike Derrett, who was doing marketing for us, and while there we went to Penang. Mike was an experienced pilot and we both joined the Penang Flying club, which had two Cessna 172s, and after a check flight we were able to fly them. We flew from Penang to Alor Setar, then to Langkawi island, back to Alor Setar and then returned to Penang over the course of three days.

The sails on the Hallberg were hard work, so I had in-mast reefing fitted to the mainsail and mizzen which worked very well. We were slowly preparing the boat for the Atlantic crossing, and I fitted a water maker and a generator.

We built a new office block to compliment the new factory, but in the middle of '98 work slowed down and I thought another recession was imminent. We lost most of the orders for passerelles to Italian manufacturers, but it started to pick up towards the end of the year.

Early in '99 Bill gave his notice to leave, as he had an issue with his Christmas bonus. He refused to discuss the issue and I was surprised at his attitude after 10 years during which I felt I had treated him very well. I planned to hand over to James and leave in July on the first leg of the trip to the Canaries, from where we were setting off across the Atlantic.

James was negotiating with the RNLI to supply a crane for the Severn class lifeboat, which carried a large inflatable boat on deck for rescues where the water was too shallow for the main lifeboat. It was a substantial crane and James was working with the RNLI on the design. Andrew Sims came to work for us as General Manager to take over from Bill Cullum. In July we had a leaving party, and all of our friends were there and most of the family.

On *Blue Jeans* everything was ready and all gear stowed ready for departure on 16th. We locked out of the marina at 0700 on 17th July 1999.

25th. July 1999. 48 43.95'N. 04 39.88' W

We are motor sailing towards Ushant along the Brittany coast. The wind is light and variable, mainly NE. I hope we don't have to motor most of the way as I don't have enough diesel. We spent a couple of nights in Guernsey waiting for a window in the weather. It was Ann's birthday yesterday and I think she was apprehensive about setting sail across Biscay.

The engine has just gone off and we are making about 5 knots in a force 4 on a dead run. In a couple of hours we will be round Ushant and into the Bay proper. The forecast is good for the next few days. I haven't got used to the watch system yet and feel very tired, but that should be easing tomorrow after another sleepless night.

The trip across Biscay took about 3 days 14 hours, which was fairly fast. The last three times I had done this trip it had taken about 4 days.

Down the Portuguese coast we sailed in company with *Shilling, Ragtime* and *Seventh Wave,* an HR 49, calling in at various ports. We sailed from Lisbon heading for the Canaries on 28th August and arrived in Lanzarote on 5th September. We spent some time sailing around the islands and flew back to UK at the end of September, leaving the boat in Pasito Blanco. We rejoined the boat on 3rd November. We were carrying a lot of spares and gear and it cost us £140 excess baggage.

Everything fitted surprisingly well and we were soon almost ready to go. There were a lot of social events and lectures and it was a great time, with everyone looking forward to the Atlantic crossing. There were about 200 boats doing the ARC. The organizers were quite strict on safety and inspected every boat to ensure that all the necessary safety measures were in place.

The night before the start, Stokey Woodall, one of organisers, broadcast over the radio a last briefing with expected weather conditions and a pep talk. The overall message was 'You are on your own now, once you are out there you need to sort yourselves out'.

24th November: At the moment we are on a run and have about 18 knots of wind. We have just reported the noon position and it seems there are quite a lot of boats around although we can only see one on the horizon. Things have settled down now. We are getting used to the watches and are sleeping well. Not much has happened. We are getting into the routine with the radio schedules and find that we seem busy all of the time. I have not picked up a book yet. I am however starting to enjoy the trip. There have been no dolphins yet or flying fish. Yesterday we ran all day with poled out twin headsails but then had a depression forecast and decided to run for 20N 22W at which position it should pass us by. This change has cost us quite a few miles and put us about 20 miles behind Ragtime and almost back with Dennis (Shilling).

The weather seems to be quite different to the norm and apparently the trades are not blowing W of 40 W. However it will be quite a time before we are there and things may have settled down. The weather and motion of the boat make it quite difficult to write.

With the ARC there seem to be an enormous number of yachts milling around at the start, and the steering rules were largely ignored. Some boats get damaged and for the first couple of hours it's a case of keeping out of everyone's way. Once past the southern tip of Grand Canaria the boats spread out and after 24 hours it is rare to sight another until approaching St. Lucia.

The trip for us took longer than expected. I had hoped to be in St Lucia in about 20 days, but it took us 24 days.

15th December: We arrived St. Lucia this morning at 02h 2min 16s. Making the trip 24 days approx. This was about five days longer than I had expected. The main reason for this was lack of wind. We had several days when we made less than 100 miles. Our worst day was only 64 miles and at times we were becalmed. The best daily run was 161 miles.

As we crossed the finish line a horn sounded and an American voice said over the radio, 'That horn was for you Forever in Blue Jeans*, congratulations on sailing the Atlantic'.*

You feel a special bond with people you have shared something as significant as an Atlantic crossing with. We would miss the daily banter on the SSB radio so we decided to sail in company with *Ragtime, Fani* and *Astolata* from St Lucia down to Bequia to spend Christmas and New Year. We then sailed to Mustique, The Grenadines and the Tobago Cays, leaving the boat in Grenada for the hurricane season.

Back in the UK the business had survived without Ann and me and was doing very well. I was thinking of changing the boat. I liked the Moody 46, which had far more comfortable accommodation than the Rassy. There was a new version of the M46 due to be launched at the 2001 boat show and I decided to sail *Blue Jeans* back to the UK in 2001and put her on the market. So towards the end of 2000 we rejoined the ship and started to work our way up to Antigua, from where we were setting off back to the UK.

We left Antigua on 10th May 2001 heading for Bermuda,

and arrived on 16th May after a very rough passage. I had promised Ann that one day I would take her to Bermuda, after being enchanted by the island when I visited it in the 60s.

We left Bermuda on 23rd May heading for the Azores. For this leg of the trip we had an extra crew member, Laurie, a sailing buddy from Shotley. From leaving Bermuda to landfall in the Azores was 14 days.

After leaving Ponta Delgado on the 23rd June we Arrived in Plymouth eight days later. The trip round to Moody's marina was uneventful and I was looking forward to seeing the new boat. We'd been advertising *Blue Jeans* in the yachting press and some viewings were imminent.

The New Moody 47, my fourth Moody, was a beautiful ship. The thing I liked about the Moodys I had owned over the years was the good accommodation and lots of stowage space. We had a large water maker fitted, a generator and air conditioning. I planned to do the ARC in November 2002, so I had plenty of time to prepare the boat and in the summer I sailed to Alderney and the Channel Islands. In the September I took the boat round to Shamrock Quay in Southampton and the company used it as accommodation for the Southampton Boat Show!

Over that winter more preparations were made for the trip to the Caribbean and we finally left Moody's Marina on 30th July 2002. On the way down we spent some time sailing around the Channel Islands, then to Northern Spain, down the Portuguese coast and across to Lanzarote.

For this ARC we had two extra crew – Laurie Mullaney, who had sailed with us in *Blue Jeans* from Bermuda to the Azores, and Terry Lovatt, a Shotley boat owner, both highly-experienced sailors. We left Las Palmas heading for St Lucia on the 24th November. It was peculiar having crew, but it made the trip less stressful for Ann and me and the watch system meant that we could sometimes turn in together!

Blue Genie was faster than *Blue Jeans* and at times we were averaging over 10 knots. The trip took 17 days compared to 24 days in *Blue Jeans*, although the weather and the extra crew helped. As we came alongside at 7am in Rodney Bay, Terry's wife Sue and Laurie's wife Jackie were waiting on the pontoon to welcome us and we all had a rum punch to celebrate.

Sailing in the Caribbean to escape the British winter and being home for the summer worked for a few years, but then we decided to sell the boat and charter, the advantage with chartering being that there is no maintenance or repairs to worry about. So in 2006 *Blue Genie* was shipped back to the UK and put on brokerage. The economy was in yet another recession, so I didn't hold out much hope of a quick sale. I was in the process of building another house on the plot next door. Cooney Marine were holding their own, although things were difficult.

We moved into Acre House around the 6th October. On Friday 13th October Fairline summoned James and Andrew and told us they were moving all their stainless supplies away from us. I was devastated. I had been a major supplier since the early seventies and always felt proud walking around marinas anywhere in the world and seeing the Fairlines with Cooney stainless on them. At that time Fairline was buying about 25% of our production. We could survive, but we would have to downsize and make some redundancies. I had a meeting with Ann, James and Andrew to decide on the strategy for the future.

That evening there was a knock on the door. It was Richard, a friend from the village, with the news that Don, one of my best mates, had been killed in a motorbike accident the day before. My business problems suddenly seemed trivial compared to the horror and grief that Don's wife George and daughter Emma must be suffering.

The loss of the Fairline work made a big difference and 2007 was the first year the company had made a loss since 1980, but luckily we had a healthy bank balance which carried us through, and in 2008 we were back into profit. Fairline were in trouble and made 90 people redundant. The new management didn't seem to have much idea. The company had run much more efficiently when it had been family owned.

Blue Genie wasn't selling, and with the general economy in a mess it would be some time before a buyer could be found. We eventually sold her in May 2009. I was sad to see her go but relieved to at last be free of the responsibility. We chartered a 35ft Beneteau for 10 days in Tortola and while there looked at some boats for sale.

We chartered a few times over the next two years. On 11th December 2009 Ann and I and friends Carl and Carol flew out to Antigua. They went off to a resort and we flew on to Tortola and picked up a 40ft moorings charter yacht. After about a week Carl and Carol joined us on board the boat and we spent Christmas and New Year sailing around the islands.

In 2010 the business did remarkably well. A lot of companies were failing, but James was running a very tight ship and we were managing to stay in profit and hold everything together. Princess and Sunseeker were weathering the recession due to their astute management, but some of the other big boatbuilders were struggling. We were manufacturing food packaging machinery and architectural stainless as well as the marine products.

We had booked a month-long trip to the Caribbean in January 2011, three weeks on a charter catamaran and a week in an apartment with our friends Alan and Karen. We flew out to Grenada on 6th January and joined the 38 ft catamaran. The plan was to sail up to Bequia and then sail around the Grenadines, Union Island and Tobago Cays. The weather was diabolical with around 30 knots of wind most of the time. On the trip from Carriacou to Bequia, Alan noticed that the floor in the port hull was afloat. The pumps were totally inadequate, the manual pump falling apart after a short time. Alan and I then had to take it in turns baling out the water with a bucket as Ann headed for Admiralty Bay, Bequia, where we were able to beach the boat and get it pumped out. The rest of the holiday wasn't too bad, but this event put us off chartering and catamarans.

Then our main competitor in the marine business, Belmar Engineering, finally went bust, causing us to be flooded with work. This was excellent for us, but a challenge to absorb it into our production.

I had decided that perhaps chartering wasn't for us and in June we flew out to Tortola to look at ex-charter boats for sale. Eventually we did a deal on an ex-charter 40 ft. Beneteau.

We still keep an eye on the business, and spend a few months a year in the Virgin Islands sailing. We now have a 43ft boat which we picked up in St. Martin and brought up to Tortola in November 2014.